THE DC COMICS ACTION FIGURE ARCHIVE

CHRONICLE BOOKS
SAN FRANCISCO

THE DC COMICS ACTION FIGURE ARCHIVE

By Scott Beatty

Library of Congress Cataloging-in-Publication Data available.

ISBN-10: 0-8118-5832-4
ISBN-13: 978-0-8118-5832-8

Manufactured in China

Designed by Mike Essl
Visual programming by Robb Irrgang/3sт
Design assistance by Alexander Tochilovsky
Photographs by Marc X. Witz
Digital silhouetting and retouching by Allison M. Chetirko

10 9 8 7 6 5 4 3 2 1

Chronicle Books LLC
680 Second Street
San Francisco, California 94107
www.chroniclebooks.com

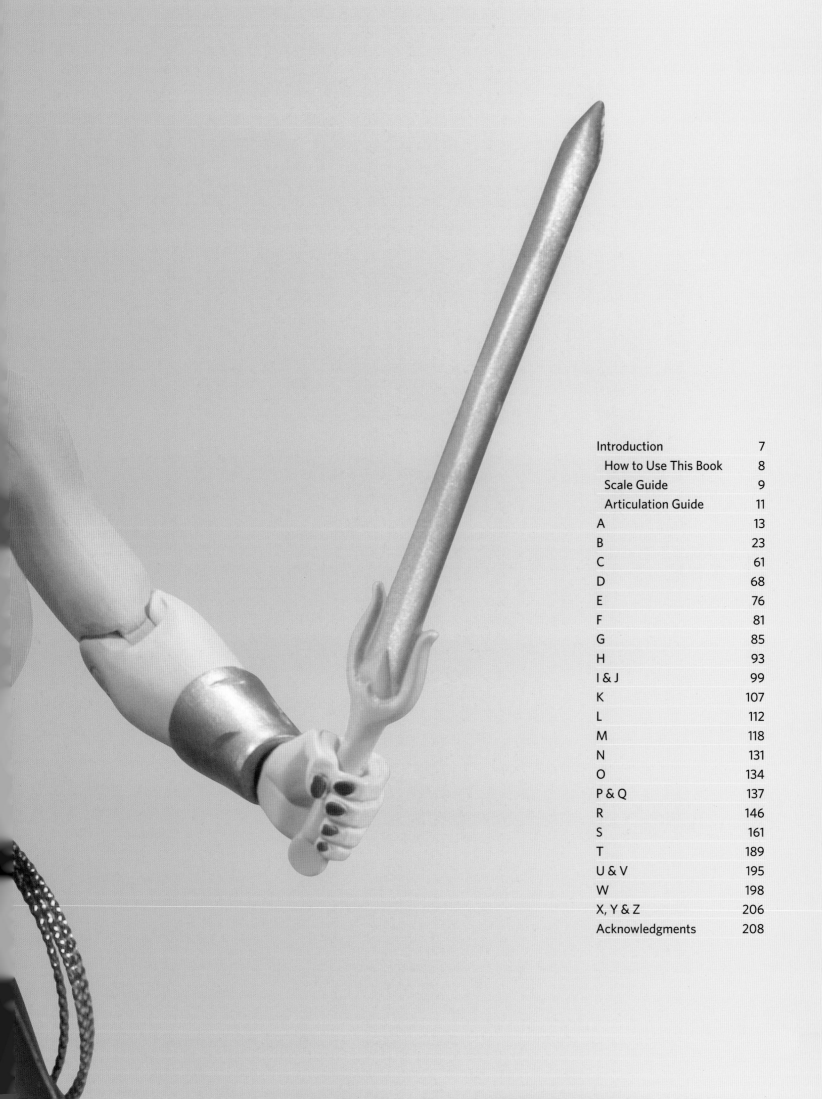

INTRODUCTION

We live in a golden age of DC Comics action figures. But it hasn't always been this way.

During the Golden Age of comic books in the 1930s and 1940s, toy figures of DC's stalwart World's Finest team of Superman and Batman were limited to little more than paper dolls, wooden figures, and wind-up tin toys in the years after the heroes' debuts in 1938 and 1939, respectively.

Action figures, by definition articulated plastic renderings, made their debut in the mid-1960s when Hasbro created the twelve-inch-scale G.I. Joe adventure hero. In 1966, the Ideal toy company released the first true DC Comics action figures when it offered various outfits to accessorize the poseable Captain Action and his sidekick, Action Boy.

Six years later, the Mego Corporation created not one but several action figure lines devoted to DC Comics heroes and villains, the longest lasting and best remembered being the company's *World's Greatest Super-Heroes!* assortments of eight-inch figures with cloth costumes.

By 1978, Mego expanded its offerings to include twelve-inch lines of its most popular heroes, including sub-sets devoted to the smash success of *Superman: The Movie* on the silver screen and Wonder Woman's transition to television.

Unfortunately, Mego's demise in the early 1980s led to the DC license lying fallow for a few years, at least until Kenner created the popular *Super Powers* line in 1984, issuing thirty-three separate DC characters in three years, at the time the largest roster of DC action figures.

Toy Biz started making DC characters in 1989, albeit in fewer numbers, while focusing on adapting toys for the soon-to-be-blockbuster *Batman* motion picture. Toy Biz's association with DC, however, would be short-lived, and the company would soon relinquish the DC license to Kenner and its future parent company Hasbro. Kenner's earlier success with *Super Powers* was nothing compared to what it would do in producing action figures based on the *Batman* movie sequels, in addition to *Batman: The Animated Series* and its antecedents on the small screen, throughout the 1990s and into the twenty-first century.

But it was the creation of DC Direct in 1998 within DC Comics itself that planted the seeds for the golden age of toys. By producing its own action figures for the direct market (primarily comic book shops and specialty stores), DC Direct started out small, but today has developed the most impressive lineup of DC toys ever molded in plastic. In addition to creating a dizzying array of characters, DC Direct also offers artist-inspired series and assortments based on specific storylines, very often listening to the collectors themselves in determining future figures.

Flash forward to the present day, and now Mattel is also releasing DC figures every month with Superman and Batman assortments, in addition to creating a lineup from the popular *Justice League Unlimited* animated series that already rivals the bygone *Super Powers*.

That creaking sound you hear is the weight of five decades of action figures on many collectors' toy shelves.

It is with appreciation of all things DC-toy-related that *The DC Comics Action Figure Archive* was conceived as a means of chronicling every DC figure ever produced. Not merely a photographic and historical record, this book can also be a checklist for the toys that remain on all of our wish lists.

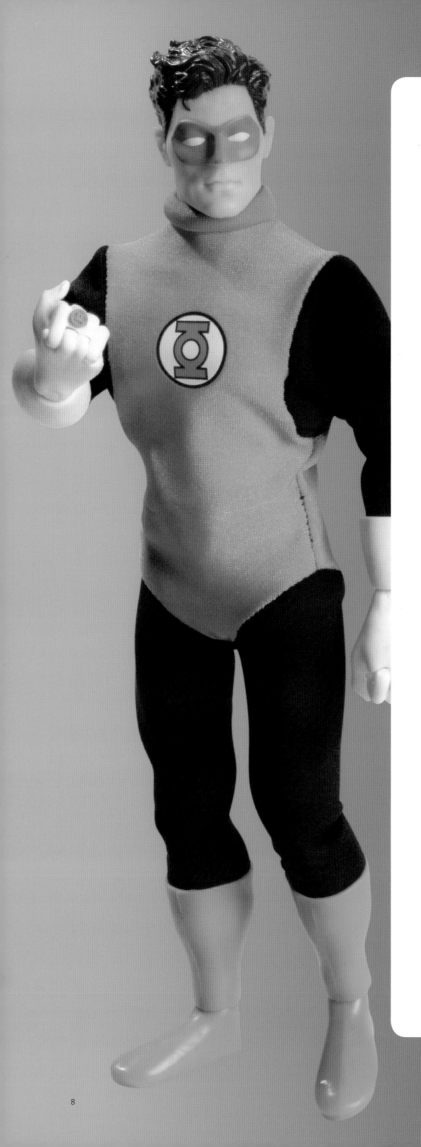

HOW TO USE THIS BOOK

The following DC Comics action figures are listed A to Z, with sub-listings for larger collections such as the many Batman and Superman toys. Excluded from the archive are fast food premium toys and foreign-only releases not readily available to American toy buyers. The action figures here are categorized by several different items of information about each figure, including the following:

NAME
The character's name. Note that in the DC Universe, often several characters have gone by a specific super hero or super-villain sobriquet.

Line
The name of the assortment or collection in which the action figure was released.

Company
The name of the company that produced and released the toy.

RELEASE DATE:
The year in which the action figure was first released.

SCALE: •• inches
The average height, in inches, of the toy collection to which the action figure belongs.

ARTICULATION: •• points
The number of movable joints or features of the action figure, counted head to toe.

ACCESSORIES:
Any weapons or removable accoutrements accompanying the figure, as well as display bases.

ACTION FEATURE:
Any sort of unique function or mechanism, such as "Power Punch" action.

VARIANTS:
Any "redecoed" versions of the same figure released after the initial offering. While the figure is merely repainted a different color scheme from the original, it may also come packaged with alternate accessories.

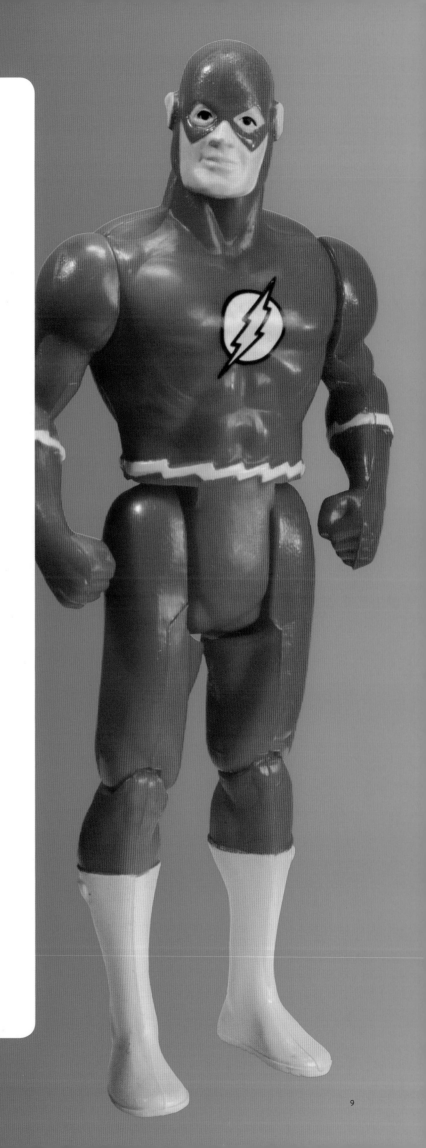

SCALE GUIDE

DC Comics action figures come in all shapes and sizes, from the very beginning of the scale—as befits a toy Atom—and well past the end of a standard ruler, where we see that DC Direct's *Deluxe Collector Figures* go all the way to thirteen inches. While *The DC Comics Action Figure Archive* depicts the various DC toys as large as possible for your viewing pleasure, we provide this lineup of some usual (and unusual) super-hero suspects to illustrate in incremental detail just how these titanic toys measure up in terms of relative scale to one another.

1 inch ("Unofficial")
The Atom (Hasbro/Mattel/DC Direct)

2–3 inches
DC Minimates (DC Direct/Art Asylum)

3¼ inches
Pocket Super Heroes (DC Direct)

3½ inches
Teen Titans (Bandai)

3¾ inches
Comic Action Heroes (Mego)
Pocket Super Heroes (Mego)
Sgt. Rock (Remco)
Super Powers Collection (Kenner)
DC Super Heroes (Toy Biz)
Batman (Toy Biz)

4¼ inches
Justice League (Mattel)
DC Super Heroes: Justice League Unlimited (Mattel)

4¾ inches
The Dark Knight Collection (Kenner)
Swamp Thing (Kenner)
Batman Returns (Kenner)
Batman: The Animated Series (Kenner)
Batman: Mask of the Phantasm (Kenner)
Superman (Hasbro)
The Adventures of Batman & Robin (Kenner)
Spectrum of the Bat (Hasbro)
Mission Masters (Hasbro)
The New Batman Adventures (Hasbro)
Batman [animated] (Hasbro)
Batman [animated] (Mattel)
Batman Beyond (Hasbro)
Batman Beyond: Batlinks (Hasbro)
Batman Beyond: Return of The Joker (Hasbro)
World of Batman (Hasbro)

5 inches
Batman Forever (Kenner)
Batman & Robin (Kenner)
Legends of Batman (Kenner)
Total Justice (Kenner)
Superman: Man of Steel (Kenner)
JLA (Hasbro)

5¼ inches
The Lost World of the Warlord (Remco)
The Batman (Mattel)
The Batman: EXP (Mattel)

5½ inches
Diecast Metal Action Figures (Mego)
Batman Begins (Mattel)
Superman Returns (Mattel)

6 inches
Batman (Mattel)
DC Super Heroes (Mattel)

6½ inches
DC Comics Action Figures (DC Direct)

7 inches
Teen Titans (Mego)
DC Super Heroes (Hasbro)
Legends of the Dark Knight (Kenner)
Justice (DC Direct)

8 inches
World's Greatest Super-Heroes! (Mego)

9 inches
Action Boy (Ideal)
DC Super Heroes (Hasbro)
JLA (Hasbro)

9½ inches
World's Greatest Super-Heroes! (Mego)

10 inches
Justice League (Mattel)
Teen Titans (Bandai)

11½ inches
Super Queens (Ideal)

12 inches
Wonder Woman (Mego)
JLA (Hasbro)

12½ inches
World's Greatest Super-Heroes! (Mego)
Superman (Mego)

13 inches
DC Comics 1:6 Scale Deluxe Collector Figures (DC Direct)

ARTICULATION GUIDE

While some toys are articulate—at least those with push-button talking features—*articulation* refers to the toy's movable parts, the joints that put the *action* in action figures. Most action figures have at least 5 points of articulation: neck (1), shoulders (2), and hips (2). Herein, articulation is identified by *number* rather than location. One of DC Direct's Superman action figures includes an impressive 21 points of articulation, identified below. As the Man of Steel illustrates, the more points of articulation, the greater the number of dynamic action poses in which a figure can be posed.

Neck (2)

Shoulders (2)

Biceps (2)

Elbows (2)

Wrist Joints (2)

Wrist Swivels (2)

Waist (1)

Hips (2)

Thighs (2)

Knees (2)

Ankles (2)

As you read this book, see if you're eagle-eyed enough to identify a figure's points of articulation based on the number shown in each listing!

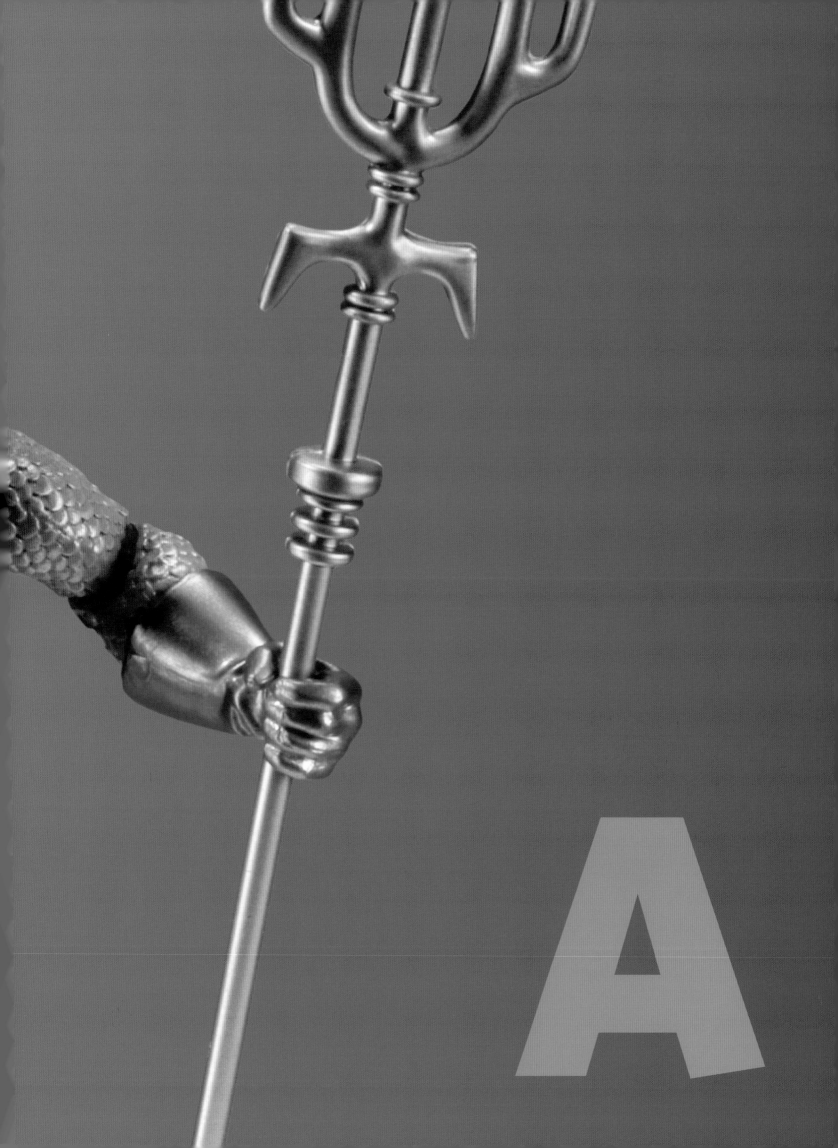

A

ACE THE BAT-HOUND
The Classic Silver Age
Bat-Girl and Batwoman
DC Direct

RELEASE DATE: **2004**
SCALE: **6½ inches**
ARTICULATION: **1 point**

ACE THE BAT-HOUND
Krypto the Superdog
Fisher-Price

RELEASE DATE: **2005**
SCALE: **6 inches**
ARTICULATION: **5 points**
ACCESSORIES: **Wrap-and-trap Batarang**

ACE THE BAT-HOUND
Krypto the Superdog
Fisher-Price

RELEASE DATE: **2005**
SCALE: **6 inches**
ARTICULATION: **5 points**
ACCESSORIES: **Batarang and launcher**
ACTION FEATURE: **Push-button talking feature**

ACE THE BAT-HOUND
Krypto the Superdog
Fisher-Price

RELEASE DATE: **2005**
SCALE: **6 inches**
ARTICULATION: **5 points**
ACCESSORIES: **Bat-sled on wheels, two hyenas,
hyena-seeking missile, net and launcher**

Adventurer Adam Strange
"commutes" from Earth to the
distant planet Rann, courtesy
of the teleporting Zeta Beam!

FIRST APPEARANCE
Showcase No. 17

ADAM STRANGE
JLA (Series 2)
DC Direct

RELEASE DATE: **2004**
SCALE: **6½ inches**
ARTICULATION: **9 points**
ACCESSORIES: **Removable jetpack, ray gun, and
JLA Logo display base**

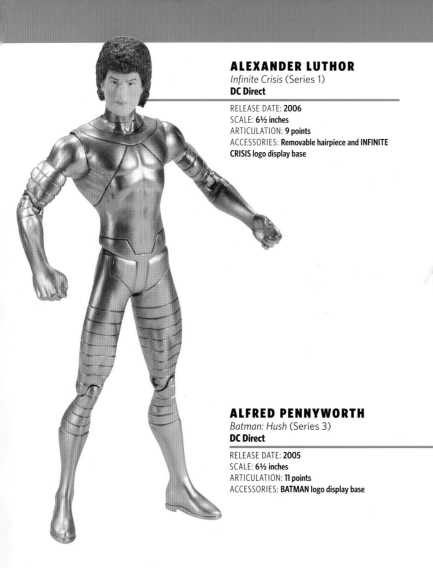

ALEXANDER LUTHOR
Infinite Crisis (Series 1)
DC Direct

RELEASE DATE: **2006**
SCALE: **6½ inches**
ARTICULATION: **9 points**
ACCESSORIES: **Removable hairpiece and INFINITE CRISIS logo display base**

ALFRED PENNYWORTH
Batman: Hush (Series 3)
DC Direct

RELEASE DATE: **2005**
SCALE: **6½ inches**
ARTICULATION: **11 points**
ACCESSORIES: **BATMAN logo display base**

ALFRED PENNYWORTH
The New Batman Adventures
Hasbro

RELEASE DATE: **1998**
SCALE: **4¾ inches**
ARTICULATION: **5 points**
ACCESSORIES: **Serving tray (w/ lobster thermidor under covered dish); four-pack only**
VARIANT: **Black-haired version released with Batcave Command Center**

ALFRED PENNYWORTH
Pocket Super Heroes (Batman Box Set)
DC Direct

RELEASE DATE: **2004**
SCALE: **3¼ inches**
ARTICULATION: **6 points**

> When he first appeared, Batman's faithful butler was named Alfred Beagle.
>
> **FIRST APPEARANCE**
> *Batman* No. 16

NEUMAN!

Beginning in 2001, DC Direct capitalized on the appeal of a *different* sort of Alfred when it released DC Comics super-hero incarnations of *MAD* magazine's titular mascot, Alfred E. Neuman. The *Just-Us League of Stupid Heroes* collection began with Alfred E. Neuman as the World's Finest duo of Batman and Superman (sold separately), each figure standing 6⅛ inches tall and including interchangeable (but certainly *ridiculous*) accessories. Releases in 2002 featured Alfred E. Neuman as the Flash, Green Arrow, Green Lantern, and Robin. His super-hero career (mercifully) short-lived, Alfred maintained his "What, me worry?" demeanor despite wearing homemade versions of classic super-hero costumes.

AMAZO
JLA: Amazing Androids
DC Direct

RELEASE DATE: **2000**
SCALE: **6½ inches**
ARTICULATION: **9 points**
ACCESSORIES: **Golden Lasso**

AMAZO
Justice League Unlimited
Mattel

RELEASE DATE: **2005**
SCALE: **4¾ inches**
ARTICULATION: **5 points**
ACCESSORIES: **Gray: none; gold (single-carded variant): Batarang, mace, and "heat vision" effect**
VARIANTS: **"Invisible" redeco released in Target-exclusive six-pack; winged variant released in three-pack**

ANIMAL MAN
52 (Series 1)
DC Direct

RELEASE DATE: **2007**
SCALE: **6½ inches**
ARTICULATION: **13 points**
ACCESSORIES: **Display base**

During DC Comics' *Crisis on Infinite Earths,* the Anti-Monitor destroyed scores of parallel Earths before his demise. Ironically, during DC's *Infinite Crisis* miniseries in 2006, the Anti-Monitor's giant remains were used to re-create the Multiverse.

FIRST APPEARANCE
Crisis on Infinite Earths No. 2

ANTI-MONITOR
Crisis on Infinite Earths (Series 2)
DC Direct

RELEASE DATE: **2006**
SCALE: **6½ inches**
ARTICULATION: **9 points**
ACCESSORIES: **CRISIS logo display base**

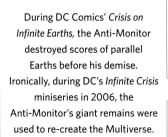

ANTON ARCANE
Swamp Thing
Kenner

RELEASE DATE: **1990**
SCALE: **5 inches**
ARTICULATION: **5 points**
ACCESSORIES: **Glow-in-the-dark spidery biomask and cane**

APOLLO
The Authority
DC Direct

RELEASE DATE: **2002**
SCALE: **6½ inches**
ARTICULATION: **11 points**

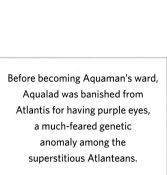

AQUALAD
Action Boy (Captain Action)
Ideal

RELEASE DATE: **1966**
SCALE: **9 inches**
ARTICULATION: **14 points**
ACCESSORIES: **Mask, cloth costume, boots, belt with sea-horse knife, seashell axe, and pet octopus Octo**

Before becoming Aquaman's ward, Aqualad was banished from Atlantis for having purple eyes, a much-feared genetic anomaly among the superstitious Atlanteans.

FIRST APPEARANCE
Adventure Comics No. 269

AQUALAD
Teen Titans
Mego

RELEASE DATE: **1976**
SCALE: **7 inches**
ARTICULATION: **14 points**
ACCESSORIES: **Removable cloth costume, plastic gloves and boots**

AQUALAD
Aquaman and Aqualad
DC Direct

RELEASE DATE: **2001**
SCALE: **6½ inches**
ARTICULATION: **11 points**
ACCESSORIES: **Interchangeable hands and swimming-wave base**

AQUALAD
Pocket Super Heroes (Series 2)
DC Direct

RELEASE DATE: **2003**
SCALE: **3¼ inches**
ARTICULATION: **6 points**
ACCESSORIES: **Display base**

AQUALAD
Teen Titans
Bandai

RELEASE DATE: **2005**
SCALE: **3½ inches**
ARTICULATION: **9 points**

AQUALAD
Teen Titans
Bandai

RELEASE DATE: **2005**
SCALE: **3½ inches**
ARTICULATION: **5 points**
ACCESSORIES: **Harpoon weapon (nonfiring)**

AQUALAD
Teen Titans
Bandai

RELEASE DATE: **2005**
SCALE: **10 inches**
ARTICULATION: **3 points**

AQUALAD
Teen Titans
Bandai

RELEASE DATE: **2006**
SCALE: **5 inches**
ARTICULATION: **13 points**
ACCESSORIES: **Spear gun**

AQUAMAN
Captain Action
Ideal

RELEASE DATE: **1966**
SCALE: **12 inches**
ARTICULATION: **13 points**
ACCESSORIES: **Mask, cloth costume (w/ fins), swordfish sword, conch horns, trident spear, and knife with sheath**

AQUAMAN
World's Greatest Super-Heroes!
Mego

RELEASE DATE: **1972–82**
SCALE: **8 inches**
ARTICULATION: **14 points**
ACCESSORIES: **Cloth costume**

Mego also released this action figure as *Aquaman vs. The Great White Shark,* a box set featuring the Sea King in mortal combat with a battery-operated propeller-driven attacking shark toy.

AQUAMAN
Comic Action Heroes
Mego

RELEASE DATE: **1975–78**
SCALE: **3¾ inches**
ARTICULATION: **5 points**
ACCESSORIES: **Display base**

AQUAMAN
Pocket Super Heroes
Mego

RELEASE DATE: **1979-82**
SCALE: **3¾ inches**
ARTICULATION: **5 points**

AQUAMAN
Super Powers (Series 1)
Kenner

RELEASE DATE: **1984–86**
SCALE: **3¾ inches**
ARTICULATION: **7 points**
ACCESSORIES: **Trident (power-action deep-sea kick)**

AQUAMAN
DC Super Heroes
Toy Biz

RELEASE DATE: **1990**
SCALE: **3¾ inches**
ARTICULATION: **7 points**
ACCESSORIES: **Trident and sea horse (fin-kick action)**

AQUAMAN
Total Justice
Hasbro

RELEASE DATE: **1996**
SCALE: **5 inches**
ARTICULATION: **5 points**
ACCESSORIES: **Fractal techgear armor and blasting hydro spear**
VARIANTS: **Gold armor chase figure in** *TJ* **series; redecoed version in Hasbro's** *JLA* **collection**

Aquaman's left hand was eaten by piranhas, thanks to the villain known as Charybdis.

FIRST APPEARANCE
More Fun Comics No. 73

AQUAMAN
JLA
Hasbro

RELEASE DATE: **1997**
SCALE: **12 inches**
ARTICULATION: **13 points**

AQUAMAN
DC Super Heroes
Hasbro

RELEASE DATE: **1998**
SCALE: **9 inches**
ARTICULATION: **27 points**
ACCESSORIES: **DC BULLET logo display base and cloth costume (nonremovable)**

AQUAMAN
Aquaman and Aqualad
DC Direct

RELEASE DATE: **2001**
SCALE: **6½ inches**
ARTICULATION: **11 points**
ACCESSORIES: **Trident and sea-horse base**
VARIANT: **Redecoed version w/ yellow gloves included in** *The Brave and the Bold* **gift set**

AQUAMAN
Pocket Super Heroes (Series 1)
DC Direct

RELEASE DATE: **2002**
SCALE: **3¼ inches**
ARTICULATION: **6 points**
ACCESSORIES: **Display base**

AQUAMAN
Super Friends!
DC Direct

RELEASE DATE: **2003**
SCALE: **6½ inches**
ARTICULATION: **9 points**
ACCESSORIES: **SUPER FRIENDS! logo display base**

AQUAMAN
JLA (Series 1)
DC Direct

RELEASE DATE: **2003**
SCALE: **6½ inches**
ARTICULATION: **11 points**
ACCESSORIES: **Trident and JLA logo display base**

AQUAMAN
JLA Gift Set
DC Direct

RELEASE DATE: **2005**
SCALE: **6½ inches**
ARTICULATION: **9 points**
ACCESSORIES: **JLA logo display base**

AQUAMAN
Justice (Series 2)
DC Direct

RELEASE DATE: **2003**
SCALE: **7 inches**
ARTICULATION: **11 points**
ACCESSORIES: **Trident and display base**

AQUAMAN
Justice League Unlimited
Mattel

RELEASE DATE: **2004–05**
SCALE: **4¾ inches**
ARTICULATION: **5 points**
ACCESSORIES: **Trident (single-carded only)**

AQUAMAN
Justice League Unlimited
Mattel

RELEASE DATE: **2005**
SCALE: **10 inches**
ARTICULATION: **5 points**

On the *Justice League Unlimited* animated series, Aquaman cut off his own hand with his A-shaped belt buckle in order to save his infant son from death by molten lava.

AQUAMAN
DC Super Heroes:
Justice League Unlimited
Mattel

RELEASE DATE: **2006**
SCALE: **4¾ inches**
ARTICULATION: **5 points**
ACCESSORIES: **Cloak**
VARIANT: **Non-hooked hand released in 2007 JLU three-pack**

AQUAMAN
JLA Classified (Series 1)
DC Direct

RELEASE DATE: **2005**
SCALE: **6½ inches**
ARTICULATION: **11 points**
ACCESSORIES: **Display base**

AQUAMAN
Elseworlds (Series 3: *Kingdom Come*)
DC Direct

RELEASE DATE: **2007**
SCALE: **6½ inches**
ARTICULATION: **3 points**
ACCESSORIES: **Display base and trident**

AQUAMAN
Aquaman 1:6 Scale Deluxe Figure
DC Direct

RELEASE DATE: **2006**
SCALE: **13 inches**
ARTICULATION: **26 points**
ACCESSORIES: **Trident, poseable hands, and display base**

ARAK, SON OF THUNDER
The Lost World of the Warlord
Remco

RELEASE DATE: **1982**
SCALE: **5¼ inches**
ARTICULATION: **6 points**
ACCESSORIES: **Knife and tomahawk**

ARES
*Wonder Woman:
Amazons and Adversaries*
DC Direct

RELEASE DATE: **2001**
SCALE: **6½ inches**
ARTICULATION: **12 points**
ACCESSORIES: **Sword and battle-axe**

ARKKIS CHUMMUCK
*DC Super Heroes:
Justice League Unlimited*
Mattel

RELEASE DATE: **2006**
SCALE: **4¾ inches**
ARTICULATION: **5 points**

Both Arkkis Chummuck and
the villainess known as Fatality
hail from the planet Xanshi,
a world accidentally destroyed by
Green Lantern John Stewart.

FIRST APPEARANCE
Green Lantern Vol. 1, No. 130

ARTEMIS
*Wonder Woman:
Amazons and Adversaries*
DC Direct

RELEASE DATE: **2001**
SCALE: **6½ inches**
ARTICULATION: **8 points**
ACCESSORIES: **Sword and bow**

THE ATOM
Pocket Super Heroes (Series 1)
DC Direct

RELEASE DATE: **2002**
SCALE: **3¼ inches**
ARTICULATION: **6 points**
ACCESSORIES: **Display base**

A former ninety-eight-pound
weakling, Al Pratt added
muscle mass and joined the
JSA to stand up to villainy
as the original Atom.

FIRST APPEARANCE
All-American Comics No. 19

THE ATOM
JSA (Series 1) *Two-Pack*
DC Direct

RELEASE DATE: **2006**
SCALE: **6½ inches**
ARTICULATION: **11 points**
ACCESSORIES: **Two different costumes (fin mask
and full-face mask) and display base**

THE ATOM II
JLA
Hasbro

RELEASE DATE: **1999**
SCALE: **5 inches**
ARTICULATION: **5 points**
ACCESSORIES: **Mini Atom figure and JLA logo
display base**

THE ATOM II
Pocket Super Heroes (JLA Box Set)
Hasbro

RELEASE DATE: **2003**
SCALE: **3¼ inches (The Atom is actually 1 inch tall)**
ARTICULATION: **3 points**
ACCESSORIES: **Display base (attached to figure)**

THE ATOM II
JLA (Series 2)
DC Direct

RELEASE DATE: **1999**
SCALE: **6½ inches**
ARTICULATION: **9 points**
ACCESSORIES: **Standing/seated mini Atom figures
(nonarticulated) and JLA logo display base**

THE ATOM II
Justice League Unlimited
Mattel

RELEASE DATE: **2004**
SCALE: **5 inches**
ARTICULATION: **5 points**
ACCESSORIES: **Mini Atom figure (nonarticulated)**

THE ATOM II
Justice League Unlimited
Mattel

RELEASE DATE: **2005**
SCALE: **10 inches**
ARTICULATION: **5 points**
ACCESSORIES: **Mini Atom figure**

Physicist Ray Palmer was able to
reduce his size and weight after
discovering the peculiar properties
of matter from a white dwarf star.

FIRST APPEARANCE
Showcase No. 34

THE PRIMAL ATOM

Interestingly, the Atom action figure from Hasbro's *JLA* collection was neither the first Atom toy ever released nor the first rendering of DC Comics' "Mighty Mite" for the Rhode Island–based company. Previously, Hasbro produced a nonarticulated Atom mini figure as part of the *DC Super-Heroes: The Flash & Blue Beetle* box set exclusive to comic-book stores. This mini figure was styled after writer/artist Dan Jurgens's costume redesign for the Atom as he appeared in the late-nineties *Teen Titans* comic book relaunch. The mini figure was altered slightly to reflect the Atom's classic costume for inclusion with the five-inch *JLA* action figure.

ATOM SMASHER
Justice League Unlimited
Mattel

RELEASE DATE: **2005**
SCALE: **5 inches**
ARTICULATION: **5 points**
ACCESSORIES: **Fist gauntlet (single-carded only)**

While the Atom is able to reduce his mass, Atom Smasher (formerly known as Nuklon) is capable of increasing his, growing to giant size.

FIRST APPEARANCE
All-Star Squadron No. 25

AZRAEL
Batman: Knight Force Ninjas
Hasbro

RELEASE DATE: **1998**
SCALE: **6½ inches**
ARTICULATION: **6 points**
ACCESSORIES: **Removable cloak, detachable gauntlet blade, and combat training accessory**
ACTION FEATURE: **Real punching action!**

AZRAEL
DC Super Heroes: Batman
Mattel

RELEASE DATE: **2006**
SCALE: **6 inches**
ARTICULATION: **19 points**

AZRAEL AS BATMAN
Batman: Knightfall (Series 1)
DC Direct

RELEASE DATE: **2006**
SCALE: **6½ inches**
ARTICULATION: **11 points**
ACCESSORIES: **KNIGHTFALL logo display base**

AZTEK
Justice League Unlimited
Mattel

RELEASE DATE: **2005**
SCALE: **5 inches**
ARTICULATION: **5 points**
ACCESSORIES: **Shield (single-carded only)**

Azrael donned the mantel of Batman for a tumultuous time after Bane broke the Dark Knight's back.

FIRST APPEARANCE
Batman: Sword of Azrael No. 1

B

BANE
The Adventures of Batman & Robin
Kenner

RELEASE DATE: **1994**
SCALE: **4¾ inches**
ARTICULATION: **5 points**
ACCESSORIES: **Steel beam and "venom" tube**

LETHAL IMPACT BANE
Legends of the Dark Knight
Kenner

RELEASE DATE: **1997**
SCALE: **7 inches**
ARTICULATION: **5 points**
ACCESSORIES: **Stinger gauntlet (venom-powered punch)**

On the island nation of Santa Prisca, Bane was sentenced to life in prison before he was even born.

FIRST APPEARANCE
Batman: Vengeance of Bane No. 1

BANE
Batman & Robin
Kenner

RELEASE DATE: **1997**
SCALE: **5 inches**
ARTICULATION: **5 points**
ACCESSORIES: **Double-attack axe and colossal crusher gauntlet**

BANE
Batman & Robin
Kenner

RELEASE DATE: **1997**
SCALE: **5 inches**
ARTICULATION: **5 points**
ACCESSORIES: **Winch-hook and cable**

BANE
Brain vs. Brawn: Batman vs. Bane Two-Pack
Kenner

RELEASE DATE: **1997**
SCALE: **5 inches**
ARTICULATION: **5 points**
ACCESSORIES: **Hook and venom tube**

BANE
The Batman
Mattel

RELEASE DATE: **2004**
SCALE: **5 inches**
ARTICULATION: **5 points**
ACTION FEATURE: **Bashing action**

BANE
DC Super Heroes: Batman
Mattel

RELEASE DATE: **2005**
SCALE: **6 inches**
ARTICULATION: **12 points**
ACCESSORIES: **"Osoito" teddy bear (chase figure only)**

BANE
Batman: Knightfall
DC Direct

RELEASE DATE: **2006**
SCALE: **6½ inches**
ARTICULATION: **13 points**
ACCESSORIES: **KNIGHTFALL logo display base**

BANE (PUMP-UP)
The Batman
Mattel

RELEASE DATE: **2006**
SCALE: **5 inches**
ARTICULATION: **8 points**

BARBIE GIRLS

Mattel's acquisition of DC Comics' master toy license in 2003 led to one particular union built specifically for a certain Dream House. Beginning in 2004, the California-based toy company released DC super-heroine versions of America's favorite fashion doll, Barbie! To date, Barbie has masqueraded as Batgirl (including a Toys R Us–exclusive release, with accessorizing Batcycle), Wonder Woman, and Supergirl, each with character-specific accoutrements and accompanying mini makeup cases. Of course, Barbie also explored her own dark side by donning the costumes of Catwoman (both Selina Kyle in classic *purr*-ple dress and Halle Berry's feature-film incarnation), Harley Quinn, and Poison Ivy!

BAT-GIRL I (BETTE KANE)
The Classic Silver Age Bat-Girl and Batwoman
DC Direct

RELEASE DATE: 2004
SCALE: 6½ inches
ARTICULATION: 9 points
ACCESSORIES: Utility purse and interlocking Gotham City rooftop display base

BATGIRL II
Super Queens
Ideal

RELEASE DATE: 1967
SCALE: 11½ inches
ARTICULATION: 5 points
ACCESSORIES: Cloth costume, Batarang, and Batrope

BATGIRL II
World's Greatest Super-Heroes!
Mego

RELEASE DATE: 1972-82
SCALE: 8 inches
ARTICULATION: 21 points
ACCESSORIES: Removable plastic cowl and Utility Belt

Inspired by the Caped Crusader to become a crime fighter in her own right, Barbara Gordon's Batgirl saved billionaire Bruce Wayne—Batman himself—from being kidnapped by the Killer Moth during her first adventure.

FIRST APPEARANCE
Detective Comics No. 359

WIND BLITZ BATGIRL
The Adventures of Batman & Robin
Kenner

RELEASE DATE: 1997
SCALE: 4¾ inches
ARTICULATION: 5 points
ACCESSORIES: Sky Glider/Wave Racer

BATGIRL
Legends of the Dark Knight
Kenner

RELEASE DATE: 1997
SCALE: 3¾ inches
ARTICULATION: 5 points
ACCESSORIES: Batarang

BATGIRL
Batman & Robin
Kenner

RELEASE DATE: 1997
SCALE: 4¾ inches
ARTICULATION: 5 points
ACCESSORIES: Battle blade blaster, strike scythe

BATGIRL
Batman & Robin
Kenner

RELEASE DATE: 1997
SCALE: 4¾ inches
ARTICULATION: 5 points
ACCESSORIES: Icestrike cycle

BATGIRL
Batman & Robin
Kenner

RELEASE DATE: **1997**
SCALE: **12 inches**
ARTICULATION: **14 points**
ACCESSORIES: **Grapnel gun**

BATGIRL
Batman & Robin
Kenner

RELEASE DATE: **1997**
SCALE: **12 inches**
ARTICULATION: **9 points**
ACCESSORIES: **Batarang**

BATGIRL
The New Batman Adventures
Kenner

RELEASE DATE: **1998**
SCALE: **12 inches**
ARTICULATION: **14 points**
ACCESSORIES: **Grapnel gun and Batarang**

BATGIRL
Batman: Alliance of Fear
Hasbro: Toys R Us Exclusive

RELEASE DATE: **2002**
SCALE: **4¾ inches**
ARTICULATION: **3 points**
ACCESSORIES: **Launcher and projectile**
VARIANT: **Also included in *Batman: Girls of Gotham City* TRU Exclusive four-pack**

SONIC STUN BATGIRL
Spectrum of the Bat
Hasbro

RELEASE DATE: **2002**
SCALE: **4¾ inches**
ARTICULATION: **5 points**
ACCESSORIES: **Sonic weapon**

BATGIRL
The Classic Silver Age Batgirl and The Joker
DC Direct

RELEASE DATE: **2003**
SCALE: **6½ inches**
ARTICULATION: **11 points**
ACCESSORIES: **Climbing Batrope, Batarang, and interlocking Gotham City rooftop display base**

BATGIRL
Batman: Rise of Sin Tzu
Mattel: UbiSoft Videogame Exclusive

RELEASE DATE: **2003**
SCALE: **4¾ inches**
ARTICULATION: **5 points**
VARIANTS: **Various redecoed versions released by Mattel**

BARBARA GORDON/ BATGIRL II
Secret Files (Series 2: *Unmasked*)
DC Direct

RELEASE DATE: **2005**
SCALE: **6½ inches**
ARTICULATION: **11 points**
ACCESSORIES: **Interchangeable heads (2: w/ cowl and unmasked), Batarang, and UNMASKED! logo display base**

BATGIRL
The Batman: EXP
Mattel

RELEASE DATE: **2005**
SCALE: **5 inches**
ARTICULATION: **4 points**
ACCESSORIES: **Batarang launcher and EXP power key**

BARBARA GORDON TO BATGIRL
The Batman
Mattel

RELEASE DATE: **2006**
SCALE: **5 inches**
ARTICULATION: **4 points**
ACCESSORIES: **Batarang launcher and power key**

BATGIRL
DC Super Heroes: Batman
Mattel

RELEASE DATE: **2006**
SCALE: **6 inches**
ARTICULATION: **23 points**
ACCESSORIES: **Batarang**

BATGIRL (THRILLKILLER)
Elseworlds (Series 1)
DC Direct

RELEASE DATE: **2005**
SCALE: **6½ inches**
ARTICULATION: **9 points**
ACCESSORIES: **Batarang and ELSEWORLDS logo display base**

BATGIRL (ELSEWORLDS FINEST)
Elseworlds (Series 3)
DC Direct

RELEASE DATE: **2006**
SCALE: **6½ inches**
ARTICULATION: **9 points**
ACCESSORIES: **Batzuka and ELSEWORLDS logo display base**

BATGIRL III
First Appearance (Series 3)
DC Direct

RELEASE DATE: **2005**
SCALE: **6½ inches**
ARTICULATION: **11 points**
ACCESSORIES: **Batarang and FIRST APPEARANCE logo display base**

As a mute child, Cassandra Cain was trained by her adoptive father, assassin David Cain, to be a silent killer.

FIRST APPEARANCE
Batman No. 567

BATGIRL III
DC Super Heroes: Batman
Mattel

RELEASE DATE: **2007**
SCALE: **6 inches**
ARTICULATION: **23 points**
ACCESSORIES: **Batarang and diorama**

With hundreds of action figures under his Utility Belt, Batman is the most prolific DC Comics action figure.

FIRST APPEARANCE
Detective Comics No. 27

BATMAN
Captain Action
Mego

RELEASE DATE: **1967**
SCALE: **12 inches**
ARTICULATION: **14 points**
ACCESSORIES: **Costume and mask, boots, Batarang, grappling hook, Batrope reel, Utility Belt (w/ two-way radio, flashlight, and laser torch)**

BATMAN
World's Greatest Super-Heroes!
Mego

RELEASE DATE: **1972–82**
SCALE: **8 inches**
ARTICULATION: **21 points**
ACCESSORIES: **Removable cloth costume, plastic boots, and vinyl gloves**
VARIANT: **Removble cowl**
VEHICLES/PLAYSETS: **Batcave, Batcopter, Batcycle, Batman's Wayne Foundation, Batmobile, and Mobile Bat Lab**

BATMAN
World's Greatest Super-Heroes!:
Fist Fighters
Mego

RELEASE DATE: **1975–76**
SCALE: **8 inches**
ARTICULATION: **21 points**
ACCESSORIES: **Removable cloth costume, plastic boots, and vinyl gloves**
ACTION FEATURE: **Power-fist fighting action**

BATMAN
Comic Action Heroes
Mego

RELEASE DATE: **1975–78**
ARTICULATION: **5 points**
ACCESSORIES: **Batarang w/ Batrope and display base**
VEHICLE/PLAYSET: **The exploding bridge, with Batmobile and activator**

BATMAN
World's Greatest Super-Heroes!
Mego

RELEASE DATE: **1978–80**
SCALE: **12½ inches**
ARTICULATION: **21 points**
ACCESSORIES: **Magnetic hands and feet**
ACTION FEATURE: **Fly-away action**

BATMAN
World's Greatest Super-Heroes!
Mego

RELEASE DATE: **1978–80**
SCALE: **12½ inches**
ARTICULATION: **21 points**
ACCESSORIES: **Cloth costume**

BATMAN
Batman (Diecast Metal)
Mego

RELEASE DATE: **1979–80**
SCALE: **5½ inches**
ARTICULATION: **12 points**

BATMAN
Pocket Super Heroes
Mego

RELEASE DATE: **1979–82**
SCALE: **3¾ inches**
ARTICULATION: **5 points**
VEHICLES/PLAYSETS: **Batcave, Batmachine, and Batmobile**

BATMAN
Super Powers (Series 1)
Kenner

RELEASE DATE: **1984**
SCALE: **3¾ inches**
ARTICULATION: **7 points**
ACTION FEATURE: **Power-action Bat Punch**

BATMAN
Legends of Batman
Kenner

RELEASE DATE: **1995**
SCALE: **5 inches**
ARTICULATION: **6 points**
ACCESSORIES: **Projectile launcher**

BATMAN
Total Justice (Series 1)
Kenner

RELEASE DATE: **1996**
SCALE: **5 inches**
ARTICULATION: **5 points**
ACCESSORIES: **Fractal Techgear flight armor and glider cape**

FRACTAL ARMOR BATMAN
Total Justice (Series 2)
Kenner

RELEASE DATE: **1996**
SCALE: **5 inches**
ARTICULATION: **5 points**
ACCESSORIES: **Fractal Techgear optical shoulder cannon system**

BATMAN
JLA (Series 2)
Kenner

RELEASE DATE: **1998**
SCALE: **5 inches**
ARTICULATION: **5 points**
ACCESSORIES: **JLA logo display base**

DARK KNIGHT BATMAN
JLA (Series 2)
Kenner

RELEASE DATE: **1998**
SCALE: **5 inches**
ARTICULATION: **5 points**
ACCESSORIES: **JLA logo display base**

BATMAN
JLA (Series 4)
Kenner

RELEASE DATE: **1998**
SCALE: **5 inches**
ARTICULATION: **5 points**
ACCESSORIES: **JLA logo display base**

BATMAN
DC Super Heroes
Hasbro: Target Exclusive

RELEASE DATE: **1999**
SCALE: **9 inches**
ARTICULATION: **27 points**
ACCESSORIES: **DC Comics BULLET logo display base**

BATMAN
The Classic Silver Age Batman and Robin
DC Direct

RELEASE DATE: **2003**
SCALE: **6½ inches**
ARTICULATION: **9 points**
ACCESSORIES: **Climbing Batrope w/ suction cup, Batarang, and interlocking Gotham City rooftop display base**

BATMAN
DC Super Heroes
Hasbro

RELEASE DATE: **1999**
SCALE: **7 inches**
ARTICULATION: **10 points**
ACCESSORIES: **Removable cape and display base**
VARIANT: **Cloth cape version released in Toys R Us exclusive four-pack**

KNIGHTFALL BATMAN
DC Super Heroes
Hasbro

RELEASE DATE: **1999**
SCALE: **7 inches**
ARTICULATION: **10 points**
ACCESSORIES: **Display base**

BATMAN
Batman: Guardian of Gotham City
Hasbro: Target Exclusive

RELEASE DATE: **2001**
SCALE: **9 inches**
ARTICULATION: **27 points**
ACCESSORIES: **Cloth outfits (2: Batman costume/ tuxedo), interchangeable heads (2: Batman/Bruce Wayne), removable belt, and wrist cuffs**

BATMAN
Super Friends!
DC Direct

RELEASE DATE: **2003**
SCALE: **6½ inches**
ARTICULATION: **9 points**
ACCESSORIES: **Batplane miniature and SUPER FRIENDS! logo display base**

BATMAN
Pocket Super Heroes (JLA Box Set)
DC Direct

RELEASE DATE: **2003**
SCALE: **3¼ inches**
ARTICULATION: **6 points**
ACCESSORIES: **Removable cape**

BATMAN
Batman
Mattel

RELEASE DATE: **2003**
SCALE: **4¾ inches**
ARTICULATION: **5 points**
VARIANTS: **All of the following two-pack releases are redecoed versions of the same figure.**

BATMAN & NIGHTWING

BATTLE SCARS BATMAN VS. CATWOMAN

BATMAN & ROBIN

TECH SUIT BATMAN VS. TWO-FACE

BATMAN VS. JOKER

BATMAN
Kingdom Come (Series 2)
DC Direct

RELEASE DATE: **2003**
SCALE: **6½ inches**
ARTICULATION: **11 points (9: figure; 2: poseable wings)**
ACCESSORIES: **Lance**

BATMAN
Justice League
Mattel

RELEASE DATE: **2003**
SCALE: **5 inches**
ARTICULATION: **5 points**
ACCESSORIES: **Display base**
VARIANTS: **Black suit release**

BATMAN
Batman: Hush (Series 1)
DC Direct

RELEASE DATE: **2004**
SCALE: **6½ inches**
ARTICULATION: **10 points**
ACCESSORIES: **Interchangeable hand (w/ grapnel gun) and BATMAN logo display base**

BATMAN
Pocket Super Heroes (Batman Box Set)
DC Direct

RELEASE DATE: **2004**
SCALE: **3¼ inches**
ARTICULATION: **6 points**
ACCESSORIES: **Removable cape and Batman's JLA chair**

BATMAN
First Appearance (Series 1)
DC Direct

RELEASE DATE: **2004**
SCALE: **6½ inches**
ARTICULATION: **13 points + wires in poseable cape**
ACCESSORIES: **Mini comic and FIRST APPEARANCE logo display base**

BATMAN
Justice League: Mission Vision
Mattel

RELEASE DATE: **2004**
SCALE: **4¾ inches**
ARTICULATION: **10 points**
ACCESSORIES: **Projectile-launching flight pack, Mission Vision Bat-Shield, and glider armor**

BATMAN
Batman: The Dark Knight Returns (Series 1)
DC Direct

RELEASE DATE: **2004**
SCALE: **6½ inches**
ARTICULATION: **11 points**
ACCESSORIES: **Batarang, string, and sidewalk display base**

STEALTH JUMPSUIT BATMAN
Batman: Hush (Series 3)
DC Direct

RELEASE DATE: **2005**
SCALE: **6½ inches**
ARTICULATION: **11 points**
ACCESSORIES: **BATMAN logo display base**

BATMAN
JLA Gift Set
DC Direct

RELEASE DATE: **2005**
SCALE: **6½ inches**
ARTICULATION: **9 points**
ACCESSORIES: **JLA logo display base**

BATMAN
Superman/Batman
(Series 1: *Public Enemies*)
DC Direct

RELEASE DATE: **2005**
SCALE: **6½ inches**
ARTICULATION: **11 points**
ACCESSORIES: **SUPERMAN/BATMAN logo display base**

BATMAN
Justice (Series 2)
DC Direct

RELEASE DATE: **2005**
SCALE: **7 inches**
ARTICULATION: **9 points**
ACCESSORIES: **Folding Batarang and display base**

BATMAN
1:6 Scale Deluxe Series
DC Direct

RELEASE DATE: **2006**
SCALE: **13 inches**
ARTICULATION: **26 points**
ACCESSORIES: **Batarangs (4) and display base**

CRIMSON MIST BATMAN
Elseworlds (Series 1)
DC Direct

RELEASE DATE: **2005**
SCALE: **6½ inches**
ARTICULATION: **13 points (including wings)**
ACCESSORIES: **Wooden dagger and display base**

THRILLKILLER BATMAN
Elseworlds (Series 1)
DC Direct

RELEASE DATE: **2005**
SCALE: **6½ inches**
ARTICULATION: **9 points**
ACCESSORIES: **Display base**

GOTHAM BY GASLIGHT BATMAN
Elseworlds (Series 2)
DC Direct

RELEASE DATE: **2006**
SCALE: **6½ inches**
ARTICULATION: **11 points**
ACCESSORIES: **Display base**

31

BATMAN
Batman: The Long Halloween (Series 1)
DC Direct

RELEASE DATE: **2006**
SCALE: **6½ inches**
ARTICULATION: **11 points**
ACCESSORIES: **Batarang and display base**

BATMAN: MASK OF TENGU
Batman: Knightfall (Series 1)
DC Direct

RELEASE DATE: **2006**
SCALE: **6½ inches**
ARTICULATION: **13 points**
ACCESSORIES: **KNIGHTFALL logo display base**

BATMAN
Identity Crisis (Series 2)
DC Direct

RELEASE DATE: **2006**
SCALE: **6½ inches**
ARTICULATION: **11 points**
ACCESSORIES: **IDENTITY CRISIS logo display base**

BATMAN
Superman/Batman
(Series 2: *The Return of Supergirl*)
DC Direct

RELEASE DATE: **2006**
SCALE: **6½ inches**
ARTICULATION: **11 points**
ACCESSORIES: **Astro-Glider, battle staves, shoulder armor, and SUPERMAN/BATMAN display base**

BATMAN
ReActivated (Series 1)
DC Direct

RELEASE DATE: **2006**
SCALE: **6½ inches**
ARTICULATION: **10 points**
ACCESSORIES: **Display base**

RED SON BATMAN
Elseworlds (Series 1)
DC Direct

RELEASE DATE: **2006**
SCALE: **6½ inches**
ARTICULATION: **11 points**
ACCESSORIES: **Batcycle, remote detonator, and display base**

BATMAN
Batman: Dark Victory (Series 1)
DC Direct

RELEASE DATE: **2006**
SCALE: **6½ inches**
ARTICULATION: **11 points**
ACCESSORIES: **Display base**

BATMAN
Crisis on Infinite Earths (Series 3)
DC Direct

RELEASE DATE: **2006**
SCALE: **6½ inches**
ARTICULATION: **11 points**
ACCESSORIES: **CRISIS logo display base**

BATMAN
DC Super Heroes (S3-Select Sculpt)
Mattel

RELEASE DATE: **2006**
SCALE: **6 inches**
ARTICULATION: **24 points**
ACCESSORIES: **Batarangs (7)**

BATMAN
Batman Armor (Justice Series 6)
DC Direct

RELEASE DATE: **2007**
SCALE: **6½ inches**
ARTICULATION: **12 points**
ACCESSORIES: **Display base**

BATMAN
Batman Through the Ages (Modern)
DC Direct

RELEASE DATE: **2007**
SCALE: **6½ inches**
ARTICULATION: **9 points**
ACCESSORIES: **Display base**

BATMAN
Batman Through the Ages (1940s)
DC Direct

RELEASE DATE: **2007**
SCALE: **6½ inches**
ARTICULATION: **11 points**
ACCESSORIES: **Display base**

BATMAN
Batman Through the Ages
(Super Friends Variant)
DC Direct

RELEASE DATE: **2007**
SCALE: **6½ inches**
ARTICULATION: **9 points**
ACCESSORIES: **Display base**

BATMAN
Batman Begins 1:6 Scale Deluxe
Collector Figure
DC Direct

RELEASE DATE: **2005**
SCALE: **3 inches**
ARTICULATION: **26 points**
ACCESSORIES: **Batarangs (3), grappling gun, cell phone, alternate hands, and display base**

KRYPTONITE BATMAN
Superman/Batman (Series 4)
DC Direct

RELEASE DATE: **2007**
SCALE: **6½ inches**
ARTICULATION: **11 points**
ACCESSORIES: **Display base**

BATMAN: THE ANIMATED SERIES (KENNER)

Batman: The Animated Series was hailed for its "cartoon noir" approach to the Dark Knight. Beginning in 1992, Kenner adapted the award-winning animation as action figures, leading off one of the longest-running Batman collections ever produced.

ACTION FIGURES

ANTI-FREEZE BATMAN
ARTICULATION: **5 points**
ACCESSORIES: **Firing Shield Blaster**

BATTLE HELMET BATMAN
(MAIL-IN EXCLUSIVE)
ARTICULATION: **5 points**
ACCESSORIES: **Snap-On Launcher w/ Launching Bat-Signal Discs**

COMBAT BELT BATMAN
ARTICULATION: **5 points**
ACCESSORIES: **Firing grappling hook and missile**

CYBER GEAR BATMAN
ARTICULATION: **5 points**
ACCESSORIES: **Hi-tech armor and power-launch weapon**

INFRARED BATMAN
ARTICULATION: **5 points**
ACCESSORIES: **Launching Bat-Signal Discs**

KNIGHT STAR BATMAN
ARTICULATION: **5 points**
ACCESSORIES: **Star Blade rocket launcher**

LIGHTNING STRIKE BATMAN
ARTICULATION: **5 points**
ACCESSORIES: **Transforming Cape Glider**

RADAR SCOPE BATMAN
ARTICULATION: **5 points**
ACCESSORIES: **Firing turbo missiles and Sky-Scan radar gear**

RAPID ATTACK BATMAN
ARTICULATION: **5 points**
ACCESSORIES: **Escape hook and Utility Belt**

SKY DIVE BATMAN
ARTICULATION: **5 points**
ACCESSORIES: **Working parachute for surprise attacks!**

TORNADO BATMAN
ARTICULATION: **5 points**
ACCESSORIES: **Whirling weapon**

TURBOJET BATMAN
ARTICULATION: **5 points**
ACCESSORIES: **Firing wrist rocket and pivoting engines**

CRIME SQUAD ACTION FIGURES

AIR ASSAULT BATMAN
ARTICULATION: **5 points**
ACCESSORIES: **Transforming Techno-Wing backpack**

LAND STRIKE BATMAN
ARTICULATION: **5 points**
ACCESSORIES: **Techno-Claw backpack**

PIRANHA BLADE BATMAN
ARTICULATION: **5 points**
ACCESSORIES: **Techno-Shield backpack**

SEA CLAW BATMAN
ARTICULATION: **5 points**
ACCESSORIES: **Techno-Dive backpack**

STEALTHWING BATMAN
ARTICULATION: **5 points**
ACCESSORIES: **Techno-Flight backpack**

TORPEDO BATMAN
ARTICULATION: **5 points**
ACCESSORIES: **Techno-Torpedo backpack**

DELUXE FIGURES

GROUND ASSAULT BATMAN
ARTICULATION: **5 points**
ACCESSORIES: **Motorized turbo-powered ground jet**

HIGH WIRE BATMAN
ARTICULATION: **5 points**
ACCESSORIES: **Quick-escape cable wire**

MECH WING BATMAN
ARTICULATION: **5 points**
ACCESSORIES: **Mechanized soaring wings**

POWER VISION BATMAN
ARTICULATION: **5 points**
ACCESSORIES: **Electric light-up eyes and firing glow-in-the-dark missile**

BATMAN: THE ANIMATED SERIES (KENNER)

TWO-PACK

NINJA POWER PACK BATMAN AND ROBIN
ARTICULATION: **5 points each**
ACCESSORIES: **Duo-power ninja weapons**

FOUR-PACK

ARKHAM ASYLUM ESCAPE: BATMAN, TWO-FACE, POISON IVY, AND HARLEY QUINN
ACCESSORIES: **Arkham gate, grappling hook (Batman), boxing glove and trick pistol (Harley Quinn), Venus flytrap and poison dart weapon (Poison Ivy), straightjacket and machine gun (Two-Face)**
NOTE: **All previously released figures.**

LARGE-SIZE FIGURE

ULTIMATE BATMAN
ARTICULATION: **2 points**
ACCESSORIES: **Light-up electric eyes and Bat-Emblem**

VEHICLES/PLAYSETS

AERO BAT
ACCESSORIES: **Escape seat and missile blaster**

BATCAVE COMMAND CENTER
ACCESSORIES: **Computer command console, Batman/Bruce Wayne chamber, breakaway skylights, sky cable, catwalk trap, and hidden vehicle entrance**

BATCYCLE
ACCESSORIES: **Nonremovable Batman**

BATMOBILE
ACCESSORIES: **Escape Jet Batplane**

BATPLANE
ACCESSORIES: **Missile launchers and hook**
VARIANTS: **Released in subsequent Hasbro *Animated Batman* assortments. Hasbro's Batplane mold was used by Mattel for its initial *Animated Batman* assortments, as well as its *Justice League* line.**

BAT-SIGNAL JET
ACCESSORIES: **Flashing Bat-Signal light**

B.A.T.V.
ACCESSORIES: **Converts from snow speeder to launching racer**
VARIANTS: **Released in subsequent Hasbro *Animated Batman* assortments**

BRUCE WAYNE STREET JET
ACCESSORIES: **Missile launchers and Bruce Wayne figure**
VARIANTS: **Bruce Wayne Custom Coupe (*Batman Returns*)**
NOTE: **The same mold was used for Clark Kent's car in Hasbro's Superman line based on the animated series.**

ELECTRONIC CRIME STALKER
ACCESSORIES: **Power laser sounds and firing missile**

HYDRO BAT
ACCESSORIES: **Water Blasts-Off accessory**
VARIANTS: **Released in subsequent Hasbro *Animated Batman* assortments**

ICE HAMMER
ACCESSORIES: **"Ice" blasting drill and firing missile**

THE JOKER MOBILE
ACCESSORIES: **Pop-up guns and Launching Smile Missile**
NOTE: **This vehicle was originally designed for *The Dark Knight Collection* but was retooled for *B:TAS* instead.**

ROBIN DRAGSTER
ACCESSORIES: **Missile launcher**
NOTE: **This vehicle was originally designed for *The Dark Knight Collection* under the name Gotham Dragster but never saw production; a factory fire during production made this the rarest *B:TAS* vehicle.**

ACCESSORIES

COLLECTOR CASE (TARA TOY CORPORATION)

BATMAN: MASK OF THE PHANTASM (KENNER)

The first full-length Batman animated film, *Batman: Mask of the Phantasm*, introduced the Dark Knight to a new vigilante in Gotham! Kenner's 1993 mini-collection included all-new figures, supplemented by a few redecoed Dark Knights.

ACTION FIGURES

DECOY BATMAN
ARTICULATION: **5 points**
ACCESSORIES: **Crime-fighting decoy disguise**

RAPID ATTACK BATMAN
ARTICULATION: **5 points**
ACCESSORIES: **Escape hook and Utility Belt Spinning battle spear**
VARIANTS: **Combat Belt Batman (*Batman: The Animated Series*), Retro Batman**

TORNADO BATMAN
ARTICULATION: **5 points**
ACCESSORIES: **Whirling weapon**
VARIANTS: **Tornado Batman (*Batman: The Animated Series*)**

TOTAL ARMOR BATMAN
ARTICULATION: **5 points**
ACCESSORIES: **Full-body armor and shield**

THE ADVENTURES OF BATMAN & ROBIN (KENNER)

By 1997, *Batman: The Animated Series* had evolved into *The Adventures of Batman & Robin.* Kenner's accompanying line added the first-ever Harley Quinn and Rā's al Ghūl action figures to its assortments, which also included the D.U.O. Force sub-assortment of Dual Usage Operation vehicles and the first Batgirl figure for the series.

ACTION FIGURES

HOVER JET BATMAN
ARTICULATION: **5 points**
ACCESSORIES: **BatStaff and Hoverjet**

PARAGLIDE BATMAN
ARTICULATION: **5 points**
ACCESSORIES: **Dive-bomb sky wing**

ROCKETPAK BATMAN
ARTICULATION: **5 points**
ACCESSORIES: **Firing turbo thrust cannon**

ACTION FIGURE BOX SET

ROGUES GALLERY (DIAMOND COMICS DISTRIBUTORS EXCLUSIVE)
Includes the following redecoed figures w/ accessories: Catwoman, Man-Bat, Killer Croc, Poison Ivy, Scarecrow, The Joker, Clayface, Phantasm

VEHICLE

NIGHTSPHERE

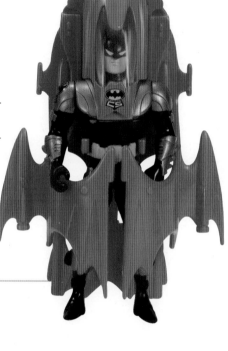

CRIME SQUAD ACTION FIGURES

BOMB CONTROL BATMAN
ARTICULATION: **5 points**
ACCESSORIES: **Techno-Armor backpack**

DISASTER CONTROL BATMAN
ARTICULATION: **5 points**
ACCESSORIES: **Techno-Rescue backpack**

FAST PURSUIT BATMAN
ARTICULATION: **5 points**
ACCESSORIES: **Techno-Bike backpack**

SUPER SONIC BATMAN
ARTICULATION: **5 points**
ACCESSORIES: **Techno-Rocket backpack**

STEALTHWING BATMAN
ARTICULATION: **5 points**
ACCESSORIES: **Transforming Techno-Flight backpack**

CRIME SQUAD DELUXE FIGURES

SKYCOPTER BATMAN
ARTICULATION: **5 points**
ACCESSORIES: **Techno-Rotor backpack**

TRI WING BATMAN
ARTICULATION: **5 points**
ACCESSORIES: **Techno-Glide backpack**

CRIME SQUAD VEHICLES

BATCYCLE: TRIPLE ATTACK JET
NOTE: **Three different vehicles in one!**

D.U.O. FORCE FIGURES

CYCLE THRUSTER BATMAN
ARTICULATION: **5 points**
ACCESSORIES: **Bat "cycle"**

TURBO SURGE BATMAN
ARTICULATION: **5 points**
ACCESSORIES: **Sky Glider/Wave Racer**

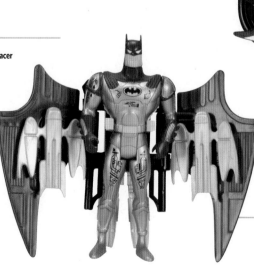

VECTOR WING BATMAN
ARTICULATION: **5 points**
ACCESSORIES: **Delta wing and land cruiser**

THE NEW BATMAN ADVENTURES (KENNER)

Beginning in 1998, Kenner's final foray into all-new animated Bat-figures was *The New Batman Adventures,* notable for including the very first toy based on DC Comics' the Creeper!

ACTION FIGURES

DETECTIVE BATMAN
ARTICULATION: **5 points**
ACCESSORIES: **Missile Flight Pack Infrared Lens Decoder Cape**
VARIANTS: **Desert Attack Batman** *(Batman: Mission Masters 1)*

KNIGHT GLIDER BATMAN
ARTICULATION: **5 points**
ACCESSORIES: **Jet Wing Pack Anti-Crime Cam: two rockets**
VARIANTS: **Sky Attack Batman** *(Batman: Mission Masters 3)*; **JetWing Batman** *(Batman: Mission Master 4)*

STREET STRIKE BATMAN
ARTICULATION: **5 points**
ACCESSORIES: **Lightning luge (sled w/ wheels) and Batarang decoder**
VARIANTS: **Ground Pursuit Batman** *(Batman: Mission Masters 3)*; **Tunnel Racer Batman** *(Batman: Mission Masters 4)*

DELUXE FIGURES

SILVER DEFENDER BATMAN
ARTICULATION: **5 points**
ACCESSORIES: **Assault force sled and multi-launching cannon.**
VARIANTS: **Golden Armor Batman** *(Batman Beyond: ROTJ)*

TWELVE-INCH FIGURES

BATMAN
ARTICULATION: **16 points**
ACCESSORIES: **Utility Belt radios, grapnel gun, and Batarangs (3)**

TWO-PACKS

BATMAN VS. TWO-FACE
ARTICULATION: **5 points each**
ACCESSORIES: **Arkham Asylum gate, machine gun and pistol, Bat Grapple, cape**

TEAM BATCYCLE (BATMAN AND NIGHTWING)
ARTICULATION: **5 points each**
ACCESSORIES: **Batcycle and sidecar**

WORLD'S FINEST TWO-PACK (BATMAN AND SUPERMAN)
ARTICULATION: **5 points each**
ACCESSORIES: **Removable cloth capes**

FOUR-PACKS (TOYS R US EXCLUSIVES)

BATMAN, ROBIN, ALFRED, AND CLAYFACE
ARTICULATION: **5 points each**
ACCESSORIES: **Serving tray w/ lobster thermidor under covered dish (Alfred); missile launcher (Batman); Redwing Skyfighter (Robin); break-open safe and dynamite (Clayface)**
NOTE: **All figures except Alfred are redecos.**

GOTHAM CITY ENFORCEMENT TEAM: BATMAN, NIGHTWING, COMMISSIONER GORDON, AND BATGIRL
ARTICULATION: **5 points each**
ACCESSORIES: **Trap Nightwing, Decoder Shield, and Grappling Hook (Batman); two pistols (Commissioner Gordon); missile launcher (Batgirl [*B:TAS* design])**
NOTE: **All figures except Commissioner Gordon are redecos.**

KNIGHT FORCE HERO COLLECTION (TARGET EXCLUSIVE): BATMAN, BATGIRL, NIGHTWING, AND ROBIN
ARTICULATION: **5 points each**
ACCESSORIES: **Disc launchers**
NOTE: **All figures are redecos.**

SUPER HEROES VS. SUPER-VILLAINS: BATMAN, SUPERMAN, THE JOKER, AND LEX LUTHOR
ARTICULATION: **5 points each**
ACCESSORIES: **Missile launcher (Batman); Funny Guns (Joker); Armor (Lex Luthor)**
NOTE: **All figures are redecos. Superman and Luthor are from Kenner's *Superman* collection.**

VEHICLES/PLAYSETS

BATMOBILE
ACCESSORIES: **Exclusive Batman figure Escape Jet pull-out front-wheel shredders**

BATMOBILE (TOYS R US EXCLUSIVE)
ACCESSORIES: **Includes Batman figure**

GOTHAM CITY BANK
ACCESSORIES: **Bust-out front doors, bending vault bars, bags of cash, gold bars, handcuffs, bending street light**

THE JOKER TOXIC LAB
ACCESSORIES: **Bubbling acid bath, capture claw, pogo stick, blue gun**

KNIGHT STRIKER BATMOBILE
ACCESSORIES: **Hidden missile launcher**

MISSION MASTERS ACTION FIGURES

ANTI-BLAZE BATMAN
ARTICULATION: **5 points**
ACCESSORIES: **Rescue pack and water cannon**

CAVE CLIMBER BATMAN
ARTICULATION: **5 points**
ACCESSORIES: **Grappling launcher and pickax**

DESERT ATTACK BATMAN
ARTICULATION: **5 points**
ACCESSORIES: **Missile flightpack**

GLIDER STRIKE BATMAN
ARTICULATION: **5 points**
ACCESSORIES: **Missile flightpack**
VARIANTS: **Knight Assault Batman** *(Batman: Mission Masters 3)*

JUNGLE TRACKER BATMAN
ARTICULATION: **5 points**
ACCESSORIES: **Electro Trap and machete**

SLALOM RACER BATMAN
ARTICULATION: **5 points**
ACCESSORIES: **Rocket skis and flame missile**

SPEEDBOAT BATMAN
ARTICULATION: **5 points**
ACCESSORIES: **Batboat racer and blasting torpedoes**

TWO-PACKS

TEAM BATCYCLE
VARIANTS: **Team Batcycle** *(The New Batman Adventures)*
NOTE: **Two-in-one vehicle with Batman and Nightwing! Jetwing sidecar converts into an aerial assault craft.**

MISSION MASTERS 2 ACTION FIGURES

INFRARED BATMAN
ARTICULATION: **5 points**
ACCESSORIES: **Photon disc backpack**

KNIGHT STRIKE BATMAN
ARTICULATION: **5 points**
ACCESSORIES: **Blastwing backpack and smoke bombs**

LANDSTRIKE BATMAN
ARTICULATION: **5 points**
ACCESSORIES: **Mech-arm claw**

RADAR BATMAN (DELUXE)
ARTICULATION: **5 points**
ACCESSORIES: **Spring-action claw**

SEA CLAW BATMAN
ARTICULATION: **5 points**
ACCESSORIES: **Spring-action claw**

SKY CHOPPER BATMAN (DELUXE)
ARTICULATION: **5 POINTS**
ACCESSORIES: **Sky chopper flight pack**

MISSION MASTERS 3 ACTION FIGURES

GOTHAM CRUSADER BATMAN
ARTICULATION: **5 points**
ACCESSORIES: **Battle shield launcher**

GROUND PURSUIT BATMAN
ARTICULATION: **5 points**
ACCESSORIES: **All-terrain Batsled and Batarang**

INFERNO EXTINCTION BATMAN
ARTICULATION: **5 points**
ACCESSORIES: **Rescue pack and extinguisher**

KNIGHT ASSAULT BATMAN
ARTICULATION: **5 points**
ACCESSORIES: **Glider and Batarang claw**

MOUNTAIN PURSUIT BATMAN
ARTICULATION: **5 points**
ACCESSORIES: **Launching Batarang hook**

SKY ATTACK BATMAN
ARTICULATION: **5 points**
ACCESSORIES: **Batwing Batpack and smoke torpedos**

> The *Mission Masters 3* line also included action figures based on Superman, the *Batman Beyond* animated series, and the comics version of Batman.

BATMAN BEYOND

CAPTURE CAPE BATMAN
ARTICULATION: **5 points**
ACCESSORIES: **Energy capture wing**

FIRE WING BATMAN (DELUXE)
ARTICULATION: **7 points**
ACCESSORIES: **Assault pack**

FREESTYLE SKATE BATMAN (DELUXE)
ARTICULATION: **7 points**
ACCESSORIES: **Batwing assault board**

HIGHWIRE ZIP-LINE BATMAN
ARTICULATION: **7 points**
ACCESSORIES: **Sliding cable gear**

QUICK ATTACK BATMAN
ARTICULATION: **5 points**
ACCESSORIES: **Batarang launcher**

MISSION MASTER 4 ACTION FIGURES

ANTI-VIRUS BATMAN (DELUXE)
ARTICULATION: **5 points**
ACCESSORIES: **Spinning light-up force ring and Netshredder suit**

LUNAR ATTACK BATMAN
ARTICULATION: **5 points**
ACCESSORIES: **Night attack wing backpack**

NIGHT SHADOW BATMAN
ARTICULATION: **5 points**
ACCESSORIES: **High speed glide**

R.A.M. BAT BATMAN (DELUXE)
ARTICULATION: **5 points**
ACCESSORIES: **Arachnotech Assault Module**
VARIANT: **Green variation**

VIRUS DELETE BATMAN
ARTICULATION: **5 points**
ACCESSORIES: **Circuit Tech Heat Blaster**

SPECTRUM OF THE BAT (KENNER)

Primarily redecoed versions of previously released figures, *Spectrum of the Bat* ended Kenner's long and successful run of Batman toys.

ACTION FIGURES

FRACTAL ARMOR BATMAN
ARTICULATION: **5 points**
ACCESSORIES: **Transmission-scrambling discs and launcher**

GAMMA BLAST BATMAN
ARTICULATION: **5 points**
ACCESSORIES: **Gamma-reflecting cruiser and Batarang**

INFRARED ARMOR BATMAN
ARTICULATION: **5 points**
ACCESSORIES: **Infrared jet pack**

SIGNAL HACKER BATMAN
ARTICULATION: **5 points**
ACCESSORIES: **Sonic-pulse missile launcher**

SUB-FREQUENCY ARMOR BATMAN
ARTICULATION: **5 points**
ACCESSORIES: **Sonic projectile launcher**

ULTRA-FREQUENCY ARMOR BATMAN
ARTICULATION: **5 points**
ACCESSORIES: **Wave-deflector cape and projectile launcher**

ULTRAVIOLET AMBUSH BATMAN
ARTICULATION: **5 points**
ACCESSORIES: **Anti-ultraviolet land-ski w/ missiles**

BATMAN (HASBRO)

Before leaving the Caped Crusader completely, Kenner produced several *Batman* multipacks and vehicles as Toys R Us Exclusives, offering a few remaining felons to round out the Dark Knight's Rogues Gallery.

TWO-PACKS

ONLY IN JEST: BATMAN VS. HARLEY QUINN
ARTICULATION: **5 points each**
ACCESSORIES: **Grappling hook (Batman); Knockout punching glove and trick pistol (Harley Quinn)**
NOTE: **All figures are redecos. See individual villain listings.**

LAUGHING MATTER: BATMAN VS. THE JOKER
ARTICULATION: **5 points each**
ACCESSORIES: **Firing projectile launcher (Batman); dynamite bundle and pistol (Joker)**
NOTE: **All figures are redecos. See individual villain listings.**

FOUR-PACKS

REVENGE OF THE PENGUIN: BATMAN, ROBIN, CATWOMAN, AND THE PENGUIN
ARTICULATION: **5 points each**
ACCESSORIES: **Glider (Batman); launcher and projectile (Robin); whip, cat, and claw gauntlets (Catwoman); umbrella (Penguin)**
NOTE: **All figures except for the Penguin are redecos. See individual villain listings.**

PUPPETS OF CRIME: BATMAN, NIGHTWING, KILLER CROC, AND THE VENTRILOQUIST W/ SCARFACE
ARTICULATION: **5 points each except for Ventriloquist (3 points)**
ACCESSORIES: **Removable cape, mask, and gauntlets (Batman); shield and grappling hook launcher (Nightwing); crocodile (Killer Croc); Scarface (Ventriloquist)**
NOTE: **All figures except for Ventriloquist are redecos. See individual villain listings.**

ALLIANCE OF FEAR: BATMAN, BATGIRL, THE JOKER, AND THE SCARECROW
ARTICULATION: **5 points each except for Batgirl (3 points)**
ACCESSORIES: **Grappling hook launcher (Batman); launcher and projectile (Batgirl); water-squirting backpack and gas mask (Joker); scythe and raven (Scarecrow)**
NOTE: **All figures except for Batgirl are redecos. See individual villain listings.**

SHADOWS OF GOTHAM CITY: BATMAN, ROBIN, RÃ'S AL GHÜL, AND TALIA
ARTICULATION: **5 points except for Talia (3 points)**
ACCESSORIES: **Photon disc backpack (Batman); Hover sled (Robin); firing projectile launcher (Rã's al Ghül); pistols (Talia)**
NOTE: **All figures except for Rã's al Ghül and Talia are redecos. See individual villain listings.**

FROZEN ASSETS: BATMAN, NIGHTWING, MR. FREEZE, AND POISON IVY
ARTICULATION: **5 points each except for Mr. Freeze (4 points)**
ACCESSORIES: **Quad missile launcher (Batman); jet wings and missile launcher (Nightwing); Venus flytrap and crossbow (Poison Ivy); freeze pack and disc launcher (Mr. Freeze)**
NOTE: **All figures except for Poison Ivy are redecos. See individual villain listings.**

GIRLS OF GOTHAM CITY: CATWOMAN, POISON IVY, TALIA, AND BATGIRL
ARTICULATION: **5 points (Catwoman and Poison Ivy); 3 points (Batgirl and Talia)**
ACCESSORIES: **Launcher and projectile (Batgirl); pistols (Talia); Venus flytrap and crossbow (Poison Ivy); whip, claw gauntlets, and cat (Catwoman)**
NOTE: **All figures are redecos. See individual villain listings.**

CLASSIC BATMAN (HASBRO)

Based on the artwork of Batman creator Bob Kane, Hasbro's *Classic Batman* collection in 1998 featured two versions of the Dark Knight dynamically posed on display bases featuring artwork from *Batman* No. 1 and No. 4, respectively, as well as Batman's stylized Golden Age comics logo.

ACTION FIGURES

BATMAN NO. 1
ARTICULATION: **5 points**
ACCESSORIES: **Display base**

BATMAN NO. 4
ARTICULATION: **5 points**
ACCESSORIES: **Display base**

THE BATMAN MASTERPIECE EDITION (HASBRO)

Designed by Alex Ross, Joe DeVito, and Chip Kidd, and based on Bob Kane's original Dark Knight, this Hasbro-produced Golden Age Batman action figure accompanied *The Batman Masterpiece Edition,* a 2000 box set from Chronicle Books spotlighting Les Daniels' history of Batman's early years.

GOLDEN AGE BATMAN
ARTICULATION: **25 points**
ACCESSORIES: **Poseable cape and Batarang**

BATMAN: LIMITED 100TH EDITION (HASBRO)

The 100th Batman action figure produced by Kenner/Hasbro featured an all-new sculpt of the Dark Knight, with a vac-metallized deco, posed heroically on a Gothic Gotham City display base.

GOLDEN AGE BATMAN
ARTICULATION: **5 points**
ACCESSORIES: **Sword and display base**

WORLD OF BATMAN (HASBRO: WAL-MART EXCLUSIVES)

Hasbro produced a limited series of Batman action figures exclusively for Wal-Mart retail stores. The figures are primarily redecos of previous figures released in various collections but with new, generic likenesses as opposed to those of Michael Keaton and Jack Nicholson as Batman and the Joker.

ACTION FIGURES

AQUA SLED BATMAN
ARTICULATION: **5 points**
ACCESSORIES: **Submarine assault sled and scuba armor**

HOVER JET BATMAN
ARTICULATION: **5 points**
ACCESSORIES: **Blasting battle sled**

RADAR SCOPE BATMAN
ARTICULATION: **5 points**
ACCESSORIES: **Pulse-Scan Blaster**

TWO-PACK

GOTHAM CITY ADVENTURES: BATMAN AND KNIGHT WATCH BATMAN
ARTICULATION: **5 points each**

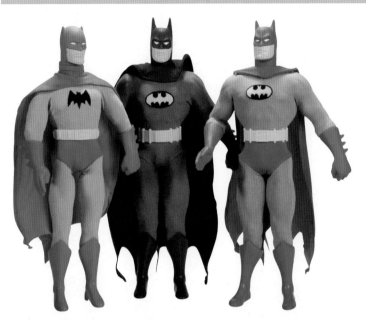

THE HISTORY OF BATMAN COLLECTION (HASBRO)

Hasbro's *The History of Batman Collection* featured three 12-inch-scale fully pose-able incarnations of the Dark Knight: Golden Age, Silver Age, and Modern Age. Interestingly, some of the box sets were released with the Silver and Modern Age Batmen's Bat-Symbols reversed, yellow bat on a black oval instead of the correct black bat on a yellow oval.

GOLDEN AGE BATMAN (FAR LEFT)
ARTICULATION: **21 points**

SILVER AGE BATMAN (MIDDLE)
ARTICULATION: **21 points**

MODERN AGE BATMAN (LEFT)
ARTICULATION: **21 points**

LEGENDS OF BATMAN (KENNER)

Kenner's *Legends of Batman* collection in 1994 included five-inch comic book adaptations of the Dark Knight and his foes, the majority of which were based on DC Comics' series of alternate-reality "Elseworlds." Most notable is the very first Nightwing action figure.

Premise: The Legends of Batman have always existed and always will, throughout history and into the future. Inspired by the timeless DC comics, the *Legends of Batman* action-figure collection features the dark super hero as he's never been seen before, "stronger and more muscular," battling crime throughout time.

ACTION FIGURES

BUCCANEER BATMAN
ARTICULATION: **5 points**
ACCESSORIES: **Cutlass and mace**
VARIANT: **Redeco released as Warner Bros. Store Exclusive**

CRUSADER BATMAN
ARTICULATION: **6 points**
ACCESSORIES: **Projectile launcher**
ACTION FEATURE: **Powerful punching action!**
VARIANT: **Redeco released as Warner Bros. Store Exclusive**

CYBORG BATMAN
ARTICULATION: **5 points**
ACCESSORIES: **Light-up eye and laser weapon (projectile launcher)**
VARIANT: **Redeco released as Warner Bros. Store Exclusive**

DARK WARRIOR BATMAN
ARTICULATION: **6 points**
ACCESSORIES: **Shield and mace**
ACTION FEATURE: **Slamming mace attack!**
VARIANT: **Redeco released as Warner Bros. Store Exclusive**

LEGENDS OF BATMAN

FUTURE BATMAN
ARTICULATION: **5 points**
ACCESSORIES: **Pop-up aero-power wings and projectile launcher**
VARIANT: **Redeco released as Warner Bros. Store Exclusive**

GLADIATOR BATMAN
ARTICULATION: **5 points**
ACCESSORIES: **Spear launcher**
VARIANT: **Redeco released as Warner Bros. Store Exclusive**

KNIGHTQUEST BATMAN
ARTICULATION: **5 points**
ACCESSORIES: **Battle wings and blazing missile (projectile launcher)**
VARIANT: **Redeco released as Warner Bros. Store Exclusive**

KNIGHTSEND BATMAN
ARTICULATION: **5 points**
ACCESSORIES: **Aerial torpedo launcher**
VARIANT: **Redeco released as Warner Bros. Store Exclusive**

LONG BOW BATMAN
ARTICULATION: **5 points**
ACCESSORIES: **Bow, quiver w/ arrows, and sword**
ACTION FEATURE: **Arrow-slinging assault!**

POWER GUARDIAN BATMAN
ARTICULATION: **6 points**
ACCESSORIES: **Sword, dagger, and shield**
ACTION FEATURE: **Real sword-fighting action!**
VARIANT: **Redeco released as Warner Bros. Store Exclusive**

SAMURAI BATMAN
ARTICULATION: **5 points**
ACCESSORIES: **Sword, spiked staff, and flag**
ACTION FEATURE: **Slashing sword and spike action!**
VARIANT: **Redeco released as Warner Bros. Store Exclusive**

ULTRA ARMOR BATMAN
ARTICULATION: **5 points**
ACCESSORIES: **Blasting battle cannon (projectile launcher)**

VIKING BATMAN
ARTICULATION: **6 points**
ACCESSORIES: **Battle-axe and shield**
ACTION FEATURE: **Swinging battle-axe action!**
VARIANT: **Redeco released as Warner Bros. Store Exclusive**

100TH EDITION BATMAN
ARTICULATION: **5 points**
ACCESSORIES: **Display base**
VARIATIONS: **1997 Hong Kong Batman**

1997 HONG KONG BATMAN (COMMEMORATIVE EDITION)
ARTICULATION: **5 points**
ACCESSORIES: **Display base**
NOTE: **Redeco of 100th Edition Batman**

DESERT KNIGHT BATMAN
ARTICULATION: **7 points**
ACCESSORIES: **Whirling scimitar swords (2) and double battle staves**

ENERGY SURGE BATMAN
ARTICULATION: **7 points**
ACCESSORIES: **Sonic stun blaster (projectile launcher)**

FLIGHTPAK BATMAN
ARTICULATION: **7 points**
ACCESSORIES: **Flightpak and weapon**
ACTION FEATURE: **Battle-ready jet wing action!**

SILVER KNIGHT BATMAN
ARTICULATION: **5 points**
ACCESSORIES: **Shield, sword, and mace**
ACTION FEATURE: **Sword-slashing action!**

TWO-PACKS

PIRATE BATMAN VS. PIRATE TWO-FACE
ARTICULATION: **6 points**
ACCESSORIES: **Swords**
NOTE: **See Two-Face villain listing for Pirate Two-Face.**

EGYPTIAN BATMAN VS. EGYPTIAN CATWOMAN
ARTICULATION: **5 points**
ACCESSORIES: **Headdress and staff**
NOTE: **See Catwoman listing for Egyptian Catwoman.**

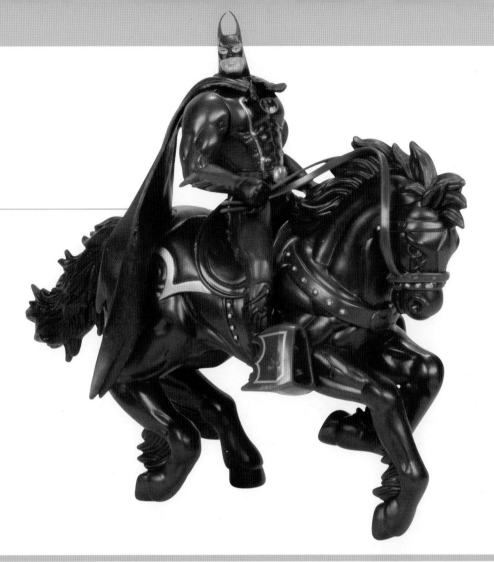

BATCYCLE W/ BATMAN FIGURE (ATTACHED)
ACTION FEATURES: Super wheelie power!

BATMOBILE
ACTION FEATURES: Missile detonator and Quick-Lift canopy
VARIANT: Knight Star Batmobile (*Batman: Knight Force Ninjas*)

DARK RIDER BATMAN: REARING BATTLE STALLION
ACTION FEATURES: Whipping arm and slashing sword action!

SKYBAT
ACTION FEATURES: Wing-mount missile and menacing jaw attack!

LARGE-SIZE FIGURES

ULTIMATE KNIGHTQUEST BATMAN
SCALE: 15 inches
ARTICULATION: 3 points
ACCESSORIES: Energy disc weapon

BATMAN VS. CATWOMAN: BATMAN
SCALE: 12 inches
ARTICULATION: 16 points

BATMAN: KNIGHT FORCE NINJAS (HASBRO)

Capitalizing on Batman's martial arts prowess, Hasbro's *Batman: Knight Force Ninjas* line sported the Dark Knight, Robin, Azrael, and several villains with fighting action features and breakaway ninja combat accessories. The card art was supplied by comic book artist Scott McDaniel, artist of Batman, Nightwing, and Robin at different times in his ongoing career.

ACTION FIGURES

ARSENAL CAPE BATMAN
ARTICULATION: 5 points
ACCESSORIES: Ninja combat weaponry
ACTION FEATURE: Blast-open weapons cape!

FIST FURY BATMAN
ARTICULATION: 7 points
ACCESSORIES: Ninja combat weaponry
ACTION FEATURE: Real spinning-fist action!

KARATE CHOP BATMAN
ARTICULATION: 9 points
ACCESSORIES: Ninja combat weaponry
ACTION FEATURE: Sword battling action!

KNIGHT BLADE BATMAN
ARTICULATION: 11 points
ACCESSORIES: Ninja combat weaponry
ACTION FEATURE: Real punching action!

POWER KICK BATMAN
ARTICULATION: 8 points
ACCESSORIES: Ninja combat weaponry
ACTION FEATURE: Real kicking action!

THUNDER KICK BATMAN
ARTICULATION: 11 points
ACCESSORIES: Ninja combat weaponry
ACTION FEATURE: Real roundhouse kick!

DELUXE FIGURE

MULTI-BLAST BATMAN
ARTICULATION: 7 points
ACCESSORIES: Swords
ACTION FEATURE: Power punch and karate kick!

VEHICLE

KNIGHT STAR BATMOBILE
ACTION FEATURE: Missile launcher
VARIANT: Batmobile (*Legends of Batman*); Knight Star Batmobile also available with a World of Batman figure

LEGENDS OF THE DARK KNIGHT

Kenner supersized Batman and his friends and foes in 1997 with the debut of the seven-inch-scale *Legends of the Dark Knight* collection. Set in a "twisted parallel Gotham City where the criminals are unimaginably deadly and in total control," *LODK* action figures featured Neural Suit and Responsive Camouflage technologies for the Dynamic Duo. Lasting just two series, *LODK* is notable for having some of the rarest Batman toys after a *ToyFare* magazine contest awarded one hundred exclusive redecos of Bat Attack Batman, Glacier Shield Batman, Laughing Gas Joker, and Panther Prowl Catwoman to twenty-five lucky readers (four figures per prize).

Premise: From a horrible nightmare, Batman has awakened in an alternate reality where the villains are in control. Batman fights back to regain control by developing Neural Suit technology that taps into his thoughts and impulses and automatically reacts to danger. Batman has now become a living, breathing weapon.

ACTION FIGURES

ASSAULT GAUNTLET BATMAN
ARTICULATION: **5 points**
ACCESSORIES: **Spike strike missile gloves**

BAT ATTACK BATMAN
ARTICULATION: **5 points**
ACCESSORIES: **Robotic Mission Bat converts into sonic surveillance armor**

DARK KNIGHT DETECTIVE BATMAN (HASBRO.COM/DIAMOND COMIC DISTRIBUTORS EXCLUSIVE)
ARTICULATION: **5 points**
ACCESSORIES: **Batarang**

GLACIER SHIELD BATMAN
ARTICULATION: **5 points**
ACCESSORIES: **Ice Shard Expansion Cape and climbing spikes**

LAVA FURY BATMAN
ARTICULATION: **5 points**
ACCESSORIES: **Solar array wings and fire-swallower blast shield**

NEURAL CLAW BATMAN
ARTICULATION: **5 points**
ACCESSORIES: **Capture grip cape and massive razor claws**

SHATTER BLADE BATMAN (HASBRO.COM/DIAMOND COMIC DISTRIBUTORS EXCLUSIVE)
ARTICULATION: **5 points**
ACCESSORIES: **Assault cape and arm swords**

SPLINE CAPE BATMAN
ARTICULATION: **5 points**
ACCESSORIES: **Spiked assault cape and arm swords**

UNDERWATER ASSAULT BATMAN
ARTICULATION: **5 points**
ACCESSORIES: **Manta cape and sea claw**

VEHICLE (W/ FIGURE)

SKYWING STREET BIKE: BATMAN
ARTICULATION: **5 points**
ACCESSORIES: **Converts from ground vehicle to air assault vehicle**

BATMAN (MATTEL)

Mattel's acquisition of the Batman master toy license in 2002 led to a small assortment of Batman toys based on the Dark Knight's animated adventures in 2003, as the company prepared for its all-out Bat-Assault.

ACTION FIGURE TWO-PACKS

BATMAN AND BATGIRL
ARTICULATION: **5 points each**
NOTE: **See Batgirl listing for figure.**

BATMAN AND ROBIN
ARTICULATION: **5 points each**
NOTE: **See Robin listing for figure.**

BATMAN AND NIGHTWING
ARTICULATION: **5 points each**
NOTE: **See Nightwing listing for figure.**

BATMAN VS. CATWOMAN
ARTICULATION: **5 points each**
NOTE: **See Catwoman listing for figure.**

BATMAN VS. THE JOKER
ARTICULATION: **5 points each**
NOTE: **See Joker listing for figure.**

BATMAN VS. TWO-FACE
ARTICULATION: **5 points each**
NOTE: **See Two-Face listing for figure.**

ACTION FIGURES (SINGLE-CARDED)

NOTE: **All except for the Penguin are redecoed figures from the previous two-packs.**

BATGIRL
ARTICULATION: **5 points**

BATMAN
ARTICULATION: **5 points**

NIGHTWING
ARTICULATION: **5 points**

PENGUIN
ARTICULATION: **5 points**

ROBIN
ARTICULATION: **5 points**

FIGURE FOUR-PACKS (TOYS R US EXCLUSIVES)

NOTE: **All except for the Penguin are redecoed figures from the previous two-packs.**

GOTHAM CITY FIGURES PACK NO. 1: BATMAN, CATWOMAN, THE JOKER, AND TWO-FACE
ARTICULATION: **5 points each**

GOTHAM CITY FIGURES PACK NO. 1: BATMAN, BATGIRL, NIGHTWING, AND ROBIN
ARTICULATION: **5 points each**

ATTACK OF THE PENGUIN FIGURE PACK: BATMAN, BATGIRL, NIGHTWING, AND THE PENGUIN
ARTICULATION: **5 points each**
ACCESSORIES: **Umbrella (Penguin)**

THE RISE OF SIN TZU VIDEO GAME EXCLUSIVES

NOTE: **Batman and Robin are redecos of previous Mattel releases. Batgirl is the first Mattel release of the character in animation-style deco.**

BATGIRL
ARTICULATION: **5 points each**

BATMAN
ARTICULATION: **5 points each**

NIGHTWING
ARTICULATION: **5 points each**

ROBIN
ARTICULATION: **5 points each**

VEHICLES/PLAYSETS (TOYS R US EXCLUSIVES)

BATMOBILE
ACTION FEATURE: **Two vehicles in one! Deploy jet from Batmobile for aerial pursuit**
ACCESSORIES: **Includes Batman figure**

BATPLANE
ACTION FEATURE: **Rotating capture hook and firing projectiles (2)**
ACCESSORIES: **Includes Batman figure**

WAYNE MANOR/THE BATCAVE PLAYSET
ACCESSORIES: **Includes Alfred figure (see individual listing)**

BATMAN (MATTEL)

In 2003, Mattel's Batman action-figure collection built on comic book likenesses in a six-inch scale, with (of course) Batman's seemingly endless costume variations and designs by the Four Horsemen.

ACTION FIGURES (SERIES 1)

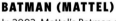

BATTLE ARMOR BATMAN
ARTICULATION: **10 points**
ACCESSORIES: **Battle armor, combat blade, and belt blade**

HYDRO SUIT BATMAN
ARTICULATION: **12 points**
ACCESSORIES: **Dive pack w/ breathing mask and missile launcher**

MARTIAL ARTS BATMAN
ARTICULATION: **10 points**
ACCESSORIES: **Dual axe staff and hand blade**

ZIPLINE BATMAN
ARTICULATION: **10 points**
ACCESSORIES: **Zipline and Batarang**

BATMAN (MATTEL)

NIGHT PATROL BATMAN
ARTICULATION: **10 points**
ACCESSORIES: **Shield and Batarang launcher**

STEALTH ARMOR BATMAN
ARTICULATION: **10 points**
ACCESSORIES: **Stealth armor, missile launcher, and jet boots**

TECH ARMOR BATMAN
ARTICULATION: **10 points**
ACCESSORIES: **Laser cannon, claw arm, and disc launcher**

ACTION FIGURES (SERIES 2)

ARCTIC SHIELD BATMAN
ARTICULATION: **10 points**
ACCESSORIES: **Arctic shield, axe launcher, backpack, and goggles**

BATTLE SPIKE BATMAN
ARTICULATION: **8 points**
ACCESSORIES: **Battle spike and combat armor**

ACTION FIGURES (SERIES 3)

CROC ARMOR BATMAN
ARTICULATION: **8 points**
ACCESSORIES: **Wing blades and spring-loaded claws**

ELECTRO NET BATMAN
ARTICULATION: **10 points**
ACCESSORIES: **Electro-Net discs, launcher, goggles, and gauntlets**

SNARE STRIKE BATMAN
ARTICULATION: **8 points**
ACCESSORIES: **Retractable snare rope and missile launcher**

ZIPLINE BATMAN
ARTICULATION: **10 points**
ACCESSORIES: **Batarang and zipline**
NOTE: **This is a re-release of the Series 1 figure.**

DELUXE FIGURES (SERIES 3)

BATTLE SLED BATMAN
ARTICULATION: **12 points**
ACCESSORIES: **Battle sled and missile launchers**

DRILL CANNON BATMAN
ARTICULATION: **8 points**
ACCESSORIES: **Drill cannon, missiles (6), battle wings, and claw**

SKY STRIKE BATMAN
ARTICULATION: **12 points**
ACCESSORIES: **Wing pack and net missiles**

TWO-PACKS (SERIES 1–2)

NOTE: Batman is a redeco of single-carded figure.

BATMAN & NIGHTWING: BATMAN
ARTICULATION: **10 points**
ACCESSORIES: **Battle shield**

BATMAN & SUPERMAN: BATMAN
ARTICULATION: **11 points**
ACCESSORIES: **Combat communicator and disc launcher**

TWO-PACKS (SERIES 3)

NOTE: All figures except for Nightwing (see individual listing) are redecos of single-carded figures.

BATMAN & NIGHTWING: BATMAN
ARTICULATION: **10 points**
ACCESSORIES: **Battle shield**
NOTE: **New packaging from Series 1-2 releases**

BATMAN & ROBIN: BATMAN
ARTICULATION: **5 points**

BATMAN VS. THE JOKER: BATMAN
ARTICULATION: **5 points**

TWO-PACKS (SERIES 4)

NOTE: All figures are redecos of single-carded figures.

BATMAN VS. MR. FREEZE: ARCTIC SHIELD BATMAN
ARTICULATION: **10 points**

BATMAN VS. KILLER CROC: BATMAN
ARTICULATION: **12 points**
ACCESSORIES: **Batshield**
NOTE: **Each figure features "battle damage" deco.**

SUMMER CONVENTION EXCLUSIVES

2003 BATMAN
ARTICULATION: **10 points**
ACCESSORIES: **Batarang, Batcuffs, and grapnel gun**
NOTE: **Redeco of Zipline Batman w/ new Utility Belt and "classic" deco, including yellow oval Bat-Symbol**

2003 BATMAN UNMASKING
ARTICULATION: **10 points**
VERSION: NO. 1: **Removing cowl**
VERSION: NO. 2: **Cowl back**
VERSION: NO. 3: **Cowl back w/ "Battle Damage" deco**
NOTE: **Redeco of Zipline Batman w/ new head sculpts (3 versions)**

12-INCH ACTION FIGURES

ULTIMATE BATMAN (2003)
Target/Toys R Us/Kay-Bee Toys
ARTICULATION: **12 points**
ACCESSORIES: **Batarang, Batcuffs, rope-launcher, torch, and display stand**

ULTIMATE BATMAN (2004)
Target/Toys R Us
ARTICULATION: **12 points**
ACCESSORIES: **Base**

VEHICLES

BATCOPTER
ACTION FEATURE: **Missile launcher**

BATCYCLE
ACTION FEATURE: **Missile launcher**

BATJET
ACTION FEATURE: **Disk launcher**

BATMOBILE
ACTION FEATURE: **Detachable street-jet, removable Bat-wing glider (for action figure), and a front grille projectile launcher**
VARIANT: **K-Mart sold an exclusive redecoed vehicle.**
NOTE: **Mattel's Batmobile release for this series was recalled shortly after its release when the attachable tail-fins were deemed poking hazards. At no cost, the company mailed replacement rounded fins to owners anxious to keep their Batmobile in play.**

BATMAN BEYOND (HASBRO)

Batman Beyond imagined the Dark Knight of the twenty-first century as teenager Terry McGinnis, who donned the mantle of the Bat in aged Bruce Wayne's stead to continue the good fight in policing Gotham City. Hasbro's action figure collection played heavily on Batman's high-tech upgrades to the Batsuits.

ACTION FIGURES (BASIC)

BALLISTIC BLADE BATMAN
ARTICULATION: **5 points**
ACCESSORIES: **Batarang disc barrage**

BAT-HANG BATMAN
ARTICULATION: **5 points**
ACCESSORIES: **Covert cape and upside-down action**

ENERGY STRIKE BATMAN
ARTICULATION: **5 points**
ACCESSORIES: **Lightning cape and neutron missiles**

FUTURE KNIGHT BATMAN
ARTICULATION: **5 points**
ACCESSORIES: **Electro-swords and glider wings**

HYDRO FORCE BATMAN
ARTICULATION: **5 points**
ACCESSORIES: **Aqua torpedo and propulsion armor**

JUSTICE FLIGHT BATMAN
ARTICULATION: **3 points**
ACCESSORIES: **Display base**
NOTE: **This 200th Edition Batman action figure marked Kenner/Hasbro's long run of Batman toys, with still more to follow.**

LASER BATMAN
ARTICULATION: **5 points**
ACCESSORIES: **Hyper-flight gear and pulse missile**

LIGHTNING STORM BATMAN
ARTICULATION: **5 points**
ACCESSORIES: **Force-field cape and lightning weapons**

MANTA RACER BATMAN
ARTICULATION: **5 points**
ACCESSORIES: **Surf sled and stinger tail**

POWER ARMOR BATMAN
ARTICULATION: **5 points**
ACCESSORIES: **Anti-gravity armor and strike R.O.B.I.N.**

POWER CAPE BATMAN
ARTICULATION: **7 points**
ACCESSORIES: **Dual Batarang and jet thrusters**

SONAR STRIKE BATMAN
ARTICULATION: **5 points**
ACCESSORIES: **Ramjet rocket pack and dual wing blaster**

SURFACE-TO-AIR BATMAN
ARTICULATION: **5 points**
ACCESSORIES: **Converting mobile assault cape**

THUNDER WHIP BATMAN
ARTICULATION: **5 points**
ACCESSORIES: **Recoiling stun flare**

ACTION FIGURES (DELUXE)

ENERGY SURGE BATMAN
ARTICULATION: **5 points**
ACCESSORIES: **Dual audio CD-ROM**

NEON-CAMO BATMAN
ARTICULATION: **5 points**
ACCESSORIES: **Pump-action launcher and combat-ready canine (Ace the Bathound)**

STRATO-DEFENSE BATMAN
ARTICULATION: **5 points**
ACCESSORIES: **Knight Hunter patrol jet and thermal disc blaster**

STRIKECYCLE BATMAN
ARTICULATION: **5 points**
ACCESSORIES: **Street armor and Batcycle**

TOMORROW ARMOR BATMAN
ARTICULATION: **5 points**
ACCESSORIES: **Water spray cannon**

VEHICLE

STREET TO SKY BATMOBILE
ACTION FEATURES: **Two-in-one vehicle and disc launcher**

LARGE-SIZE FIGURES

BATMAN
SCALE: **9 inches**
ARTICULATION: **27 points (including wings)**
ACCESSORIES: **Retractable Batarang and line (in back of figure)**

AFTER BURNER BATMAN
SCALE: **12 inches**
ARTICULATION: **7 points**
ACCESSORIES: **Electronic talking feature**

BATMAN BEYOND: BATLINK

ACTION FIGURES

CODEBUSTER BATMAN
ARTICULATION: **5 points**
ACCESSORIES: **Shield cape and retriever missile**

PARTICLE BURST BATMAN
ARTICULATION: **5 points**
ACCESSORIES: **Quantumizer Batarang**

POWER GRID BATMAN
ARTICULATION: **5 points**
ACCESSORIES: **Five-finger booster shield**

SEARCH ENGINE BATMAN
ARTICULATION: **5 points**
ACCESSORIES: **Cyber-scope vision**

VIRTUAL BAT (DELUXE)
ACCESSORIES: **Plug-in and light-up interface**

VEHICLES/PLAYSETS

NET ESCAPE PLAYSET
ACTION FEATURES: **Includes firing turbo missiles (2) and exclusive Batman Beyond action figure**

NET RUNNER BATMOBILE
ACTION FEATURES: **Launching "delete" missile**

BATMAN BEYOND: RETURN OF THE JOKER (HASBRO)

Batman Beyond: Return of the Joker was a full-length animated film featuring the future Dark Knight's first appearance with his namesake's worst nemesis: The Clown Prince of Crime! Hasbro continued the *BB* collection with *Return of the Joker* action figures, mixing the Batmen of today and tomorrow. However, although fans clamored for a futuristic Joker or Bruce Wayne, the line consisted solely of redecoes.

ACTION FIGURES

GOTHAM DEFENDER BATMAN
ARTICULATION: **5 points**
ACCESSORIES: **Bat-pack missile launcher**

GOTHAM KNIGHT BATMAN
ARTICULATION: **5 points**
ACCESSORIES: **Jet-booster cape and ion swords**

ACTION FIGURES (DELUXE)

GOLDEN ARMOR BATMAN
ARTICULATION: **5 points**
ACCESSORIES: **Mobile assault cannon**

BATMAN (TOY BIZ)

Toy Biz's 1989 *Batman* collection was fairly conservative, given the mega-success of the Dark Knight's first cinematic endeavor since 1966. Critics who scoffed at the choice of comedian Michael Keaton to play Batman nevertheless hailed director Tim Burton's gothic vision of Gotham City and its Dark Knight protector. With just Batman, the Joker, and Joker's henchman Bob the Goon, the following assortment focused on the Dark Knight's vehicles (only the Batmobile and Batwing were actually seen in the film) and playsets rather than endless variations on Batman.

ACTION FIGURES

BATMAN (MICHAEL KEATON LIKENESS)
ARTICULATION: **7 points**
ACCESSORIES: **Batarang, Batrope, and grapnel gun**

BATMAN (SQUARE JAW)
ARTICULATION: **7 points**
ACCESSORIES: **Batarang, Batrope, and grapnel gun**

BATMAN (ROUND JAW)
ARTICULATION: **7 points**
ACCESSORIES: **Batarang, Batrope, and grapnel gun**

VEHICLES/PLAYSETS

BATCAVE
ACTION FEATURE: **Five action-packed movie scenes!**

BATCYCLE
ACTION FEATURE: **Drop-down Batwings**

BATMOBILE
ACTION FEATURE: **Rocket launcher (w/ 2 concealed rockets)**

BATMOBILE (W/ COCOON)
ACTION FEATURE: **Rocket launcher (w/ 2 concealed rockets) and cocoon**

BATWING
ACTION FEATURE: **Villain cruncher**

JOKER CYCLE
ACTION FEATURE: **Detachable launching sidecar**

JOKER VAN
ACTION FEATURE: **Water-shooting cannon**

THE DARK KNIGHT COLLECTION (KENNER)

Kenner's acquisition of the Batman master toy license in 1990 predated the second Batman movie, *Batman Returns*. But ramping up to its movie toy releases, Kenner offered the following action figures in *The Dark Knight Collection*, playing on Batman's vast arsenal of gadgetry with a Caped Crusader for every occasion.

ACTION FIGURES

CRIME ATTACK BATMAN
ARTICULATION: **5 points**
ACCESSORIES: **Batarang and claw (w/ launcher)**

IRON WINCH BATMAN
ARTICULATION: **5 points**
ACCESSORIES: **Batarang winch**

SHADOW WING BATMAN
ARTICULATION: **5 points**
ACCESSORIES: **Handcuffs**
ACTION FEATURE: **Cape-spreading pop-up arms**

TEC-SHIELD BATMAN
ARTICULATION: **5 points**
ACCESSORIES: **Flight pack and shield suit**
VARIANT: **While the common version featured a black pulley mechanism, a rarer version featured gold.**

THUNDERWHIP BATMAN
ARTICULATION: **5 points**
ACCESSORIES: **Weapons**
ACTION FEATURE: **Spinning arm**

DELUXE FIGURES

BLAST SHIELD BATMAN
ARTICULATION: **5 points**
ACCESSORIES: **Double barrel bola missile**

CLAW CLIMBER BATMAN
ARTICULATION: **5 points**
ACCESSORIES: **Moving wings and firing missile**

NIGHT GLIDER BATMAN
ARTICULATION: **5 points**
ACCESSORIES: **Giant glider (w/ moveable wings and capture hook)**

VEHICLES/PLAYSETS

BATCAVE COMMAND CENTER
ACTION FEATURE: **Computer command console, Batman/Bruce Wayne chamber, breakaway skylights, sky cable, catwalk trap, and hidden vehicle entrance**

BATCOPTER
ACTION FEATURE: **Launching missile cone, capture winch, and criminal spinner**

BATCYCLE
ACTION FEATURE: **Rapid-action rocket**

BATJET
ACTION FEATURE: **Blast-off missile and spring action wings**

BATMOBILE
ACTION FEATURE: **Firing nose missile and pop-up machine guns**

GOTHAM CITY DRAGSTER
ACTION FEATURE: **Suspension and launching Batarang**

THE JOKER CYCLE
ACTION FEATURE: **Firing Joker mask**

THE JOKER MOBILE
ACTION FEATURE: **Anti-aircraft machine guns and firing Joker teeth**

SKYBLADE
ACTION FEATURE: **Ejecting cockpit**

STRIKE WING
ACTION FEATURE: **Firing heat-seeking missile**

TURBOJET BATWING
ACTION FEATURE: **Three vehicles in one!**

ACCESSORIES

COLLECTORS CASE (TARA TOY CORP.)
NOTE: **Holds twelve figures**

BATMAN RETURNS (KENNER)

The Dark Knight returned to movie screens in 1992, with Michael Keaton reprising his role as Batman and facing both Catwoman (Michelle Pfeiffer) and the Penguin (Danny DeVito) in *Batman Returns*. Kenner's toy assortments based on the film continued to build on Batman having a Batsuit or vehicle for every occasion. Interestingly, the toy depiction of the Penguin is based on his comic book incarnation and not DeVito's on-screen character. In addition, Robin was added to the mix, although the character would not appear in the Batman film series until the subsequent sequel.

ACTION FIGURES

AERO STRIKE BATMAN
ARTICULATION: **5 points**
ACCESSORIES: **Ultrasonic armor and firing rocket**

AIR ATTACK BATMAN
ARTICULATION: **5 points**
ACCESSORIES: **Camouflage artillery gear**

ARCTIC BATMAN
ARTICULATION: **5 points**
ACCESSORIES: **Polar armor and ice blaster weapon**

CRIME ATTACK BATMAN
ARTICULATION: **5 points**
ACCESSORIES: **Firing claw and Batarang**

DEEP DIVE BATMAN
ARTICULATION: **5 points**
ACCESSORIES: **Torpedo-launching scuba gear**

HYDRO CHARGE BATMAN
ARTICULATION: **5 points**
ACCESSORIES: **Water-blast missile**

JUNGLE TRACKER BATMAN
ARTICULATION: **5 points**
ACCESSORIES: **Shoulder-mount launcher**

LASER BATMAN
ARTICULATION: **5 points**
ACCESSORIES: **Missile-firing radar dish**
NOTE: While all basic Batman figures of *Batman Returns* and *DKC* shared the same body, Laser Batman's was retooled with a grid pattern.

NIGHT CLIMBER BATMAN
ARTICULATION: **5 points**
ACCESSORIES: **Quick-climbing hook**

POWERWING BATMAN
ARTICULATION: **5 points**
ACCESSORIES: **Firing wing**

SKY WINCH BATMAN
ARTICULATION: **5 points**
ACCESSORIES: **Batarang winch**

THUNDERWHIP BATMAN
ARTICULATION: **5 points**
ACCESSORIES: **Turbo weapon spinning arm**

DELUXE FIGURES

**BOLA STRIKE BATMAN
(TOYS R US EXCLUSIVE)**
ARTICULATION: **5 points**
ACCESSORIES: **Firing double-barrel bola missile**

**CLAW CLIMBER BATMAN
(TOYS R US EXCLUSIVE)**
ARTICULATION: **5 points**
ACCESSORIES: **Moveable wings and firing missile**
ACTION FEATURE: **Climbs like a bat!**

FIREBOLT BATMAN
ARTICULATION: **5 points**
ACTION FEATURE: **Deploy weapon to activate light beam and light electronic sounds!**

**POLAR BLAST BATMAN
(TOYS R US EXCLUSIVE)**
ARTICULATION: **5 points**
ACCESSORIES: **Giant glider (w/ moveable wings and capture hook)**

ROCKET BLAST BATMAN
ARTICULATION: **5 points**
ACCESSORIES: **Deployable wings**
ACTION FEATURE: **Electronic blast-off and laser sounds**

LARGE-SIZE FIGURE

BATMAN
SCALE: **15 inches**
ARTICULATION: **2 points**

VEHICLES/PLAYSETS

ALL-TERRAIN BATSKIBOAT
ACTION FEATURE: **Retractable skis and firing torpedoes**

BATCAVE COMMAND CENTER
ACTION FEATURE: **Computer command console, Batman/Bruce Wayne chamber, breakaway skylights, sky cable, catwalk trap, and hidden vehicle entrance**
NOTE: This was originally designed for Series 2 of *DKC* but never saw production. Its success would allow multiple redecoed versions in future lines.

BATMAN SKYBLADE
ACTION FEATURE: **Ejecting cockpit**

LASER BLADE CYCLE
ACTION FEATURE: **Converts to fighter jet!**

THE PENGUIN UMBRELLA JET
ACCESSORIES: **Spraying "knock out" gas; umbrella bombs**

ROBIN JET FOIL
ACCESSORIES: **Firing ground-level assault missile**

SKY DROP AIRSHIP
ACCESSORIES: **Hidden compartment for surprise attacks**

SKY BLADE
ACCESSORIES: **Hidden compartment for surprise attacks**

TURBOJET BATWING
ACTION FEATURE: **Converts to street racer and Turbo Glider**
NOTE: Collectors' case (Tara Toy Corporation) holds 12 figures

BATMOBILE
ACCESSORIES: **Special-edition Batman figure**
ACTION FEATURE: **Firing nose missile, pop-up machine guns**
VARIANTS: Batmobile (*The Dark Knight Collection*); Batmobile (*Batman Returns*)

BATMISSILE BATMOBILE
ACCESSORIES: **Machine guns**
ACTION FEATURE: **Divides into three vehicle assemblies**

BRUCE WAYNE CUSTOM COUPE
ACCESSORIES: **Special-edition Bruce Wayne action figure**
ACTION FEATURE: **"Changes" Bruce Wayne into Batman and converts to a sleek fighting machine**

CAMO ATTACK BATMOBILE
ACCESSORIES: **Firing nose missile and pop-up machine guns; special-edition Batman figure**
VARIANTS: Batmobile (*The Dark Knight Collection*); Batmobile (*Batman Returns*)

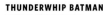

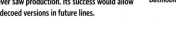

BATMAN FOREVER (KENNER)

Batman Forever introduced the Teen Wonder, Robin (Chris O'Donnell), as the Dark Knight (now played by Val Kilmer) battled the Riddler (Jim Carrey) and Two-Face (Tommy Lee Jones) for the fate of Gotham City. This series broke away from the recyled *DKC* figure sculpts used in *Batman Returns* and featured a gimmick known as the B.A.T. : Body Adaptive Techsuit.

Premise: Developed exclusively for Batman's ultimate showdown with Two-Face and the Riddler, the scientifically advanced Body Adaptive Techsuit—code name B.A.T.—actually senses and assesses danger, instantly providing from within the weaponry that Batman needs for each threat. It's not just a B.A.T. suit—it's an automatic crime-fighting arsenal!

NIGHT FLIGHT BATMAN
ARTICULATION: **5 points**
ACCESSORIES: **Bat-attack action**

NIGHT HUNTER BATMAN
ARTICULATION: **5 points**
ACCESSORIES: **Claw glider wing and night-vision goggles**

POWER BEACON BATMAN
ARTICULATION: **5 points**
ACCESSORIES: **Light-force suit and flash-fire weapon**

SOLAR SHIELD BATMAN
ARTICULATION: **5 points**
ACCESSORIES: **Heat-deflection cape**

SONAR SENSOR BATMAN
ARTICULATION: **5 points**
ACCESSORIES: **Flying disc blaster and pop-up sonar scope**

WING BLAST BATMAN
ARTICULATION: **5 points**
ACCESSORIES: **Sudden-alert bio wings**

BATARANG BATMAN
ARTICULATION: **5 points**
ACCESSORIES: **Spinning Batarang and radar system**

BLAST CAPE BATMAN
ARTICULATION: **5 points**
ACCESSORIES: **Assault blades and launching attack cape**

FIREGUARD BATMAN
ARTICULATION: **5 points**
ACCESSORIES: **Spinning attack-cape action!**

ICE BLADE BATMAN
ARTICULATION: **5 points**
ACCESSORIES: **Quick-deploy ski sled and blade runners**

MANTA RAY BATMAN
ARTICULATION: **5 points**
ACCESSORIES: **Firing sea sled and pop-out breathing gear**

NEON ARMOR BATMAN
ARTICULATION: **5 points**
ACCESSORIES: **Snap-on armor shield**

ATTACK WING BATMAN
ARTICULATION: **5 points**
ACCESSORIES: **Power-flex attack cape**

LASER DISC BATMAN
ARTICULATION: **5 points**
ACCESSORIES: **Flashing color "laser" launcher**

LIGHTWING BATMAN
ARTICULATION: **5 points**
ACCESSORIES: **Electro-glow wings and lightning launcher**

GUARDIANS OF GOTHAM CITY (BATMAN & ROBIN): BATMAN
ARTICULATION: **5 points**
ACCESSORIES: **Batarang**

RECON HUNTER BATMAN
ARTICULATION: **5 points**
ACCESSORIES: **Missile-firing surveillance drone**

STREET RACER BATMAN
ARTICULATION: **5 points**
ACCESSORIES: **Missile-firing pursuit cycle**

BATBOAT
ACTION FEATURE: **Instantly converts from racing boat to land attack vehicle**

BATCAVE PLAYSET
ACCESSORIES: **Bruce Wayne/Batman transforming elevator, computer control console, rotating Batmobile ramp, missile-firing station, villain-trapping spikes, Batwing docking station, quick-attack cable, and easy-storage feature**

BATWING
ACCESSORIES: **Hidden battle cockpit and "explosive" rocket launcher**

ELECTRONIC BATMOBILE
ACCESSORIES: **Light-up chassis and firing long-range missile**

ROBIN CYCLE
ACCESSORIES: **Ripcord racing power and sonic speed sound**

TRIPLE ACTION VEHICLE SET
ACTION FEATURE: **Makes three "real" movie vehicles: a Batwing, Batmobile, or Batboat!**

WAYNE MANOR BATCAVE COMPOUND
ACCESSORIES: **Breakaway skylights, computer command console, Batman/Bruce Wayne chamber, the Riddler's hideout, Batcave secret entrance, and much, much more!**

ULTIMATE BATMAN
SCALE: **12½ inches**
ARTICULATION: **3 points**
ACCESSORIES: **Batarang and Bat-Symbol display base**

BATMAN & ROBIN (KENNER)

The fourth *Batman* feature film was chock-full of action and characters ready-made for action figures. Joining Batman (now played by George Clooney) and Robin (Chris O'Donnell) this time around was Batgirl (Alicia Silverstone), with villains Mr. Freeze (Arnold Schwarzenegger), Poison Ivy (Uma Thurman), and Bane (Jeep Swenson) laying siege to Gotham City. By far, Kenner's *Batman & Robin* collection was the most expansive Bat-Toy collection up to that point.

Premise: The cold front moving through the streets of Gotham City lately is the diabolical doings of Mr. Freeze, Poison Ivy, and Bane planning to put the Dynamic Duo on ice! Batman and Robin respond immediately by using the Batcomputer to develop Covert Strike Cape technology—specially designed assault capes that reveal secret arsenals of cutting edge weaponry! Discover this new, secret technology that gives Batman, Robin, and Batgirl the power to bring these fiendish foes to justice!

ACTION FIGURES

AMBUSH ATTACK BATMAN
ARTICULATION: **5 points**
ACCESSORIES: **Arsenal cape and restraint rockets**

BATMAN (FUJIFILM MAIL-AWAY EXCLUSIVE)
ARTICULATION: **5 points**
NOTE: **This is a re-release of Hover Attack Batman, with cape and no accessories.**

BATTLE BOARD BATMAN
ARTICULATION: **5 points**
ACCESSORIES: **Flight conversion cape and ionic blaster**

HEAT SCAN BATMAN
ARTICULATION: **5 points**
ACCESSORIES: **Opti-scope launcher and laser-ray emitters**

HOVER ATTACK BATMAN
ARTICULATION: **5 points**
ACCESSORIES: **Blasting battle sled and sickle shields**

ICE BLADE BATMAN
ARTICULATION: **5 points**
ACCESSORIES: **Quick-deploy ski sled and blade runners**

LASER CAPE BATMAN
ARTICULATION: **5 points**
ACCESSORIES: **Wing-mounted torpedo launcher**

NEON ARMOR BATMAN
ARTICULATION: **5 points**
ACCESSORIES: **Snap-on armor shield and grapnel hook**
VARIANT: **W/o bonus Batman ring; redecoed body from *Batman Forever*'s Neon Armor Batman**

ROTOR BLADE BATMAN
ARTICULATION: **5 points**
ACCESSORIES: **Bonus Batman ring!**

SKY ASSAULT BATMAN
ARTICULATION: **5 points**
ACCESSORIES: **Blasting battle sled, sickle shields, and bonus Batman ring!**
NOTE: **Redeco of Hover Attack Batman**

SNOW TRACKER BATMAN
ARTICULATION: **5 points**
ACCESSORIES: **Snow tracker wings and missile launcher**

THERMAL SHIELD BATMAN
ARTICULATION: **5 points**
ACCESSORIES: **Heat-blast cape, Flying Disc Blaster, and bonus Batman ring**

WING BLAST BATMAN
ARTICULATION: **5 points**
ACCESSORIES: **Bonus Batman ring**
VARIANT: **W/o bonus Batman ring**

DELUXE FIGURES

BLAST WING BATMAN
ARTICULATION: **5 points**
ACCESSORIES: **Ice-chopper hoverpack and freeze-seeker missile**

ROOFTOP PURSUIT BATMAN
ARTICULATION: **5 points**
ACCESSORIES: **Night hunter jet and heat blast torpedo**

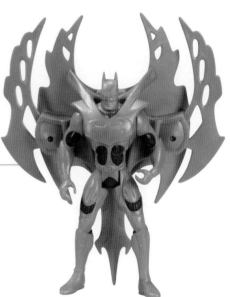

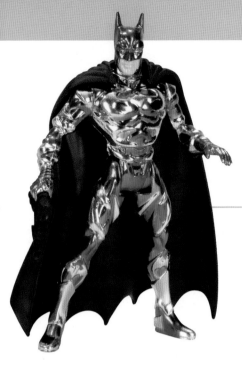

BATMAN & ROBIN (KENNER)

TWO-PACKS

BRAIN VS. BRAWN: BATMAN VS. BANE
ARTICULATION: 5 points
ACCESSORIES: Batarang launcher

**CHALLENGERS OF THE NIGHT:
BATMAN & ROBIN**
ARTICULATION: 5 points
ACCESSORIES: Hand weapons

**GUARDIANS OF GOTHAM CITY:
BATMAN & ROBIN**
ARTICULATION: 5 points
ACCESSORIES: Batarang launcher

**A COLD NIGHT IN GOTHAM CITY:
BATMAN VS. MR. FREEZE**
ARTICULATION: 5 points
ACCESSORIES: Chestplate

ACTION FIGURES W/ VEHICLES

AERIAL COMBAT BATMAN
ACCESSORIES: Twin targeting torpedos

AERIAL DEFENDER ROBIN
ACCESSORIES: Duel interceptor missiles

BATGIRL'S ICESTRIKE CYCLE
ARTICULATION: 5 points
ACCESSORIES: Snow assault mode and razor wheel
launcher

ROBIN'S REDBIRD CYCLE
ARTICULATION: 5 points
ACCESSORIES: Night strike missile; ice slice blades

LARGE-SIZE FIGURES

BATMAN
SCALE: 12 inches
ARTICULATION: 9 points
ACCESSORIES: Heat ray

ULTIMATE BATMAN
SCALE: 15 inches
ARTICULATION: 5 points
ACCESSORIES: Batarang and Bat-Symbol display base

VEHICLES/PLAYSETS

BATMOBILE
ACCESSORIES: Ice shatter missile and vine attack
blades

CRYO-FREEZE CHAMBER
ACCESSORIES: Cryo-freeze laboratory and working
capture claw

ICE FORTRESS
ACTION FEATURE: Mr. Freeze battles Batman from
his frozen command center

ICEGLOW BATHAMMER
ACCESSORIES: Missile launchers and electronic lights

JET BLADE
ACTION FEATURE: Two vehicles in one!

SONIC BATMOBILE
ACTION FEATURE: Pull the rip stick and watch the
Sonic Batmobile zoom into action

TRIPLE ACTION VEHICLE SET
ACTION FEATURE: Makes three vehicles: Batwing,
Batmobile, Batboat

WAYNE MANOR BATCAVE
FEATURES: Computer Command Console, Batman/
Bruce Wayne Chamber, Breakaway Skylights, Sky
Cable, Villain Hideout, and Batcave Secret Entrance
NOTE: Redeco of Batcave playset released in other
Kenner/Hasbro Batman Animated and Batman Film
collections.

BATMAN BEGINS (MATTEL)

For the fifth Batman feature film in 2005, the Dark Knight was taken back to his
roots in a movie and action figure collection that spotlighted Batman's origins and
martial arts background. This time, Mattel was the toy company producing action
figures based on the highly successful *Batman Begins*.

ACTION FIGURES

2005 BATMAN (TOYS R US EXCLUSIVE)
ARTICULATION: 10 points
ACCESSORIES: Batarang

**"PRE-SUIT" BATMAN
(SDCC 2005 EXCLUSIVE)**
ARTICULATION: 10 points
ACCESSORIES: Carrying case, grapnel gun,
folding Batarang, and night-vision goggles
VARIANT: Masked

BATTLE GEAR BATMAN
ARTICULATION: 10 points
ACCESSORIES: Carrying case, grapnel gun, folding
Batarang, and night-vision goggles

BOMB BLAST BATMAN
ARTICULATION: 10 points
ACCESSORIES: Bombs, bomb dropper, and
sighting scope

NINJA BRUCE TO BATMAN
ARTICULATION: 10 points
ACCESSORIES: Dual blade, armor, and forearm blade

POWER PUNCH BATMAN
ARTICULATION: 10 points
ACCESSORIES: Power fists

ROTOBLADE BATMAN
ARTICULATION: 10 points
ACCESSORIES: Roto-blade armament

ZIPLINE ATTACK BATMAN
ARTICULATION: 10 points
ACCESSORIES: Zipline launcher, zipline, and missiles

DELUXE FIGURES

BATTLE CAPE BATMAN
ARTICULATION: 15 points
ACCESSORIES: Light-up battle cape and two missile
launchers

ELECTRO STRIKE BATMAN
ARTICULATION: 10 points
ACCESSORIES: Twin gauntlet light-up electro blasters

LASER BLASTER BATMAN
ARTICULATION: 10 points
ACCESSORIES: Twin gauntlet laser missile launchers

LIGHT SUIT BATMAN
ARTICULATION: 10 points
ACCESSORIES: Light-up feature and Batwings

TOTAL CONTROL FIGURES (7-INCH SCALE)

BATMAN
ARTICULATION: 6 points
ACCESSORIES: Spinning star disk launcher, grapnel
hooks, and nunchaku

LARGE-SIZE FIGURES

ACTION CAPE BATMAN
SCALE: 14 inches
ARTICULATION: 13 points
ACCESSORIES: Action cape and Batarang
VARIANT: Bronze Utility Belt and Batarang

BATMAN (WAL-MART EXCLUSIVE)
SCALE: 30 inches
ARTICULATION: 5 points

VEHICLES/PLAYSETS

ARMORED SPEEDBIKE
ACCESSORIES: Batman figure

BATCOPTER
ACCESSORIES: Batman figure and missiles

BATMOBILE
ACCESSORIES: Projectiles
VARIANTS: Purple "battle-damaged" deco, all-black
deco, and "accurate" black and gold deco

DISC SHOOTING JET
ACCESSORIES: Batman figure and disks

TRANSFORMING BATMOBILE PLAYSET
ACCESSORIES: Zipline with barred room

THE BATMAN (MATTEL)

Batman returned to animation in 2004 with *The Batman,* a look at a younger Dark Knight new to crimefighting. Mattel's action figure collection appeals to the series' anime inspirations.

ACTION FIGURES

ANTI-FREEZE BATMAN
ARTICULATION: **10 points**
ACCESSORIES: **Dual flame-thrower Batarang launchers, and removable mask**

ANTI-FREEZE BATMAN NO. 2
ARTICULATION: **10 points**
ACCESSORIES: **Twin anti-freeze missiles**

AQUA ATTACK BATMAN
ARTICULATION: **10 points**
ACCESSORIES: **Skim board, propellers, diving mask, and harpoon gun**

BATARANG CRUSADER BATMAN
ARTICULATION: **10 points**
ACCESSORIES: **Power key and Batarang launcher**

BATMAN (CAMPBELL'S SOUP MAIL-AWAY EXCLUSIVE)
ARTICULATION: **10 points**
ACCESSORIES: **Batarang on zipline**
NOTE: **"Camo" redeco of Zip Action Batman**

BRUCE TO BATMAN
ARTICULATION: **10 points**
ACCESSORIES: **Power key, Batarang-launcher, snap-on gloves, boots, cape, cowl, and Utility Belt**
VARIANT: **Redeco of same figure with different color applications**

CAMO TECH BATMAN
ARTICULATION: **10 points**
ACCESSORIES: **Power key, Batarang launcher, camo cape with hood**

COMBAT CRASH BATMAN
ARTICULATION: **8 points**
ACCESSORIES: **Cup wall hanger w/ power key air release**

CRIMINAL CAPTURE BATMAN
ARTICULATION: **9 points**
ACCESSORIES: **Criminal capture gun**

DISC ATTACK BATMAN
ARTICULATION: **10 points**
ACCESSORIES: **Disk launcher and Batarang**

EXP ENEMY CONTROL BATMAN
ARTICULATION: **10 points**
ACCESSORIES: **EXP Power Key**

HOVER ATTACK BATMAN
ARTICULATION: **7 points**
ACCESSORIES: **Launcher and glider**

KNIGHT SHADOW BATMAN
ARTICULATION: **10 points**
ACCESSORIES: **Clamp capture weapon**

KNIGHT STRIKE BATMAN
ARTICULATION: **9 points**
ACCESSORIES: **Power key and Batarang launcher**

MEGA CLAW BATMAN
ARTICULATION: **8 points**
ACCESSORIES: **Claw, key, and missile launcher**

POWER NET BATMAN
ARTICULATION: **10 points**
ACCESSORIES: **Capture net**

RAZOR WHIP BATMAN
ARTICULATION: **6 points**
ACCESSORIES: **Razor whip and buzzsaw**

BATMAN BEGINS (MATTEL)

SONIC DISRUPTOR BATMAN
ARTICULATION: **10 points**
ACCESSORIES: **Disruptor Batwings**

TRAP JAW BATMAN
ARTICULATION: **10 points**
ACCESSORIES: **Trap jaw clamp**

TRIPLE SHOT BATMAN
ARTICULATION: **9 points**
ACCESSORIES: **Snap-on armor w/ triple-missile launcher**

ULTIMATE DEFENDER BATMAN
ARTICULATION: **10 points**
ACCESSORIES: **Disk launcher**

ZIP ACTION BATMAN
ARTICULATION: **8 points**
ACCESSORIES: **Batarang and disk launcher**

DELUXE FIGURES

BATBOT BATMAN
ARTICULATION: **7 points**
ACCESSORIES: **Shield, Batarang, and missile launcher**

BATMAN TO BATBOT (BATBOT NO. 2)
ARTICULATION: **10 points**
ACCESSORIES: **Batbot suit, missile launcher, and missile**

BATTLE PUNCH BATMAN
ARTICULATION: **9 points**
ACCESSORIES: **Dual battle punchers**

BATTLE WING BATMAN
ARTICULATION: **10 points**
ACCESSORIES: **Twin battle wing missile launchers**

FIRE ARMOR BATMAN
ARTICULATION: **9 points**
ACCESSORIES: **Detachable fire armor wings and fire stand**

INLINE ATTACK BATMAN
ARTICULATION: **10 points**
ACCESSORIES: **Inline skates, helmet, Batshield, and twin shoulder-mounted missile launchers**

MAGNA DETECTIVE BATMAN
ARTICULATION: **8 points**
ACCESSORIES: **Power key w/ magnet and magnet detector**

POWER PROP BATMAN
ARTICULATION: **10 points**
ACCESSORIES: **Helicoptor backpack, twin gauntlet missiles, and launcher**

ROCKET SHIELD BATMAN
ARTICULATION: **10 points**
ACCESSORIES: **Shield wings and defensive missile launcher w/ missile**

MULTIPACKS

NOTE: See individual listings for villains—all figures are redecoes. Accessories are the same as the single-carded figures, except where noted.

FOUR-PACK NO. 1 (TOYS R US EXCLUSIVE): MR. FREEZE, THE JOKER, ANTI-FREEZE BATMAN, AND POWER DISC BATMAN

FOUR-PACK NO. 2 (TOYS R US EXCLUSIVE): FIREFLY, ZIP ACTION BATMAN, HAMMER STRIKE THE JOKER, AND HOVER ATTACK BATMAN

FOUR-PACK NO. 3 (TOYS R US EXCLUSIVE): CATWOMAN, KNIGHT STRIKE BATMAN, MIDNIGHT NINJA BATMAN, AND THE PENGUIN
ACCESSORIES: **Whip, clear idol, and stand**

ARKHAM ASYLUM SIX-PACK (TARGET EXCLUSIVE): CRIMINAL CAPTURE BATMAN, THE RIDDLER, POISON IVY, MR. FREEZE, CLAYFACE, AND VENTRILOQUIST W/ SCARFACE

VEHICLES/PLAYSETS

BATCAVE
ACCESSORIES: **Launching projectiles, elevator, and adjustable zipline**

BATCAVE POWER KEY PLAYSET
ACCESSORIES: **Batman figure**

BATCYCLE
ACCESSORIES: **Missile**

BATMOBILE
ACCESSORIES: **Missile**
ACTION FEATURE: **Electronic sound effects**

EXP BATMOBILE

EXP STRIKE CYCLE
ACCESSORIES: **Missile**

HYPERJET

3-IN-1 BATJET

TRIPLE MISSION BATMOBILE
ACCESSORIES: **Missiles and missile towline**

Wealthy circus owner Kathy Kane adopted the identity of Batwoman in order to woo and win the heart of Batman.

FIRST APPEARANCE
Detective Comics No. 233

BATMAN BEYOND
Superman/Batman (Series 4)
DC Direct

RELEASE DATE: **2007**
SCALE: **6½ inches**
ARTICULATION: **9 points**
ACCESSORIES: **Display base**

BATMITE
The Classic Silver Age Bat-Girl and Batwoman
DC Direct

RELEASE DATE: **2004**
SCALE: **6½ inches**
ARTICULATION: **5 points**

BATWOMAN
The Classic Silver Age Bat-Girl and Batwoman
DC Direct

RELEASE DATE: **2004**
SCALE: **6½ inches**
ARTICULATION: **9 points**
ACCESSORIES: **Utility purse and interlocking Gotham City rooftop display base**

BATWOMAN III
52 (Series 1)
DC Direct

RELEASE DATE: **2007**
SCALE: **6½ inches**
ARTICULATION: **9 points**
ACCESSORIES: **Display base**

BATZARRO
Superman/Batman (Series 4)
DC Direct

RELEASE DATE: **2007**
SCALE: **6½ inches**
ARTICULATION: **9 points**
ACCESSORIES: **Display base**

BAYOU JACK
Swamp Thing
Kenner

RELEASE DATE: **1990**
SCALE: **5 inches**
ARTICULATION: **5 points**
ACCESSORIES: **Swamp water blaster**

> Beast Boy was adopted by
> Mento and Elasti-Girl,
> his teammates
> in the Doom Patrol.
>
> **FIRST APPEARANCE**
> *Doom Patrol* Vol. 1, No. 99

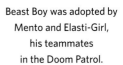

BEAST BOY
The Classic Teen Titans Gift Set
DC Direct

RELEASE DATE: **2004**
SCALE: **6½ inches**
ARTICULATION: **9 points**
ACCESSORIES: **Beast Boy in his monkey form (2 points of articulation: arms)**

BEAST BOY
Teen Titans
Bandai

RELEASE DATE: **2004**
SCALE: **3½ inches**
ARTICULATION: **7 points**
ACCESSORIES: **Weapon**

BEAST BOY
Teen Titans
Bandai

RELEASE DATE: **2004**
SCALE: **5 inches**
ARTICULATION: **12 points**
ACCESSORIES: **Weapon**

BEAST BOY
Teen Titans
Bandai

RELEASE DATE: **2006**
SCALE: **5 inches**
ARTICULATION: **11 points**
ACCESSORIES: **Moped**

BEPPO THE SUPERMONKEY
Silver Age Superman
DC Direct

RELEASE DATE: **2006**
SCALE: **6½ inches**
ARTICULATION: **6 points (including tail)**
NOTE: **Packaged with Superman**

BIG BARDA
Mister Miracle and Big Barda
DC Direct

RELEASE DATE: **2000**
SCALE: **6½ inches**
ARTICULATION: **7 points**
ACCESSORIES: **Mega-rod and removable helmet**
NOTE: **Packaged with Mister Miracle and Oberon figures**

BIG BARDA
*DC Super Heroes:
Justice League Unlimited*
Mattel

RELEASE DATE: **2007**
SCALE: **4¾ inches**
ARTICULATION: **5 points**

BILLY BATSON
Shazam! Gift Set
DC Direct

RELEASE DATE: **2000**
SCALE: **6½ inches**
ARTICULATION: **7 points**
ACCESSORIES: **Reproduction newspaper and free-standing WHIZ Radio microphone**
NOTE: **Packaged with Captain Marvel figure**

Before marrying Scott Free,
a.k.a. Mister Miracle,
Barda led Granny Goodness's
Female Furies on Apokolips.

FIRST APPEARANCE
Mister Miracle Vol. 1, No. 4

BIZARRO
Superman
**Kenner: Diamond Comics Distributors
Exclusive**

RELEASE DATE: **1998**
SCALE: **4¾ inches**
ARTICULATION: **6 points**
ACCESSORIES: **Tire and drive-shaft; removable cape**
ACTION FEATURE: **Tantrum attack!**
NOTE: **Listed on package as Evil Bizarro**

BIZARRO
Superman (Series 1)
DC Direct

RELEASE DATE: **2003**
SCALE: **6½ inches**
ARTICULATION: **21 points**
ACCESSORIES: **Bizarro No. 1 medal and Superman S-shield insignia display base**

BIZARRO
Pocket Super Heroes (Series 2)
DC Direct

RELEASE DATE: **2003**
SCALE: **3¼ inches**
ARTICULATION: **6 points**
ACCESSORIES: **Bizarro No. 1 medal, removable cape, and display base**

As an imperfect duplicate
of Superman, Bizarro does
everything opposite of the
Man of Steel.

FIRST APPEARANCE
Action Comics No. 254

BIZARRO
Justice (Series 1)
DC Direct

RELEASE DATE: **2005**
SCALE: **7 inches**
ARTICULATION: **11 points**
ACCESSORIES: **Display base**

BIZARRO
Justice League Unlimited
Mattel: Target Exclusive

RELEASE DATE: **2005**
SCALE: **5 inches**
ARTICULATION: **5 points**

BIZARRO
DC Super Heroes: Superman
Mattel

RELEASE DATE: **2006**
SCALE: **6 inches**
ARTICULATION: **23 points**
ACCESSORIES: **Truck tire and axle**

BIZARRO
Superman/Batman (Series 4)
DC Direct

RELEASE DATE: **2007**
SCALE: **6½ inches**
ARTICULATION: **9 points**
ACCESSORIES: **Display base**

BLACK ADAM
Shazam!
DC Direct

RELEASE DATE: **2002**
SCALE: **6½ inches**
ARTICULATION: **9 points**
ACCESSORIES: **Mystical scarab necklace**

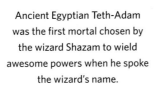

Ancient Egyptian Teth-Adam was the first mortal chosen by the wizard Shazam to wield awesome powers when he spoke the wizard's name.

FIRST APPEARANCE
Marvel Family No. 1

BLACK ADAM
Justice (Series 4)
DC Direct

RELEASE DATE: **2003**
SCALE: **7 inches**
ARTICULATION: **11 points**
ACCESSORIES: **Display base**

BLACK CANARY
Hard-Traveling Heroes
DC Direct

RELEASE DATE: **2000**
SCALE: **6½ inches**
ARTICULATION: **7 points**
ACCESSORIES: **Interchangeable heads (2: Black Canary/Dinah Lance) and cloth skirt disguise**

BLACK CANARY
Pocket Super Heroes (Series 2)
DC Direct

RELEASE DATE: **2003**
SCALE: **3¾ inches**
ARTICULATION: **6 points**
ACCESSORIES: **Display base**

BLACK CANARY
Birds of Prey Box Set
DC Direct

RELEASE DATE: **2003**
SCALE: **6½ inches**
ARTICULATION: **12 points**
ACCESSORIES: **Removable belt**
NOTE: **Packaged with Huntress and Oracle figures**

BLACK CANARY
Justice League Unlimited
Mattel: Target Exclusive

RELEASE DATE: **2005**
SCALE: **4¾ inches**
ARTICULATION: **5 points**

> Black Canary's
> superpower is an
> ear-shattering hypersonic
> "canary cry."
>
> **FIRST APPEARANCE**
> *Justice League of America* Vol. 1, No. 75

BLACK CANARY
Justice (Series 2)
DC Direct

RELEASE DATE: **2005**
SCALE: **7 inches**
ARTICULATION: **11 points**
ACCESSORIES: **Real fishnet stockings and display base**

BLACK CANARY
Identity Crisis (Series 2)
DC Direct

RELEASE DATE: **2006**
SCALE: **6½ inches**
ARTICULATION: **9 points**
ACCESSORIES: **IDENTITY CRISIS logo display base**

> Blackfire is the traitorous sister
> of Tamaran's Princess Koriand'r,
> better known as Starfire of
> the Teen Titans.
>
> **FIRST APPEARANCE**
> *The New Teen Titans* Vol. 1, No. 23

BLACKFIRE
Contemporary Teen Titans (Series 1)
DC Direct

RELEASE DATE: **2004**
SCALE: **6½ inches**
ARTICULATION: **9 points**
ACCESSORIES: **TEEN TITANS logo display base**

BLACK HAND
Green Lantern (Series 1)
DC Direct

RELEASE DATE: **2005**
SCALE: **6½ inches**
ARTICULATION: **11 points**
ACCESSORIES: **Green Lantern insignia display base**

BLACKHAWK
Blackhawk
Dreams & Visions

RELEASE DATE: **2004**
SCALE: **12 inches**
ARTICULATION: **21 points**
ACCESSORIES: **Removable uniform, cap, and sidearm**
NOTE: **Blackhawk was packaged with two alternate costumes and equipment trays: Air Rescue uniform jacket, uniform pants, belt, boots, submachine gun, and parachute with pack; and Ice Troops hooded thermal parka, thermal pants, thermal gloves, goggles, boots, and radio with headset.**

BLACKHAWK
DC: The New Frontier (Series 1)
DC Direct

RELEASE DATE: **2006**
SCALE: **6½ inches**
ARTICULATION: **14 points**
ACCESSORIES: **Pistol, ammo clips (2), and display base**

> Blackhawk lends his name to
> a squadron of international
> flying aces who soared into
> action against the Axis during
> World War II.
>
> **FIRST APPEARANCE**
> *Military Comics* No. 1

BLACK LIGHTNING
Total Justice (Series 3)
Kenner

RELEASE DATE: **1996**
SCALE: **5 inches**
ARTICULATION: **5 points**
ACCESSORIES: **Fractal Techgear armor and Electrobolt strike cannon**

Black Lightning's Oath:
Justice, like lightning, should ever appear to some men hope, to other men fear!

FIRST APPEARANCE
Black Lightning Vol. 1, No. 1

BLACK MANTA
Super Friends!
DC Direct

RELEASE DATE: **2003**
SCALE: **6½ inches**
ARTICULATION: **9 points**
ACCESSORIES: **Neutron eraser gun, Black Manta's Manta-Sub miniature w/ removable stand, and SUPER FRIENDS! logo display base**

To become a more formidable foe, the human Black Manta sold his soul to the devilish Neron and was transformed into a true aquatic adversary.

FIRST APPEARANCE
Aquaman No. 35

BLACK MANTA
Pocket Super Heroes (Series 1)
DC Direct

RELEASE DATE: **2002**
SCALE: **3¼ inches**
ARTICULATION: **6 points**
ACCESSORIES: **Display base**

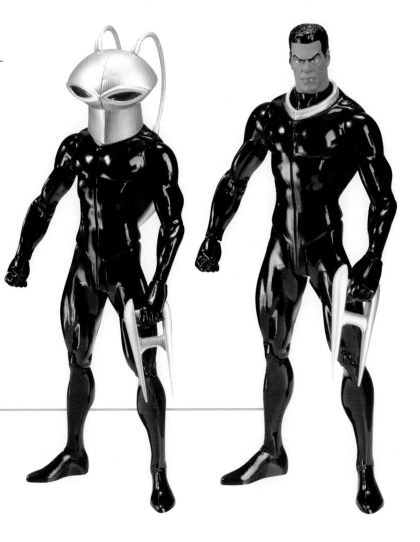

BLACK MANTA
Justice (Series 2)
DC Direct

RELEASE DATE: **2005**
SCALE: **7 inches**
ARTICULATION: **11 points**
ACCESSORIES: **Removable helmet, hand-held blaster, and display base**

BLACK MASK
Secret Files
(Series 1: *Batman Rogues' Gallery*)
DC Direct

RELEASE DATE: **2005**
SCALE: **6½ inches**
ARTICULATION: **11 points**
ACCESSORIES: **Construction helmet, power drill, hacksaw, and display base**

BLIGHT
Batman Beyond
Hasbro

RELEASE DATE: **1999**
SCALE: **4¾ inches**
ARTICULATION: **5 points**
ACCESSORIES: **Radiation blaster and plasma missile**
ACTION FEATURE: **Glow-in-the-dark skeleton**

BLUE BEETLE II
DC Super Heroes
Hasbro

RELEASE DATE: **1999**
SCALE: **5 inches**
ARTICULATION: **5 points**

> Unlike his predecessor or successor, Ted Kord possessed no true superpowers as the Blue Beetle, instead relying on his scientific expertise for a variety of high-tech tricks.
>
> **FIRST APPEARANCE**
> *Captain Atom* No. 83

BLUE BEETLE II
Classic Heroes
DC Direct

RELEASE DATE: **2002**
SCALE: **6½ inches**
ARTICULATION: **9 points**
ACCESSORIES: **Air gun and climbing cable w/ suction cup**

BLUE BEETLE III
First Appearance: Brave New World
DC Direct

RELEASE DATE: **2006**
SCALE: **6½ inches**
ARTICULATION: **11 points**
ACCESSORIES: **Shield**
VARIANT: **"Stealth Mode" redeco**

> Booster Gold hails from the twenty-fourth century, where he was a famed college quarterback before being banished from the game for gambling.
>
> **FIRST APPEARANCE**
> *Booster Gold* No. 1

BOB THE GOON
Batman
Toy Biz

RELEASE DATE: **1989**
ARTICULATION: **7 points**
ACCESSORIES: **Removable hat, pistol, and knife**
ACTION FEATURE: **Button-activated power kick!**

BOOSTER GOLD
Justice League Unlimited
Mattel

RELEASE DATE: **2005**
SCALE: **4¾ inches**
ARTICULATION: **5 points**
ACCESSORIES: **Skeets mini robot (single-carded only)**

BOOSTER GOLD
52 (Series 1)
DC Direct

RELEASE DATE: **2007**
SCALE: **6½ inches**
ARTICULATION: **11 points**
ACCESSORIES: **Skeets**

BRAINIAC
Pocket Super Heroes (Series 2)
DC Direct

RELEASE DATE: **2003**
SCALE: **3¼ inches**
ARTICULATION: **6 points**
ACCESSORIES: **Ray gun and display base**

> Brainiac abandoned his humanoid body for a more fearsome visage: a silver skeletal frame mirroring his skull-faced spaceship.
>
> **FIRST APPEARANCE**
> *Action Comics* No. 242

BRAINIAC
Super Powers (Series 2)
Kenner

RELEASE DATE: **1985**
SCALE: **3¾ inches**
ARTICULATION: **5 points**
ACTION FEATURE: **Power-action computer kick**

BRAINIAC
Crisis on Infinite Earths (Series 2)
DC Direct

RELEASE DATE: **2006**
SCALE: **6½ inches**
ARTICULATION: **12 points**
ACCESSORIES: **CRISIS logo display base**

BRAINIAC
DC Super Heroes: Superman
Mattel

RELEASE DATE: **2006**
SCALE: **6 inches**
ARTICULATION: **23 points**

BRAINIAC
Superman (Series 1)
Kenner

RELEASE DATE: **1998**
SCALE: **4¾ inches**
ARTICULATION: **6 points**
ACCESSORIES: **Blasting space sled**
NOTE: **Single-carded as Evil Alien Brainiac**

BRAINIAC
Justice (Series 5)
DC Direct

RELEASE DATE: **2007**
SCALE: **7 inches**
ARTICULATION: **11 points**
ACCESSORIES: **Koko the monkey and display base**

BRAINIAC
Justice League Unlimited
Mattel

RELEASE DATE: **2004**
SCALE: **4¾ inches**
ARTICULATION: **5 points**
ACCESSORIES: **Ray weapon (single-carded only)**

> Despite being a direct descendant of the evil Brainiac, Querl Dox was a member in good standing of the Legion of Super-Heroes.
>
> **FIRST APPEARANCE**
> *Action Comics* No. 276

BRAINIAC 5
Legion of Super-Heroes (Series 2)
DC Direct

RELEASE DATE: **2002**
SCALE: **6½ inches**
ARTICULATION: **11 points**

BRAINIAC 13
Superman (Series 1)
DC Direct

RELEASE DATE: **2003**
SCALE: **6½ inches**
ARTICULATION: **11 points**
ACCESSORIES: **Removable flexible tendrils (6) and Superman S-shield insignia display base**

BROTHER BLOOD
Contemporary Teen Titans (Series 2)
DC Direct

RELEASE DATE: **2005**
SCALE: **6½ inches**
ARTICULATION: **9 points**
ACCESSORIES: **TEEN TITANS logo display base**

BRUCE WAYNE
World's Greatest Super-Heroes!
(Alter Egos)
Mego

RELEASE DATE: **1974**
SCALE: **8 inches**
ARTICULATION: **21 points**
ACCESSORIES: **Removable clothing**

QUICK CHANGE BRUCE WAYNE
The Dark Knight Collection
Kenner

RELEASE DATE: **1990**
SCALE: **3¾ inches**
ARTICULATION: **5 points**
ACCESSORIES: **Quick-change suit and Communicator**

BRUCE WAYNE
Batman: The Animated Series
Kenner

RELEASE DATE: **1992**
SCALE: **4¾ inches**
ARTICULATION: **5 points**
ACCESSORIES: **Snap-on Batman armor**

BRUCE WAYNE
Batman Returns
Kenner

RELEASE DATE: **1992**
SCALE: **4¾ inches**
ARTICULATION: **5 points**
ACCESSORIES: **Quick-change Batman armor; communicator**

BATTLE GEAR BRUCE WAYNE
Batman & Robin
Kenner

RELEASE DATE: **1997**
SCALE: **5 inches**
ARTICULATION: **5 points**
ACCESSORIES: **Ice block armor suit and cryo claw shooter**

BRUCE WAYNE
Batman
Hasbro: Target Exclusive

RELEASE DATE: **2000**
SCALE: **9 inches**
ARTICULATION: **27 points**
ACCESSORIES: **Interchangeable heads and removable clothing (Bat-costume and tuxedo)**

BRUCE WAYNE/BATMAN
Batman
Mattel

RELEASE DATE: **2004**
SCALE: **6 inches**
ARTICULATION: **8 points**
ACCESSORIES: **Attachable Batman costume and weapon**

BULL DOG
Krypto the Superdog
Fisher-Price

RELEASE DATE: **2006**
SCALE: **6 inches**
ARTICULATION: **4 points plus tail and horns**

BUMBLEBEE
Teen Titans
Bandai

RELEASE DATE: **2005**
SCALE: **3½ inches**
ARTICULATION: **5 points**

BRUCE WAYNE/BATMAN (TARGET EXCLUSIVE)
Batman Forever
Kenner

RELEASE DATE: **1995**
SCALE: **4¾ inches**
ARTICULATION: **5 points**
ACCESSORIES: **Snap-on crime-fighting armor and side swords**

UNDERCOVER BRUCE WAYNE
The New Batman Adventures
Kenner

RELEASE DATE: **1998**
SCALE: **4¾ inches**
ARTICULATION: **5 points**
ACCESSORIES: **Overcoat, mask w/ attached cape, battle armor, and villain decoder**
VARIANTS: **Rapid Switch Bruce Wayne** (*Batman Beyond: ROTJ*)

QUICK-CHANGE BRUCE WAYNE
World of Batman
Hasbro: Wal-Mart Exclusive

RELEASE DATE: **2000**
SCALE: **4¾ inches**
ARTICULATION: **5 points**
ACCESSORIES: **Bat-Steel armor and decoding unit**

BRUCE WAYNE
Secret Files (Series 2: *Unmasked!*)
DC Direct

RELEASE DATE: **2005**
SCALE: **6½ inches**
ARTICULATION: **10 points**
ACCESSORIES: **Interchangeable heads (2: w/ cowl and unmasked) and UNMASKED Logo display base**

BULLDOZER
Sgt. Rock
Dreams & Visions

RELEASE DATE: **2004**
SCALE: **12 inches**
ARTICULATION: **21 points**
ACCESSORIES: **Removable clothing (uniform and lace-up boots, field jacket, helmet) and loadable rifle w/ separate ammo clips**

TRANSFORMING BRUCE WAYNE
Batman Forever
Kenner

RELEASE DATE: **1995**
SCALE: **4¾ inches**
ARTICULATION: **5 points**
ACCESSORIES: **Quick-change Bat-Suit and battle blades**

BRUCE WAYNE
JLA (Series 3)
Hasbro

RELEASE DATE: **1998**
SCALE: **5 inches**
ARTICULATION: **5 points**
ACCESSORIES: **JLA logo display base**

RAPID SWITCH BRUCE WAYNE
Batman Beyond: Return of the Joker
Hasbro

RELEASE DATE: **2001**
SCALE: **4¾ inches**
ARTICULATION: **5 points**
ACCESSORIES: **Quick-change outfit and disc launcher**

READY FOR ACTION!

Ideal's *Captain Action* collection was an attempt to one-up toy rival G.I. Joe for maximum play potential. Where Joe had access to scores of accessories suited to specific missions, the good Captain was intended as a platform for kids to reinvent the hero as thirteen of their favorite characters from comics or pulp fiction. Captain Action had his own styl-ized costume and accessories, with a series of adventures published by DC Comics. But by purchasing special character-specific uniform and equipment packs, Captain Action could take on the appearance and abilities of DC's Aquaman, Batman, or Superman in order to defeat his blue-skinned adversary, the diabolical Dr. Evil. Captain Action even had a sidekick, Action Boy, who could adopt the guises of Aqualad, Robin, and Superboy (see individual listings for all). Though outsold and out-lasted by G.I. Joe, Captain Action remains a nostalgic favorite for many toy aficionados and earns the distinction of being the first true DC Comics action figure offering.

CAPTAIN ATOM
Superman/Batman
(Series 1: *Public Enemies*)
DC Direct

RELEASE DATE: **2005**
SCALE: **6½ inches**
ARTICULATION: **13 points**
ACCESSORIES: **SUPERMAN/BATMAN logo display base**

> To contain his quantum energies, Captain Atom's body is covered in an alien alloy.
>
> **FIRST APPEARANCE**
> *Space Adventures* No. 33

CAPTAIN COLD
The Flash Rogues Gallery
DC Direct

RELEASE DATE: **2001**
SCALE: **6½ inches**
ARTICULATION: **11 points**
ACCESSORIES: **Cold gun**

> Captain Cold's sister is the Golden Glider, a speed-skating nemesis of the Flash.
>
> **FIRST APPEARANCE**
> *Showcase* No. 8

CAPTAIN BOOMERANG II
Identity Crisis (Series 2)
DC Direct

RELEASE DATE: **2006**
SCALE: **6½ inches**
ARTICULATION: **11 points**
ACCESSORIES: Boomerangs (6) and **IDENTITY CRISIS logo display base**

CAPTAIN COLD
Pocket Super Heroes (Series 1)
DC Direct

RELEASE DATE: **2002**
SCALE: **3¾ inches**
ARTICULATION: **6 points**
ACCESSORIES: **Cold gun, removable hood, and display base**

CASSIDY
Preacher
DC Direct

RELEASE DATE: **2000**
SCALE: **6½ inches**
ARTICULATION: **11 points**
ACCESSORIES: **Pint of blood**

CATWOMAN
World's Greatest Super-Heroes!
Mego

RELEASE DATE: **1972-82**
SCALE: **8 inches**
ARTICULATION: **21 points**
ACCESSORIES: **Removable cloth costume**

CATWOMAN
Batman Returns
Kenner

RELEASE DATE: **1991**
SCALE: **4¾ inches**
ARTICULATION: **5 points**
ACCESSORIES: **Whip and taser gun**
ACTION FEATURE: **Whip-action arm**

CATWOMAN
Batman: The Animated Series
Kenner

RELEASE DATE: **1993**
SCALE: **4¾ inches**
ARTICULATION: **5 points**
ACCESSORIES: **Whip, pet cat, and cat claws (2)**

CATWOMAN
Legends of Batman
Kenner

RELEASE DATE: **1995**
SCALE: **5 inches**
ARTICULATION: **5 points**
ACCESSORIES: **Quick-climb claw, capture net, and bullwhip**
VARIANT: **Redeco released as Warner Bros. Store Exclusive**

Since her debut, Catwoman has been romantically linked to Batman.

FIRST APPEARANCE
Batman No. 1

EGYPTIAN CATWOMAN
Legends of Batman
Kenner

RELEASE DATE: **1995**
SCALE: **5 inches**
ARTICULATION: **5 points**
ACCESSORIES: **Headdress and staff**

CATWOMAN
Batman and Catwoman
Hasbro

RELEASE DATE: **1996**
SCALE: **12 inches**
ARTICULATION: **14 points**
ACCESSORIES: **Bullwhip**

PANTHER PROWL CATWOMAN
Legends of the Dark Knight
Kenner

RELEASE DATE: **1997**
SCALE: **7 inches**
ARTICULATION: **5 points**
ACCESSORIES: **Battle stalker panther/exoskeleton armor; whip**

TECHNOCAST CATWOMAN
The New Batman Adventures: Mission Masters 4
Hasbro

RELEASE DATE: **2002**
SCALE: **4¾ inches**
ARTICULATION: **5 points**
ACCESSORIES: **Whip arm action**

CATWOMAN
Batman
Mattel

RELEASE DATE: **2002**
SCALE: **4¾ inches**
ARTICULATION: **5 points**
VARIANT: **Redecoed version in Toys R Us Exclusive four-pack**

CATWOMAN
The Classic Silver Age Catwoman and The Penguin
DC Direct

RELEASE DATE: **2004**
SCALE: **6½ inches**
ARTICULATION: **9 points**
ACCESSORIES: **Cat-o'-nine-tails, pet cat, and interlocking Gotham City rooftop display base**

CATWOMAN
Pocket Super Heroes
(Batman Box Set)
DC Direct

RELEASE DATE: **2004**
SCALE: **3¼ inches**
ARTICULATION: **6 points**
ACCESSORIES: **Removable cape and cloth skirt**

CATWOMAN
Pocket Super Heroes
(Convention Giveaway)
DC Direct

RELEASE DATE: **2004**
SCALE: **3¼ inches**
ARTICULATION: **6 points**

IDOL WORSHIP

Mattel's 2005 summer comic-book convention Catwoman exclusive-action figure had nine lives when it came to variants. Specifically, the figure was offered with nine different decos of the lion idol that DC Comics' feline fatale wants to steal. Naturally, the vac-metallized gold idol proved to be the rarest variant, followed by idols decoed in brown (with a yellow mane), jade, fuzzy flocked pink, maroon, black, gray, silver, and a very patriotic red-white-and-blue. Unfortunately, Mattel kept no record of the distribution for any of the idol variants, and we can't assume that all others after the gilded lion were produced in equal numbers. The idols were sold in sealed boxes overlying the window-box packaging, and curiosity killed many a collector dying to see just which idol came with Catty.

CATWOMAN
The Batman
Mattel: Summer Convention Exclusive

RELEASE DATE: **2005**
SCALE: **5 inches**
ARTICULATION: **4 points**
ACCESSORIES: **Whip and idol**
VARIANTS: **Purple costume redeco released in Toys R Us Exclusive four-pack**

SELINA KYLE CATWOMAN
The Batman
Mattel (Diamond Comics Distributor Exclusive)

RELEASE DATE: **2005**
SCALE: **5 inches**
ARTICULATION: **4 points**
ACCESSORIES: **Whip and idol**
NOTE: **This is a "maskless" version of the preceding figure.**

CATWOMAN
Batman: The Long Halloween (Series 1)
DC Direct

RELEASE DATE: **2006**
SCALE: **6½ inches**
ARTICULATION: **11 points**
ACCESSORIES: **Whip and sidewalk display base**

CATWOMAN
Batman: Knightfall (Series 1)
DC Direct

RELEASE DATE: **2006**
SCALE: **6½ inches**
ARTICULATION: **9 points**
ACCESSORIES: **Cat-o'-nine-tails and KNIGHTFALL logo display base**

CHAMELEON BOY
Legion of Super-Heroes (Series 3)
DC Direct

RELEASE DATE: **2003**
SCALE: **6½ inches**
ARTICULATION: **11 points**

Like his fellow Durlans, Chameleon Boy can shape-shift into any object or being.

FIRST APPEARANCE
Adventure Comics No. 267

CHEETAH
Pocket Super Heroes (Series 1)
DC Direct

RELEASE DATE: **2002**
SCALE: **3¼ inches**
ARTICULATION: **6 points**
ACCESSORIES: **Display base**

CHEETAH
*Wonder Woman:
Amazons and Adversaries*
DC Direct

RELEASE DATE: **2001**
SCALE: **6½ inches**
ARTICULATION: **9 points**
ACCESSORIES: **Tree trunk display base**

CHEETAH
Super Friends!
DC Direct

RELEASE DATE: **2003**
SCALE: **6½ inches**
ARTICULATION: **9 points**
ACCESSORIES: **Bag of money and SUPER FRIENDS!**
logo display base

> Jealous of Wonder Woman's fame, socialite Priscilla Rich donned the costume of the Cheetah to thwart the Amazing Amazon.
>
> **FIRST APPEARANCE**
> *Wonder Woman* Vol. 1, No. 6

CHEETAH
Justice (Series 1)
DC Direct

RELEASE DATE: **2005**
SCALE: **6½ inches**
ARTICULATION: **10 points (including tail)**
ACCESSORIES: **Display base**

CINDERBLOCK
Teen Titans
Bandai

RELEASE DATE: **2005**
SCALE: **3½ inches**
ARTICULATION: **5 points**
ACCESSORIES: **Weapon**

CLARK KENT
World's Greatest Super-Heroes!
(Alter Egos)
Mego

RELEASE DATE: **1974**
SCALE: **8 inches**
ARTICULATION: **14 points**
ACCESSORIES: **Removable clothing, hat, and glasses**

> To avoid melting down from his heat-vision, the lenses of Clark Kent's glasses were made from the shattered canopy of baby Kal-El's Earthbound rocket ship.
>
> **FIRST APPEARANCE**
> *Action Comics* No. 1

CLARK KENT
Super Powers (Mail-Away Exclusive)
Kenner

RELEASE DATE: **1985**
SCALE: **3¾ inches**
ARTICULATION: **7 points**

CLARK KENT
Superman: Man of Steel
Kenner

RELEASE DATE: **1995**
SCALE: **5 inches**
ARTICULATION: **5 points**
NOTE: **Released with Matrix Conversion
Coupe vehicle**

CLARK KENT
Superman
Hasbro: Target Exclusive

RELEASE DATE: **2000**
SCALE: **9 inches**
ARTICULATION: **27 points**
ACCESSORIES: **Removable Superman uniform and
Clark Kent's clothing**

CLARK KENT
Pocket Super Heroes (Series 2)
DC Direct

RELEASE DATE: **2003**
SCALE: **3¼ inches**
ARTICULATION: **6 points**
ACCESSORIES: **Display base**

CLARK KENT
Secret Files (Series 2: *Unmasked!*)
DC Direct

RELEASE DATE: **2005**
SCALE: **6½ inches**
ARTICULATION: **9 points**
ACCESSORIES: **Removable faux shirt panel disguise,
removable glasses, and UNMASKED! logo display base**

CLARK KENT
DC Super Heroes
Mattel: Target Exclusive

RELEASE DATE: **2007**
SCALE: **6 inches**
ARTICULATION: **12 points**
ACCESSORIES: **Folder**

CLARK KENT
Smallville
DC Direct

RELEASE DATE: **2002**
SCALE: **6½ inches**
ARTICULATION: **7 points**
ACCESSORIES: **Backpack, kryptonite meteor, and alternate pair of hands w/ kryptonite-poisoned veins**

CLAYFACE
Batman: The Animated Series
Kenner

RELEASE DATE: **1993**
SCALE: **4¾ inches**
ARTICULATION: **2 points**
ACCESSORIES: **Squeeze-action launching mace hand**
VARIANT: **Redecoed figure included with Diamond Comic Distributors' Arkham Asylum box set**

> The Clayface from *The Batman* animated series is actually Bruce Wayne's best friend, detective Ethan Bennett, transformed by the Joker into a muck monster.
>
> **FIRST APPEARANCE**
> *Detective Comics* No. 40

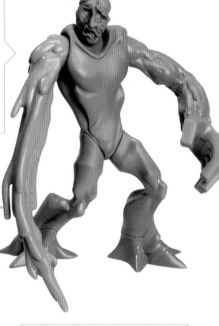

CLAYFACE
Batman: Legends of the Dark Knight
Kenner: Hasbro.com/Diamond Comics Distributors Exclusive

RELEASE DATE: **1997**
SCALE: **7 inches**
ARTICULATION: **5 points**
ACTION FEATURE: **Rotating head w/ three expressions**

CLAYFACE
The Batman
Mattel

RELEASE DATE: **2005**
SCALE: **5 inches**
ARTICULATION: **5 points**
ACTION FEATURE: **Pull-back flinging whip arm**
VARIANTS: **Re-released in 2006 with different head sculpts**

COLOSSAL BOY
Legion of Super-Heroes (Series 4)
DC Direct

RELEASE DATE: **2004**
SCALE: **6½ inches**
ARTICULATION: **11 points**

> Gotham City police commissioner James Gordon began his law enforcement career with the Chicago P. D.
>
> **FIRST APPEARANCE**
> *Detective Comics* No. 27

COMMISSIONER GORDON
The New Batman Adventures (Gotham City Enforcement Team)
Hasbro

RELEASE DATE: **2001**
SCALE: **4¾ inches**
ARTICULATION: **5 points**
ACCESSORIES: **Pistols (2)**

COMMISSIONER GORDON
Batman: Dark Victory (Series 1)
DC Direct

RELEASE DATE: **2006**
SCALE: **6½ inches**
ARTICULATION: **13 points**
ACCESSORIES: **Pistol, flashlight, and display base**

COMMISSIONER GORDON
Batman: Hush (Series 3)
DC Direct

RELEASE DATE: **2005**
SCALE: **6½ inches**
ARTICULATION: **11 points**
ACCESSORIES: **Pistol molded to hand and BATMAN logo display base**

COMPOSITE SUPERMAN
First Appearance (Series 3)
DC Direct

RELEASE DATE: **2005**
SCALE: **6½ inches**
ARTICULATION: **9 points**
ACCESSORIES: **FIRST APPEARANCE logo display base**

CONDUIT
Superman: Man of Steel
Kenner

RELEASE DATE: **1995**
SCALE: **5 inches**
ARTICULATION: **7 points**
ACCESSORIES: **Removable mask and gauntlets w/ cables**
ACTION FEATURE: **Spinning kryptonite attack cables**

COPPERHEAD
DC Super Heroes:
Justice League Unlimited
Mattel

RELEASE DATE: **2005**
SCALE: **4¾ inches**
ARTICULATION: **6 points (including tail)**
ACCESSORIES: **Serpent (single-carded release only)**

> Copperhead's serpentine tail
> is prehensile and can crush the
> life out of his victims.
>
> **FIRST APPEARANCE**
> *The Brave and the Bold* No. 78

COSMIC BOY
Pocket Super Heroes (Series 1)
DC Direct

RELEASE DATE: **2002**
SCALE: **3¼ inches**
ARTICULATION: **6 points**
ACCESSORIES: **Display base**

THE CREEPER
The New Batman Adventures
Kenner

RELEASE DATE: **1998**
SCALE: **4¾ inches**
ARTICULATION: **5 points**
ACCESSORIES: **Converting camera launcher**

COSMIC BOY
Legion of Super-Heroes (Series 1)
DC Direct

RELEASE DATE: **2005**
SCALE: **6½ inches**
ARTICULATION: **10 points**
ACCESSORIES: **Magnetic hands, steel magno balls (2), removable flight belt, and one-size-fits-all Legion Flight ring**

CYBORG
Super Powers (Series 3)
Kenner

RELEASE DATE: **1986**
SCALE: **4¾ inches**
ARTICULATION: **5 points**
ACCESSORIES: **Interchangeable action arms (3)**
ACTION FEATURE: **Power-action thrusting arms**

CYBORG
The New Teen Titans (Series 2)
DC Direct

RELEASE DATE: **2001**
SCALE: **6½ inches**
ARTICULATION: **16 points**
ACCESSORIES: **Interchangeable hands (2 sets) and sonic weapon**
VARIANT: **Redecoed figure, included in the *Classic Teen Titans* gift set (shown)**

> Victor Stone's human body was
> nearly destroyed when his father
> accidentally unleashed a creature
> from another dimension that killed
> Vic's mother and left Vic in need of
> some heavy metal upgrades.
>
> **FIRST APPEARANCE**
> *DC Comics Presents* No. 26

CYBORG
Teen Titans
Bandai

RELEASE DATE: **2004**
SCALE: **3½ inches**
ARTICULATION: **7 points**
ACCESSORIES: **Weapon**

CYBORG
Teen Titans
Bandai

RELEASE DATE: **2005**
SCALE: **3½ inches**
ARTICULATION: **7 points**
ACCESSORIES: **Interchangeable arm**

CYBORG
Teen Titans
Bandai

RELEASE DATE: **2005**
SCALE: **3½ inches**
ARTICULATION: **7 points**
ACCESSORIES: **Sword, helmet, and armor**

CYBORG SUPERMAN
Superman (Series 1)
DC Direct

RELEASE DATE: **2003**
SCALE: **6½ inches**
ARTICULATION: **18 points**
ACCESSORIES: **Superman S-shield insignia display base**

CYCLOTRON
Super Powers (Series 3)
Kenner

RELEASE DATE: **1986**
SCALE: **3¾ inches**
ARTICULATION: **8 points**
ACCESSORIES: **Removable faceplate**
ACTION FEATURE: **Power-action cyclo-spin**

D

DANIEL
The Sandman
DC Direct

RELEASE DATE: **2001**
SCALE: **6½ inches**
ARTICULATION: **5 points**
ACCESSORIES: **Orchid**

DARKSEID
Super Powers (Series 2)
Kenner

RELEASE DATE: **1985–86**
SCALE: **3¾ inches**
ARTICULATION: **7 points**
ACCESSORIES: **Removable cloth cape and mini comic**
ACTION FEATURE: **Power-action raging motion**

TOWER OF DARKNESS

Perhaps the second-most anticipated playset for *Super Powers* collectors after the Hall of Justice was the Tower of Darkness, a massive monolithic fortress carved in the fearsome image of dread Darkseid himself. With twin gun-port epaulets, giant grabbing arms to snag super heroes, and a dank dungeon to imprison captured Justice League members, the Tower of Darkness would have been the planet Apokolips' own "Hall of Injustice." Unfortunately, as the *Super Powers* line wound down in popularity, the Tower of Darkness never made it past the prototype stage, despite being pictured on *Super Powers* card backs and Kenner toy catalogs in 1986.

DARKSEID
Total Justice
Kenner

RELEASE DATE: **1996**
SCALE: **5 inches**
ARTICULATION: **5 points**
ACCESSORIES: **"Omega Effect" capture claw**
ACTION FEATURE: **Push-button opening claw (nonremovable)**

> Darkseid's "Omega Effect" eye blasts can teleport you anywhere the Dread Lord of Apokolips chooses... or disintegrate you where you stand!
>
> **FIRST APPEARANCE**
> *Superman's Pal Jimmy Olsen* No. 134

OMEGA BLAST DARKSEID
Superman
Kenner

RELEASE DATE: **1998**
SCALE: **4¾ inches**
ARTICULATION: **6 points**
ACCESSORIES: **Galactic laser blaster**

DARKSEID
Orion and Darkseid
DC Direct

RELEASE DATE: **2001**
SCALE: **6½ inches**
ARTICULATION: **6 points**
ACTION FEATURE: **Battery-operated "Omega Effect" light-up eyes**

DARKSEID
DC Super Heroes: Superman
Mattel

RELEASE DATE: **2006**
SCALE: **6 inches**
ARTICULATION: **23 points**
ACCESSORIES: **Mother Box**

DARKSEID
Justice League: Mission Vision
Mattel

RELEASE DATE: **2004**
SCALE: **4¾ inches**
ARTICULATION: **9 points**
ACCESSORIES: **Mission vision blaster and removable armor**

DARKSEID
Superman/Batman
(Series 2: *The Return of Supergirl*)
DC Direct

RELEASE DATE: **2006**
SCALE: **6½ inches**
ARTICULATION: **9 points**
ACCESSORIES: **SUPERMAN/BATMAN logo**
display base

DEADMAN
Other Worlds
DC Direct

RELEASE DATE: **2001**
SCALE: **6½ inches**
ARTICULATION: **11 points**
ACTION FEATURE: **Glow-in-the-dark features**

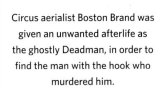

DEADMAN
Kingdom Come (Series 3)
DC Direct

RELEASE DATE: **2003**
SCALE: **6 inches**
ARTICULATION: **5 points**
ACCESSORIES: **Display base**

Circus aerialist Boston Brand was given an unwanted afterlife as the ghostly Deadman, in order to find the man with the hook who murdered him.

FIRST APPEARANCE
Strange Adventures No. 205

DEADSHOT
Identity Crisis (Series 1)
DC Direct

RELEASE DATE: **2005**
SCALE: **6½ inches**
ARTICULATION: **11 points**
ACCESSORIES: **IDENTITY CRISIS logo display base**

DEADSHOT
DC Super Heroes:
Justice League Unlimited
Mattel

RELEASE DATE: **2007**
SCALE: **4¾ inches**
ARTICULATION: **5 points**
ACCESSORIES: **Wrist blasters**

DEATH
The Sandman
DC Direct

RELEASE DATE: **1999**
SCALE: **6½ inches**
ARTICULATION: **11 points**
ACCESSORIES: **Umbrella**
VARIANT: **Alternate release w/ floppy hat accessory**

One of the Endless, Death is the sister of Dream (better known as the Sandman Morpheus) and fellow siblings Delirium, Desire, Despair, Destiny, and Destruction.

FIRST APPEARANCE
Sandman No. 8

Most humans use only 10 percent of their brain capacity. Slade Wilson uses 90 percent!

FIRST APPEARANCE
The New Teen Titans No. 2

DEATHSTROKE
Contemporary Teen Titans (Series 1)
DC Direct

RELEASE DATE: **2004**
SCALE: **6½ inches**
ARTICULATION: **9 points**
ACCESSORIES: **Sword, sawed-off shotgun,**
and TEEN TITANS logo display base
NOTE: **See also Slade.**

DEIMOS
The Lost World of the Warlord
Remco

RELEASE DATE: **1982**
SCALE: **5½ inches**
ARTICULATION: **6 points**
ACCESSORIES: **Mystic talisman**

DELIRIUM
The Sandman
DC Direct

RELEASE DATE: **2001**
SCALE: **6½ inches**
ARTICULATION: **3 points**
ACCESSORIES: **Goldfish balloon**

THE DEMON (ETRIGAN)
Other Worlds
DC Direct

RELEASE DATE: **2004**
SCALE: **6½ inches**
ARTICULATION: **11 points**
ACCESSORIES: **Cloth cape**

THE DEMON (ETRIGAN)
DC Super Heroes:
Justice League Unlimited
Mattel

RELEASE DATE: **2006**
SCALE: **4¾ inches**
ARTICULATION: **5 points**

> "Gone, gone the form of man! Rise the demon Etrigan!" Etrigan was bonded to his human host, Jason Blood, by none other than Merlin the Magician.
>
> **FIRST APPEARANCE**
> *The Demon* Vol. 1, No. 1

DESAAD
Super Powers (Series 2)
Kenner

RELEASE DATE: **1985–86**
SCALE: **3¾ inches**
ARTICULATION: **4 points**
ACCESSORIES: **Vibro-shocker (nonremovable)**
ACTION FEATURE: **Power-action shock squeeze**

> Darkseid's master torturer can't be trusted. Many times, he has plotted to overthrow Darkseid and rule Apokolips himself.
>
> **FIRST APPEARANCE**
> *The Forever People* Vol. 1, No. 2

DESIRE
The Sandman
DC Direct

RELEASE DATE: **2001**
SCALE: **6½ inches**
ARTICULATION: **3 points**

DESPERO
Total Justice
Kenner

RELEASE DATE: **1996**
SCALE: **5 inches**
ARTICULATION: **6 points**
ACCESSORIES: **Laser cannon and sword**
ACTION FEATURE: **Galactic body-blow attack**

DICK GRAYSON
World's Greatest Super-Heroes!
(Alter Egos)
Mego

RELEASE DATE: **1974**
SCALE: **8 inches**
ARTICULATION: **21 points**
ACCESSORIES: **Removable clothing**

DICK GRAYSON/ROBIN
Batman: The Animated Series
Kenner

RELEASE DATE: **1992**
SCALE: **4¾ inches**
ARTICULATION: **5 points**
ACCESSORIES: **Transforms into Robin with high-tech gear!**

TRANSFORMING DICK GRAYSON
Batman Forever
Kenner

RELEASE DATE: **1995**
SCALE: **4¾ inches**
ARTICULATION: **5 points**
ACCESSORIES: **Crime-fighting suit and sudden-reveal mask**
VARIANT: **A rarer gold-caped version was also released.**

DR. DEEMO
Swamp Thing
Kenner

RELEASE DATE: **1990**
SCALE: **5 inches**
ARTICULATION: **5 points**
ACCESSORIES: **Glow-in-the-dark serpent biomask and Swamp Thing voodoo doll**

> Next to the Spectre, Dr. Fate is the DC Universe's most powerful mystical character. Fate's helmet whispers magical incantations to him.
>
> **FIRST APPEARANCE**
> *More Fun Comics* No. 55

DR. FATE
Super Powers (Series 2)
Kenner

RELEASE DATE: **1985–86**
SCALE: **3¾ inches**
ARTICULATION: **7 points**
ACCESSORIES: **Removable cloth cape**
ACTION FEATURE: **Power-action mystic spell cast**

DR. FATE
Mages, Mystics & Magicians
DC Direct

RELEASE DATE: **2000**
SCALE: **6½ inches**
ARTICULATION: **11 points**
ACCESSORIES: **Alternate removable helmets (2)**

DR. FATE
Justice League Unlimited
Mattel

RELEASE DATE: **2004**
SCALE: **4¾ inches**
ARTICULATION: **5 points**
ACCESSORIES: **Mystic energy bolt (single-carded only)**

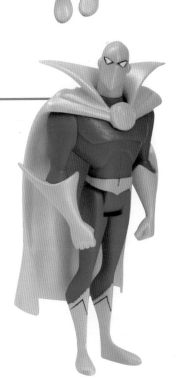

DR. FATE
Pocket Super Heroes (Series 1)
DC Direct

RELEASE DATE: **2002**
SCALE: **3¼ inches**
ARTICULATION: **6 points**
ACCESSORIES: **Removable cape and display base**

> In addition to being a frequent adversary of the JLA, Dr. Light was also a member of the Fearsome Five, foes of the New Teen Titans.
>
> **FIRST APPEARANCE**
> *Justice League of America* Vol. 1, No. 12

DR. LIGHT I
Identity Crisis (Series 1)
DC Direct

RELEASE DATE: **2005**
SCALE: **6½ inches**
ARTICULATION: **13 points**
ACCESSORIES: **IDENTITY CRISIS logo display base**

DR. LIGHT II
DC Super Heroes:
Justice League Unlimited
Mattel

RELEASE DATE: **2006**
SCALE: **4¾ inches**
ARTICULATION: **5 points**
ACCESSORIES: **Light blast (single-carded only)**

Scientist and single mom
Kimiyo Hoshi gained her mastery
over light during DC Comics'
Crisis on Infinite Earths.

FIRST APPEARANCE
Crisis on Infinite Earths No. 4

DR. LIGHT II
Crisis on Infinite Earths (Series 3)
DC Direct

RELEASE DATE: **2006**
SCALE: **6½ inches**
ARTICULATION: **9 points**
ACCESSORIES: **CRISIS logo display base**

Dr. Mid-Nite's signature weapon
was his "blackout bomb,"
which released an all-enshrouding
cloud of pitch-black smoke.

FIRST APPEARANCE
All-American Comics No. 25

DR. MID-NITE
Justice Society of America (Series 2)
DC Direct

RELEASE DATE: **2001**
SCALE: **6½ inches**
ARTICULATION: **10 points**
ACCESSORIES: **Interchangeable right hand w/ pet owl Hooty (attached)**

DR. MID-NITE
Pocket Super Heroes (Series 1)
DC Direct

RELEASE DATE: **2002**
SCALE: **3¼ inches**
ARTICULATION: **6 points**
ACCESSORIES: **Removable cape and display base**

DR. MID-NITE III
JSA (Series 1)
DC Direct

RELEASE DATE: **2006**
SCALE: **6½ inches**
ARTICULATION: **9 points**
ACCESSORIES: **Removable pet owl Charlie and JSA logo display base**

Like his predecessors,
the present Dr. Mid-Nite
is blind in daylight but can see
clearly in darkness.

FIRST APPEARANCE
Doctor Mid-Nite No. 1

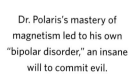

Dr. Polaris's mastery of
magnetism led to his own
"bipolar disorder," an insane
will to commit evil.

FIRST APPEARANCE
Green Lantern Vol. 1, No. 21

DR. POLARIS
DC Super Heroes
(Green Lantern vs. Dr. Polaris)
Hasbro

RELEASE DATE: **1999**
SCALE: **5 inches**
ARTICULATION: **5 points**

DONNA TROY
Identity Crisis (Series 2)
DC Direct

RELEASE DATE: **2007**
SCALE: **6½ inches**
ARTICULATION: **13 points**
ACCESSORIES: **Display base, orb**

DOOMSDAY
Superman: Man of Steel Box Set
Kenner

RELEASE DATE: **1995**
SCALE: **5 inches**
ARTICULATION: **5 points**

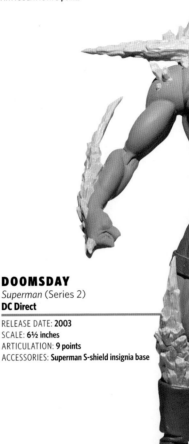

Genetic engineering
has ensured that the
monster Doomsday cannot
be defeated or killed the
same way twice.

FIRST APPEARANCE
Superman: The Man of Steel No. 17

DOOMSDAY
Superman (Series 2)
DC Direct

RELEASE DATE: **2003**
SCALE: **6½ inches**
ARTICULATION: **9 points**
ACCESSORIES: **Superman S-shield insignia base**

DOOMSDAY
DC Super Heroes: Superman
Mattel

RELEASE DATE: **2006**
SCALE: **6 inches**
ARTICULATION: **16 points**

DOOMSDAY
*DC Super Heroes:
Justice League Unlimited*
Mattel: Target Exclusive

RELEASE DATE: **2007**
SCALE: **4¾ inches**
ARTICULATION: **5 points**

DOVE
Justice League Unlimited
Mattel

RELEASE DATE: **2005**
SCALE: **4¾ inches**
ARTICULATION: **5 points**
ACCESSORIES: **Shield (single-carded only)**

Unlike his belligerent
brother, Hawk, Dove is a
self-proclaimed pacifist.

FIRST APPEARANCE
Showcase No. 75

THE DRUMMER
Planetary
DC Direct

RELEASE DATE: **2001**
SCALE: **6½ inches**
ARTICULATION: **5 points**
ACCESSORIES: **Drumsticks (2) and PLANETARY
logo display base**
NOTE: **See also Elijah Snow and Jakita Wagner.**

DUCARD
Batman Begins
Mattel

RELEASE DATE: **2005**
SCALE: **5 inches**
ARTICULATION: **10 points**
ACCESSORIES: **Gauntlet, sword, nunchaku, and
sword launcher**
VARIANT: **Green tunic deco**

ECLIPSO
Eclipso
DC Direct

RELEASE DATE: **2001**
SCALE: **6½ inches**
ARTICULATION: **9 points**
ACCESSORIES: **Life-size translucent purple "Black Diamond"**

EFFIGY
Green Lantern Corps
DC Direct

RELEASE DATE: **2003**
SCALE: **6½ inches**
ARTICULATION: **11 points**
ACCESSORIES: **Flaming sword**

> Martyn Van Wyck's fire powers were granted to him by the Controllers, aliens who descended from the same ancestors as the Guardians of the Universe, creators of the Green Lantern Corps.
>
> **FIRST APPEARANCE**
> *Green Lantern* Vol. 2, No. 110

ELIJAH SNOW
Planetary
DC Direct

RELEASE DATE: **2001**
SCALE: **6½ inches**
ARTICULATION: **5 points**
ACCESSORIES: **PLANETARY logo display base**
NOTE: **See also The Drummer and Jakita Wagner.**

ELONGATED MAN
JLA (Series 2)
DC Direct

RELEASE DATE: **2004**
SCALE: **6½ inches**
ARTICULATION: **10 points**
ACCESSORIES: **Removable "elongated" neck and JLA logo display base**

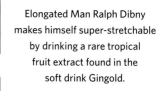

> Elongated Man Ralph Dibny makes himself super-stretchable by drinking a rare tropical fruit extract found in the soft drink Gingold.
>
> **FIRST APPEARANCE**
> *The Flash* Vol. 1, No. 112

ELONGATED MAN
Justice League Unlimited
Mattel

RELEASE DATE: **2005-06**
SCALE: **4¾ inches**
ARTICULATION: **5 points**
ACCESSORIES: **Gauntlet blaster (single-carded only)**

ELONGATED MAN
Identity Crisis (Series 2)
DC Direct

RELEASE DATE: **2006**
SCALE: **6½ inches**
ARTICULATION: **11 points**
ACCESSORIES: **Interchangeable arms (2 sets: articulated nonelongated/bendable elongated) and IDENTITY CRISIS logo display base**

ENEMY ACE
Enemy Ace
DC Direct

RELEASE DATE: **2002**
SCALE: **6½ inches**
ARTICULATION: **11 points**
ACCESSORIES: **Removable helmet, black wolf, and Fokker DR-1 triplane replica**

ENEMY ACE
Enemy Ace
Dreams & Visions

RELEASE DATE: **2003**
SCALE: **12 inches**
ARTICULATION: **21 points**
ACCESSORIES: **Dress jacket, dress pants, leather belt, boots, cap, helmet, great coat, medal, goggles, Luger w/ holster, shirt, T-shirt, pants, foil, German ceremonial sword, and wolf**

> German airman Hans von Hammer was the most feared pilot of World War I.
>
> **FIRST APPEARANCE**
> *Our Army at War* No. 151

THE ENGINEER
The Authority
DC Direct

RELEASE DATE: **2002**
SCALE: **6½ inches**
ARTICULATION: **10 points**

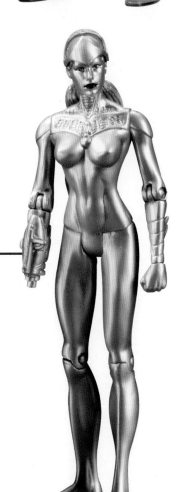

ERADICATOR
Superman: Man of Steel
Hasbro: ToyFare Exclusive

RELEASE DATE: **1999**
SCALE: **5 inches**
ARTICULATION: **5 points**
ACCESSORIES: **Removable cape**

ERADICATOR
Return of Superman (Series 1)
DC Direct

RELEASE DATE: **2004**
SCALE: **6½ inches**
ARTICULATION: **11 points**
ACCESSORIES: **Superman S-shield insignia display base**

> The Eradicator began his existence as a Kryptonian super-weapon built to preserve the planet Krypton's cultural integrity at all costs.
>
> **FIRST APPEARANCE**
> *Action Comics* No. 693

F

FATALITY
Green Lantern
DC Direct

RELEASE DATE: **2002**
SCALE: **6½ inches**
ARTICULATION: **7 points**
ACCESSORIES: **Removable gun and fighting staff**

> Fatality swore to destroy all Green Lanterns after GL John Stewart accidentally destroyed her homeworld of Xanshi.
>
> **FIRST APPEARANCE**
> *Green Lantern* Vol. 2, No. 83

FIRESTORM
Pocket Super Heroes (Series 1)
DC Direct

RELEASE DATE: **2002**
SCALE: **3¾ inches**
ARTICULATION: **6 points**
ACCESSORIES: **Display base**

FIRESTORM
JLA (Series 2)
DC Direct

RELEASE DATE: **2004**
SCALE: **6½ inches**
ARTICULATION: **9 points**
ACCESSORIES: **JLA logo display base**

FERRO LAD
Legion of Super-Heroes (Series 4)
DC Direct

RELEASE DATE: **2004**
SCALE: **6½ inches**
ARTICULATION: **11 points**

FIRESTORM
Super Powers (Series 2)
Kenner

RELEASE DATE: **1985**
SCALE: **3¾ inches**
ARTICULATION: **7 points**
ACTION FEATURE: **Power-action atomic punch**

> Teenager Ronnie Raymond fused with the body of physicist Martin Stein in a nuclear accident, which transformed the two into Firestorm the Nuclear Man!
>
> **FIRST APPEARANCE**
> *Firestorm* No. 1

FIRESTORM II
Infinite Crisis (Series 2)
DC Direct

RELEASE DATE: **2007**
SCALE: **6½ inches**
ARTICULATION: **11 points**
ACCESSORIES: **Display base**

THE FLASH I
Justice Society of America (Series 1)
DC Direct

RELEASE DATE: **2000**
SCALE: **6½ inches**
ARTICULATION: **9 points**
ACCESSORIES: **Removable helmet and Flash insignia display base**
VARIANT: **Re-released w/ JSA display base**

FIREFLY
The Batman
Mattel

RELEASE DATE: **2005**
SCALE: **5 inches**
ARTICULATION: **9 points**
ACCESSORIES: **Removable helmet and jetpack**
ACTION FEATURE: **Sparking jetpack**

THE FLASH I
Pocket Super Heroes (Series 2)
DC Direct

RELEASE DATE: **2003**
SCALE: **3¾ inches**
ARTICULATION: **6 points**
ACCESSORIES: **Removable helmet and display base**

> Jay Garrick, the first hero to be called the Flash, gained super-speed after inhaling the fumes of experimental "heavy water."
>
> **FIRST APPEARANCE**
> *Flash Comics* No. 1

THE FLASH I
First Appearance (Series 1)
DC Direct

RELEASE DATE: **2004**
SCALE: **6½ inches**
ARTICULATION: **11 points**
ACCESSORIES: **Mini comic and FIRST APPEARANCE logo display base**

THE FLASH II
Super Powers (Series 1)
Kenner

RELEASE DATE: **1984**
SCALE: **3¾ inches**
ARTICULATION: **7 points**
ACTION FEATURE: **Power-action lightning legs**

THE FLASH II
Pocket Super Heroes (Series 1)
DC Direct

RELEASE DATE: **2002**
SCALE: **3¼ inches**
ARTICULATION: **6 points**
ACCESSORIES: **Display base**

THE FLASH II
The Silver Age Flash and Kid Flash
DC Direct

RELEASE DATE: **2001**
SCALE: **6½ inches**
ARTICULATION: **9 points**
ACCESSORIES: Cosmic treadmill and one-size-fits-all
Flash ring w/ secret costume compartment
VARIANT: Redecoed version included with *First
Appearance: JLA (The Brave and the Bold No. 28)*
gift set.

THE FLASH II
Justice (Series 1)
DC Direct

RELEASE DATE: **2005**
SCALE: **7 inches**
ARTICULATION: **9 points**
ACCESSORIES: **Display base and mega-rod**

> Barry Allen made his final run
> to save the universe in DC Comics'
> *Crisis on Infinite Earths* No. 8,
> in 1985.
>
> **FIRST APPEARANCE**
> *Showcase* No. 4

THE FLASH II
DC Super Heroes/The Flash
Toy Biz

RELEASE DATE: **1989/1990**
SCALE: **3¾ inches**
ARTICULATION: **7 points**
ACCESSORIES: **Turbo platform (the Flash)**
ACTION FEATURE: **Accelerated running arm
movement**

THE FLASH II
Crisis on Infinite Earths (Series 2)
DC Direct

RELEASE DATE: **2006**
SCALE: **6½ inches**
ARTICULATION: **9 points**
ACCESSORIES: **Interchangeable heads (2: alive/
dying) and CRISIS logo display base**

THE FLASH II
The Flash 1:6 Deluxe Collector Figure
DC Direct

RELEASE DATE: **2007**
SCALE: **12 inches**
ARTICULATION: **28 points**
ACCESSORIES: **Display base**

THE FLASH III
Total Justice (Series 1)
Kenner

RELEASE DATE: **1996**
SCALE: **5 inches**
ARTICULATION: **5 points**
ACCESSORIES: **Fractal Techgear velocity power suit**
VARIANTS: **Various redecoed versions in Hasbro's
JLA collection**

THE FLASH III
JLA
Kenner: Kay-Bee Toys Exclusive

RELEASE DATE: **1997**
SCALE: **12 inches**
ARTICULATION: **18 points**

THE FLASH III
DC Super Heroes
(The Flash & Blue Beetle Box Set)
Hasbro

RELEASE DATE: **1999**
SCALE: **5 inches**
ARTICULATION: **5 points**
ACCESSORIES: **The Atom mini figure (nonarticulated)**

THE FLASH III
JLA (Series 1)
DC Direct

RELEASE DATE: **2003**
SCALE: **6½ inches**
ARTICULATION: **9 points**
ACCESSORIES: **One-size-fits-all Flash ring and JLA logo display base (w/ foot pegs)**

> Wally West was granted his superspeed after being bathed in lightning-charged chemicals, an accident exactly mirroring the origin of his uncle Barry Allen, the Flash II.
>
> **FIRST APPEARANCE**
> *The Flash* Vol. 1, No. 110

THE FLASH III
Pocket Super Heroes (JLA Box Set)
DC Direct

RELEASE DATE: **2003**
SCALE: **3¼ inches**
ARTICULATION: **6 points**

THE FLASH III
Justice League
Mattel

RELEASE DATE: **2003**
SCALE: **4¾ inches**
ARTICULATION: **5 points**
ACCESSORIES: **Display base with lenticular card**

THE FLASH III
Justice League
Mattel

RELEASE DATE: **2003**
SCALE: **10 inches**
ARTICULATION: **5 points**

THE FLASH III
Justice League: Mission Vision
Mattel

RELEASE DATE: **2004**
SCALE: **4¾ inches**
ARTICULATION: **5 points**
ACCESSORIES: **Shield, missile launcher, and wings**

THE FLASH III
Justice League: Mission Vision
Mattel

RELEASE DATE: **2004**
SCALE: **4¾ inches**
ARTICULATION: **10 points**
ACCESSORIES: **Spinning stand, shield, and wrist weapons**

THE FLASH III
Identity Crisis (Series 2)
DC Direct

RELEASE DATE: **2006**
SCALE: **6½ inches**
ARTICULATION: **11 points**
ACCESSORIES: **IDENTITY CRISIS logo display base**

THE FLASH III
JLA Classified (Series 1)
DC Direct

RELEASE DATE: **2006**
SCALE: **6½ inches**
ARTICULATION: **13 points**
ACCESSORIES: **Display base**

THE FLASH
Kingdom Come (Series 3)
DC Direct

RELEASE DATE: **2003**
SCALE: **6½ inches**
ARTICULATION: **5 points**

FROSTBITE
Batman & Robin
Kenner

RELEASE DATE: **1997**
SCALE: **5 inches**
ARTICULATION: **5 points**
ACCESSORIES: **Ice-assault luge and self-shielding hockey armor**

GANTHET
Green Lantern (Series 1)
DC Direct

RELEASE DATE: **2005**
SCALE: **6½ inches**
ARTICULATION: **11 points**
ACCESSORIES: **Green Lantern insignia display base**

GENERAL ZOD
Superman
Mego

RELEASE DATE: **1978–81**
SCALE: **12 inches**
ARTICULATION: **21 points**
ACCESSORIES: **Removable cloth costume and plastic boots**

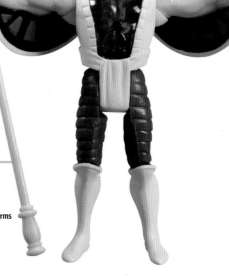

GENERAL ZOD
Pocket Super Heroes
Mego

RELEASE DATE: **1979–82**
SCALE: **3¾ inches**
ARTICULATION: **5 points**

GIZMO
Teen Titans
Bandai

RELEASE DATE: **2005**
SCALE: **3½ inches**
ARTICULATION: **5 points**
ACCESSORIES: **Wings and punching glove gizmo**

GOLDEN PHARAOH
Super Powers (Series 3)
Kenner

RELEASE DATE: **1986**
SCALE: **3¾ inches**
ARTICULATION: **7 points**
ACCESSORIES: **Staff**
ACTION FEATURE: **Power-action soaring arms**

> Superman's father, Jor-El, banished the traitorous General Zod to the Phantom Zone. Thus, Zod has sworn to destroy any surviving member of the House of El!
>
> **FIRST APPEARANCE**
> *Adventure Comics* No. 283

GORILLA GRODD
The Flash Rogues Gallery
DC Direct

RELEASE DATE: **2001**
SCALE: **6½ inches**
ARTICULATION: **7 points**
ACCESSORIES: **Calipers and human skull**

> Grodd hails from Gorilla City, a haven for a race of super-gorillas hidden deep within African jungles.
>
> **FIRST APPEARANCE**
> *The Flash* Vol. 1, No. 106

GREEN ARROW
Pocket Super Heroes (Series 2)
DC Direct

RELEASE DATE: **2003**
SCALE: **3¾ inches**
ARTICULATION: **6 points**
ACCESSORIES: **Bow, quiver, and display base**

GREEN ARROW
DC Super Heroes
Hasbro

RELEASE DATE: **1999**
SCALE: **9 inches**
ARTICULATION: **27 points**
ACCESSORIES: **Bow, arrow, cap, and quiver**

GREEN ARROW
The Silver Age Green Arrow and Speedy
DC Direct

RELEASE DATE: **2001**
SCALE: **6½ inches**
ARTICULATION: **11 points**
ACCESSORIES: **Bow, trick arrows, miniature Arrowcar, and miniature Arrowplane**

GREEN ARROW
DC: The New Frontier (Series 1)
DC Direct

RELEASE DATE: **2006**
SCALE: **6½ inches**
ARTICULATION: **14 points**
ACCESSORIES: **Bow, arrow, and display base**

> After finding himself stranded on deserted Starfish Island, wealthy playboy Oliver Queen mastered archery in order to survive, a skill he later aimed at villainy as the Green Arrow.
>
> **FIRST APPEARANCE**
> *More Fun Comics* No. 73

GREEN ARROW
World's Greatest Super-Heroes!
Mego

RELEASE DATE: **1972–82**
SCALE: **8 inches**
ARTICULATION: **21 points**
ACCESSORIES: **Removable cloth costume, plastic cap and boots, vinyl gloves, bow, and quiver**
VEHICLE: **Green Arrowcar**

GREEN ARROW
Super Powers (Series 2)
Kenner

RELEASE DATE: **1985**
SCALE: **3¾ inches**
ARTICULATION: **7 points**
ACCESSORIES: **Bow and arrows (3)**
ACTION FEATURE: **Power-action archery pull**

GREEN ARROW
Hard-Traveling Heroes/Green Arrow
DC Direct

RELEASE DATE: **2000**
SCALE: **6½ inches**
ARTICULATION: **11 points**
ACCESSORIES: **Bow and trick arrows (3: drill arrow, handcuff arrow, and boxing-glove arrow)**
NOTE: **See Red Arrow.**

After parting ways with his kid sidekick, Speedy, Green Arrow donned a new costume in *The Brave and the Bold* No. 85.

GREEN ARROW
Justice League Unlimited
Mattel

RELEASE DATE: **2005**
SCALE: **4¾ inches**
ARTICULATION: **5 points**
ACCESSORIES: **Bow and trick arrow (single-carded only)**

GREEN ARROW
Justice League Unlimited
Mattel

RELEASE DATE: **2005**
SCALE: **10 inches**
ARTICULATION: **5 points**
ACCESSORIES: **Bow**

GREEN ARROW
Identity Crisis (Series 2)
DC Direct

RELEASE DATE: **2006**
SCALE: **6½ inches**
ARTICULATION: **11 points**
ACCESSORIES: **Bow, alternate quiver arrow insert, and IDENTITY CRISIS logo display base**

GREEN ARROW
Justice (Series 5)
DC Direct

RELEASE DATE: **2007**
SCALE: **7 inches**
ARTICULATION: **9 points**
ACCESSORIES: **Bow**

GREEN ARROW II
Total Justice (Series 3)
Kenner

RELEASE DATE: **1996**
SCALE: **5 inches**
ARTICULATION: **5 points**
ACCESSORIES: **Bow and arrow**
VARIANT: **Redecoed version released in Hasbro's *JLA* collection**

Connor Hawke is the son of the original Green Arrow, Oliver Queen. Connor is one of the DC Universe's foremost martial artists.

FIRST APPEARANCE
Green Arrow Vol. 2, No. 0

GREEN LANTERN I
Justice Society of America (Series 1)
DC Direct

RELEASE DATE: **2000**
SCALE: **6½ inches**
ARTICULATION: **9 points**
ACCESSORIES: **Power battery and one-size-fits-all power ring**

Green Lantern Alan Scott's power ring was formed from a piece of "enchanted" train lantern and is powerless against wood.

FIRST APPEARANCE
All-American Comics No. 16

GREEN LANTERN I
Pocket Super Heroes (Series 1)
DC Direct

RELEASE DATE: **2002**
SCALE: **3¾ inches**
ARTICULATION: **6 points**
ACCESSORIES: **Removable cape and display base**

GREEN LANTERN I
Kingdom Come (Series 1)
DC Direct

RELEASE DATE: **2003**
SCALE: **6½ inches**
ARTICULATION: **5 points**
ACCESSORIES: **Power sword**

GREEN LANTERN I
First Appearance (Series 2)
DC Direct

RELEASE DATE: **2004**
SCALE: **6½ inches**
ARTICULATION: **11 points**
ACCESSORIES: **Power battery, removable cloth cape, mini comic, and FIRST APPEARANCE logo display base**

GREEN LANTERN II
Super Powers (Series 1)
Kenner

RELEASE DATE: **1984**
SCALE: **3¾ inches**
ARTICULATION: **7 points**
ACCESSORIES: **Power battery**
ACTION FEATURE: **Power-action ring thrust**

> Air Force test pilot Hal Jordan is fearless, a necessary character trait in becoming a member of the Green Lantern Corps.
> **FIRST APPEARANCE**
> *Showcase* No. 22

> Hal Jordan's Green Lantern Oath:
> *In brightest day, in blackest night,*
> *no evil shall escape my sight.*
> *Let those who worship evil's might,*
> *beware my power*
> *Green Lantern's light!*

GREEN LANTERN II
DC Super Heroes
Toy Biz

RELEASE DATE: **1989**
SCALE: **3¾ inches**
ARTICULATION: **7 points**
ACCESSORIES: **Power battery and water jet (power) ring**

GREEN LANTERN II
DC Super Heroes
Hasbro

RELEASE DATE: **1999**
SCALE: **9 inches**
ARTICULATION: **27 points**
ACCESSORIES: **DC Comics BULLET logo display base**

GREEN LANTERN II
Hard-Traveling Heroes
DC Direct

RELEASE DATE: **2000**
SCALE: **6½ inches**
ARTICULATION: **9 points**
ACCESSORIES: **Power battery and one-size-fits-all power ring**
VARIANT: **Redecoed version included with *First Appearance: JLA (The Brave and the Bold No. 28)* gift set**

GREEN LANTERN II
Pocket Super Heroes (Series 1)
DC Direct

RELEASE DATE: **2002**
SCALE: **3¾ inches**
ARTICULATION: **6 points**
ACCESSORIES: **Display base**

GREEN LANTERN II
Green Lantern Corps
DC Direct

RELEASE DATE: **2003**
SCALE: **6½ inches**
ARTICULATION: **11 points**
ACCESSORIES: **Power battery and one-size-fits-all power ring**
FEATURES: **Resealable packaging**

GREEN LANTERN II
Super Friends!
DC Direct

RELEASE DATE: **2003**
SCALE: **6½ inches**
ARTICULATION: **9 points**
ACCESSORIES: **Power battery, one-size-fits-all power ring, Hall of Justice miniature, and SUPER FRIENDS! logo display base**

GREEN LANTERN II
Green Lantern (Series 1)
DC Direct

RELEASE DATE: **2005**
SCALE: **6½ inches**
ARTICULATION: **13 points**
ACCESSORIES: **Power battery and Green Lantern insignia display base**

EMERALD SHIELD GREEN LANTERN
Green Lantern (Series 1)
DC Direct: ToyFare Exclusive

RELEASE DATE: **2005**
SCALE: **6½ inches**
ARTICULATION: **13 points**
ACCESSORIES: **Power battery, simulated flight stand, and Green Lantern insignia display base**

GREEN LANTERN II
Green Lantern 1:6 Scale Deluxe Collector Figure
DC Direct

RELEASE DATE: **2006**
SCALE: **13 inches**
ARTICULATION: **24 points**
ACCESSORIES: **Battery-operated light-up power battery, removable mask, and interchangeable hands w/ fully articulated fingers**

GREEN LANTERN II
Justice (Series 4)
DC Direct

RELEASE DATE: **2006**
SCALE: **7 inches**
ARTICULATION: **11 points**
ACCESSORIES: **Display base**

GREEN LANTERN II
DC: The New Frontier (Series 1)
DC Direct

RELEASE DATE: **2006**
SCALE: **6½ inches**
ARTICULATION: **13 points**
ACCESSORIES: **Power battery, interchangeable head, and display base**

SEEING GREEN

There are only one hundred of them in the world, and chances are, you're not one of the lucky few who has one. Designed by *Justice League Unlimited* cartoon producer Bruce Timm, this one-of-a-kind *JLU*-style Hal Jordan Green Lantern figure was offered as a holiday gift in 2005 from Mattel to just one hundred lucky contacts. The mold was destroyed thereafter, preserving the figure's limited-edition status forever. When news of the ultra-rare figure hit the Internet, *JLU* toy collectors were naturally green with envy, scurrying en masse to eBay with the hopes that Hal just might fly by for auction.

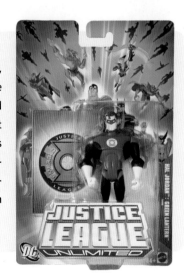

RED SON GREEN LANTERN
Elseworlds (Series 3)
DC Direct

RELEASE DATE: **2007**
SCALE: **6½ inches**
ARTICULATION: **11 points**
ACCESSORIES: **Power battery**

GREEN LANTERN III
Green Lantern Corps
DC Direct

RELEASE DATE: **2002**
SCALE: **6½ inches**
ARTICULATION: **9 points**
ACCESSORIES: **Power battery and one-size-fits-all power ring**
VARIANT: **Redecoed version features John Stewart in a "standard" Green Lantern uniform.**

After Guy Gardner, John Stewart was the second "replacement" Green Lantern chosen by Hal Jordan's power ring to serve the Green Lantern Corps if Hal were incapacitated or otherwise unavailable.

FIRST APPEARANCE
Green Lantern Vol. 1, No. 87

GREEN LANTERN III

Pocket Super Heroes
(Green Lantern Box Set)
DC Direct

RELEASE DATE: **2004**
SCALE: **3¼ inches**
ARTICULATION: **6 points**

GREEN LANTERN III

Justice League
Mattel

RELEASE DATE: **2003**
SCALE: **4¾ inches**
ARTICULATION: **5 points**
ACCESSORIES: **Display base**
VARIANT: **ATTACK ARMOR** release includes power
battery and Emerald Energy attack armor

GREEN LANTERN III

Justice League: Mission Vision
Mattel

RELEASE DATE: **2004**
SCALE: **4¾ inches**
ARTICULATION: **10 points**
ACCESSORIES: **Giant fist, helmet, and shield**

GREEN LANTERN III

JLA Gift Set
DC Direct

RELEASE DATE: **2005**
SCALE: **6½ inches**
ARTICULATION: **9 points**
ACCESSORIES: **Power battery and JLA logo display
base (w/ foot pegs)**

> Hand-picked by the Guardian
> known as Ganthet, Kyle Rayner
> became the universe's only
> Green Lantern following
> Hal Jordan's transformation
> into the villainous Parallax.
>
> **FIRST APPEARANCE**
> *Green Lantern* Vol. 1, No. 48

GREEN LANTERN III

Justice League Unlimited
Mattel

RELEASE DATE: **2005**
SCALE: **4¾ inches**
ARTICULATION: **10 points**
ACCESSORIES: **Display stand**

GREEN LANTERN IV

Total Justice (Series 1)
Kenner

RELEASE DATE: **1996**
SCALE: **5 inches**
ARTICULATION: **5 points**
ACCESSORIES: **Fractal Techgear armor and Ring-
Energy disc launcher**
VARIANTS: **Redecoed versions released in Hasbro's
JLA collection**

GREEN LANTERN IV

JLA
Hasbro

RELEASE DATE: **1998**
SCALE: **12 inches**
ARTICULATION: **18 points**
ACCESSORIES: **Power battery and emerald energy
weapon w/ ammo belt**

GREEN LANTERN IV
DC Super Heroes
(Green Lantern vs. Dr. Polaris)
Kenner

RELEASE DATE: **1999**
SCALE: **5 inches**
ARTICULATION: **5 points**

GREEN LANTERN IV
Green Lantern Corps
Kenner

RELEASE DATE: **2002**
SCALE: **6½ inches**
ARTICULATION: **9 points**
ACCESSORIES: **Power battery and one-size-fits-all power ring**

GREEN LANTERN IV
JLA (Series 1)
DC Direct

RELEASE DATE: **2003**
SCALE: **6½ inches**
ARTICULATION: **9 points**
ACCESSORIES: **Power battery and JLA logo display base**

Following the events of DC Comics' *The Rann-Thanagar War* mini series, Kyle Rayner is now known as the intergalactic hero Ion.

GREEN LANTERN IV
Pocket Super Heroes (JLA Box Set)
DC Direct

RELEASE DATE: **2003**
SCALE: **3¼ inches**
ARTICULATION: **6 points**

GREEN LANTERN IV
Pocket Super Heroes
(Green Lantern Box Set)
DC Direct

RELEASE DATE: **2004**
SCALE: **3¼ inches**
ARTICULATION: **6 points**

GREEN LANTERN IV
DC Super Heroes:
Justice League Unlimited
Mattel

RELEASE DATE: **2006-07**
SCALE: **4¾ inches**
ARTICULATION: **5 points**
ACCESSORIES: **Power battery (single-carded only)**

GUARDIAN OF THE UNIVERSE
Pocket Super Heroes (Series 2)
DC Direct

RELEASE DATE: **2003**
SCALE: **3¼ inches**
ARTICULATION: **6 points**
ACCESSORIES: **Cloth robe and display base**

GUARDIAN OF THE UNIVERSE
Green Lantern (Series 1)
DC Direct

RELEASE DATE: **2005**
SCALE: **6½ inches**
ARTICULATION: **7 points**
ACCESSORIES: **Green Lantern insignia display base**
NOTE: **See also Ganthet.**

GUY GARDNER
Green Lantern Corps
DC Direct

RELEASE DATE: **2003**
SCALE: **6½ inches**
ARTICULATION: **11 points**
ACCESSORIES: **Power battery and one-size-fits-all power ring**

GUY GARDNER
Pocket Super Heroes (Series 2)
DC Direct

RELEASE DATE: **2003**
SCALE: **3¼ inches**
ARTICULATION: **6 points**
ACCESSORIES: **Power battery and display base**

Guy Gardner became a full-time Green Lantern during DC Comics' *Crisis on Infinite Earths.*

FIRST APPEARANCE
Green Lantern Vol. 1, No. 59

GUY GARDNER
Pocket Super Heroes
(Green Lantern Box Set)
DC Direct

RELEASE DATE: **2004**
SCALE: **3¼ inches**
ARTICULATION: **6 points**

GUY GARDNER
Green Lantern (Series 2)
DC Direct

RELEASE DATE: **2006**
SCALE: **6½ inches**
ARTICULATION: **9 points**
ACCESSORIES: **Green Lantern insignia display base**

HARBINGER
Crisis on Infinite Earths (Series 1)
DC Direct

RELEASE DATE: **2005**
SCALE: **6½ inches**
ARTICULATION: **9 points**
ACCESSORIES: **CRISIS logo display base**

As a child, Harbinger was rescued by the Monitor and granted superpowers. She aided him in recording information about the heroes and villains of infinite Earths.

FIRST APPEARANCE
The New Teen Titans Annual Vol. 1, No. 2

HARD LIGHT STORY
Hasbro teamed with Diamond Comic Distributors in 1997 to offer a story-specific take on the former company's *JLA* assortment of action figures. Using the "Rock of Ages" storyline from DC Comics' *JLA* No. 10 to 15 as figure fodder, Hasbro produced seven "holographic" versions of the JLA peppered throughout four 5-pack box sets released by Diamond. These toys—cast in translucent plastic—were based on the JLA Revenge Squad created by Lex Luthor's Injustice Gang to harangue the Justice League. All are redecos of existing JLA figure sculpts, but with the added play value of adapting characters not seen before or since "Rock of Ages."

HARLEY QUINN
The Adventures of Batman & Robin
Kenner

RELEASE DATE: **1997**
SCALE: **4¾ inches**
ARTICULATION: **5 points**
ACCESSORIES: **Knockout punching glove and trick pistol**

HARLEY QUINN
Batman: Hush (Series 2)
DC Direct

RELEASE DATE: **2004**
SCALE: **6½ inches**
ARTICULATION: **11 points**
ACCESSORIES: **Gun molded to hand, mallet, and BATMAN logo display base**

Before becoming murderous moll to the Clown Prince of Crime, Dr. Harleen Quinzel was the Joker's psychotherapist in Arkham Asylum.

FIRST APPEARANCE
Batman: Harley Quinn No. 1

HARLEY QUINN
The New Batman Adventures
Hasbro

RELEASE DATE: **1998**
SCALE: **12 inches**
ARTICULATION: **19 points**
ACCESSORIES: **Harley's pet hyenas (2)**

HAWKGIRL
Hawkman and Hawkgirl
DC Direct

RELEASE DATE: **2000**
SCALE: **6½ inches**
ARTICULATION: **15 points (including wings)**
ACCESSORIES: **Golden Age and Silver Age–style removable helmets and shield**
ACTION FEATURE: **Push-button flapping wings**

HAWKGIRL
Pocket Super Heroes (Series 2)
DC Direct

RELEASE DATE: **2003**
SCALE: **3¼ inches**
ARTICULATION: **8 points (including wings)**
ACCESSORIES: **Display base**

HAWKGIRL
Justice League
Mattel

RELEASE DATE: **2003**
SCALE: **4¾ inches**
ARTICULATION: **5 points**
ACCESSORIES: **Mace**

HAWKGIRL
Justice League
Mattel

RELEASE DATE: **2004**
SCALE: **10 inches**
ARTICULATION: **5 points**
ACCESSORIES: **Mace**

HAWKGIRL
*DC Super Heroes:
Justice League Unlimited*
Mattel

RELEASE DATE: **2006**
SCALE: **4¾ inches**
ARTICULATION: **5 points**

Kendra Saunders' body
is inhabited by the
soul of the ancient
Egyptian princess Chay-Ara.

FIRST APPEARANCE
JSA Secret Files and Origins No. 1

HAWKGIRL (SHAYERA HOL)
*DC Super Heroes:
Justice League Unlimited 2007
Comic Convention Exclusive*
Mattel

RELEASE DATE: **2007**
SCALE: **4¾ inches**
ARTICULATION: **5 points**
NOTE: **Convention exclusive three-pack also included new Ray II and Green Lantern (John Stewart) re-release**

HAWKGIRL III
JSA (Series 1)
DC Direct

RELEASE DATE: **2006**
SCALE: **6½ inches**
ARTICULATION: **13 points (including wings)**
ACCESSORIES: **Removable mask, belt, mace, and JSA logo display base**

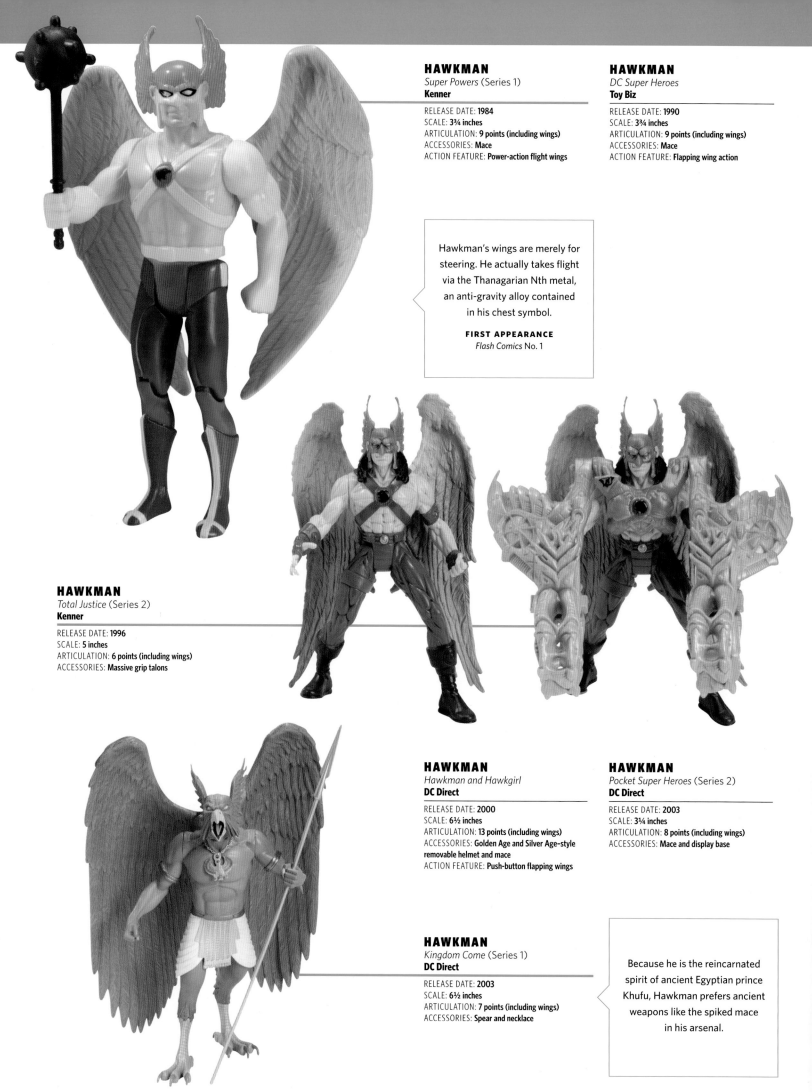

HAWKMAN
Super Powers (Series 1)
Kenner

RELEASE DATE: **1984**
SCALE: **3¾ inches**
ARTICULATION: **9 points (including wings)**
ACCESSORIES: **Mace**
ACTION FEATURE: **Power-action flight wings**

HAWKMAN
DC Super Heroes
Toy Biz

RELEASE DATE: **1990**
SCALE: **3¾ inches**
ARTICULATION: **9 points (including wings)**
ACCESSORIES: **Mace**
ACTION FEATURE: **Flapping wing action**

Hawkman's wings are merely for steering. He actually takes flight via the Thanagarian Nth metal, an anti-gravity alloy contained in his chest symbol.

FIRST APPEARANCE
Flash Comics No. 1

HAWKMAN
Total Justice (Series 2)
Kenner

RELEASE DATE: **1996**
SCALE: **5 inches**
ARTICULATION: **6 points (including wings)**
ACCESSORIES: **Massive grip talons**

HAWKMAN
Hawkman and Hawkgirl
DC Direct

RELEASE DATE: **2000**
SCALE: **6½ inches**
ARTICULATION: **13 points (including wings)**
ACCESSORIES: **Golden Age and Silver Age–style
removable helmet and mace**
ACTION FEATURE: **Push-button flapping wings**

HAWKMAN
Pocket Super Heroes (Series 2)
DC Direct

RELEASE DATE: **2003**
SCALE: **3¼ inches**
ARTICULATION: **8 points (including wings)**
ACCESSORIES: **Mace and display base**

HAWKMAN
Kingdom Come (Series 1)
DC Direct

RELEASE DATE: **2003**
SCALE: **6½ inches**
ARTICULATION: **7 points (including wings)**
ACCESSORIES: **Spear and necklace**

Because he is the reincarnated spirit of ancient Egyptian prince Khufu, Hawkman prefers ancient weapons like the spiked mace in his arsenal.

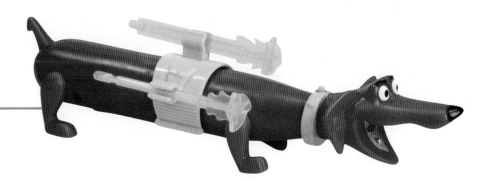

HAWKMAN
First Appearance (Series 2)
DC Direct

RELEASE DATE: **2004**
SCALE: **6½ inches**
ARTICULATION: **13 points (including wings)**
ACCESSORIES: **Glass dagger, shield, mini comic, and FIRST APPEARANCE logo display base**

HAWKMAN
Identity Crisis (Series 1)
DC Direct

RELEASE DATE: **2005**
SCALE: **6½ inches**
ARTICULATION: **13 points (including wings)**
ACCESSORIES: **Mace and IDENTITY CRISIS logo display base**

HAWKMAN
Justice (Series 4)
DC Direct

RELEASE DATE: **2006**
SCALE: **7 inches**
ARTICULATION: **13 points (including wings)**
ACCESSORIES: **Mace and display base**

HAWKMAN
Superman/Batman
(Series 3: *Public Enemies*)
DC Direct

RELEASE DATE: **2007**
SCALE: **6½ inches**
ARTICULATION: **11 points**
ACCESSORIES: **Horus power gauntlet and mace**

> The famed demigod of Greek mythology wandered a post-apocalyptic Earth in DC Comics' short-lived *Hercules Unbound* series.
>
> **FIRST APPEARANCE**
> *Hercules Unbound* No. 1

HERCULES UNBOUND
The Lost World of the Warlord
Remco

RELEASE DATE: **1982**
SCALE: **5¼ inches**
ARTICULATION: **6 points**
ACCESSORIES: **Staff**

HOT DOG
Krypto the Superdog
Fisher-Price

RELEASE DATE: **2006**
SCALE: **6 inches**
ARTICULATION: **5 points**
ACCESSORIES: **Ice creatures**

HOT SPOT
Teen Titans
Bandai

RELEASE DATE: **2005**
SCALE: **3½ inches**
ARTICULATION: **5 points**
ACCESSORIES: **Fireball**

HOURMAN I
Justice Society of America (Series 2)
DC Direct

RELEASE DATE: **2001**
SCALE: **6½ inches**
ARTICULATION: **10 points**
ACCESSORIES: **Hourglass**

> By swallowing a "Miraclo Pill," chemist Rex "Tick-Tock" Tyler gained superpowers for a duration of one hour.
>
> **FIRST APPEARANCE**
> *Adventure Comics* No. 48

HOURMAN I
Pocket Super Heroes (Series 2)
DC Direct

RELEASE DATE: **2003**
SCALE: **3¼ inches**
ARTICULATION: **6 points**
ACCESSORIES: **Removable cape/hood, hourglass, and display base**

> Rick Tyler became dependent on his father's Miraclo formula and had to develop a nonaddictive form of the super-pill to remain a costumed adventurer.
>
> **FIRST APPEARANCE**
> *Infinity Inc.* No. 20

HOURMAN II
JSA (Series 1)
DC Direct

RELEASE DATE: **2006**
SCALE: **6½ inches**
ARTICULATION: **9 points**
ACCESSORIES: **JSA logo display base**

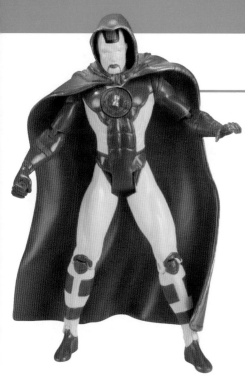

HOURMAN III
JLA: Amazing Androids
DC Direct

RELEASE DATE: **2000**
SCALE: **6½ inches**
ARTICULATION: **12 points**
ACTION FEATURE: **Rotating "Timer" hourglass chest symbol**

THE HUNTRESS
Total Justice (Series 3)
Kenner

RELEASE DATE: **1998**
SCALE: **5 inches**
ARTICULATION: **5 points**
ACCESSORIES: **Fractal Techgear barbed-arrow crossbow, halter armor, and crossbow pistol**

THE HUNTRESS
Birds of Prey
DC Direct

RELEASE DATE: **2003**
SCALE: **6½ inches**
ARTICULATION: **12 points**
ACCESSORIES: **Crossbow pistols (2)**

THE HUNTRESS
Batman: Hush (Series 1)
DC Direct

RELEASE DATE: **2004**
SCALE: **6½ inches**
ARTICULATION: **11 points**
ACCESSORIES: **Pistol molded to hand, staff, and BATMAN logo display base**

Helena Bertinelli became the costumed Huntress to avenge her murdered family.

FIRST APPEARANCE
The Huntress No. 1

Helena Wayne, the Huntress of Earth-2, is the daughter of that parallel world's Batman and Catwoman.

FIRST APPEARANCE
All-Star Comics No. 69

THE HUNTRESS
DC Super-Heroes: Justice League Unlimited
Mattel

RELEASE DATE: **2006/2007**
SCALE: **4¾ inches**
ARTICULATION: **5 points**
ACCESSORIES: **Crossbow (single-carded only)**

THE HUNTRESS (EARTH-2)
Crisis on Infinite Earths (Series 3)
DC Direct

RELEASE DATE: **2006**
SCALE: **6½ inches**
ARTICULATION: **9 points**
ACCESSORIES: **Crossbow and CRISIS logo display base**

HUSH
Batman: Hush (Series 1)
DC Direct

RELEASE DATE: **2004**
SCALE: **6½ inches**
ARTICULATION: **11 points**
ACCESSORIES: **Guns molded to hands and BATMAN logo display base**
NOTE: **See Jason Todd.**

IMPULSE
JLA (Series 3)
Hasbro

RELEASE DATE: **1998**
SCALE: **5 inches**
ARTICULATION: **5 points**
ACCESSORIES: **JLA logo display base**

IMPULSE
Impulse
DC Direct

RELEASE DATE: **2000**
SCALE: **6½ inches**
ARTICULATION: **11 points**
ACCESSORIES: **Flash insignia display base**

Super-speedster Bart Allen is the grandson of Barry Allen, a.k.a. the Flash II. Bart later became Kid Flash II. Prematurely aged to adulthood, Bart is presently the Flash IV.

FIRST APPEARANCE
The Flash Vol. 2, No. 91

INVISIBLE KID
Legion of Super-Heroes (Series 4)
DC Direct

RELEASE DATE: **2004**
SCALE: **6½ inches**
ARTICULATION: **11 points**

Lyle Norg became the Invisible Kid after inventing an invisibility serum, his unique power subsequently earning him membership in the Legion of Super-Heroes.

FIRST APPEARANCE
Action Comics No. 267

ISIS
52 (Series 1)
DC Direct

RELEASE DATE: **2007**
SCALE: **6½ inches**
ARTICULATION: **5 points**
ACCESSORIES: **Display base**

JACKIE JOHNSON
Sgt. Rock
Dreams & Visions

RELEASE DATE: **2002**
SCALE: **12 inches**
ARTICULATION: **21 points**
ACCESSORIES: **Removable uniform, boots, dog tags, field jacket, helmet, and rifle w/ ammo clips (2)**

JADE
Pocket Super Heroes
(Green Lantern Box Set)
DC Direct

RELEASE DATE: **2006**
SCALE: **3¼ inches**
ARTICULATION: **6 points**

> Jade was the daughter of Green Lantern Alan Scott and his arch-foe, Thorn. She inherited her father's emerald energies and wielded a "power pulse" via a star-shaped birthmark on her right palm.
>
> **FIRST APPEARANCE**
> *All-Star Squadron* No. 25

JADE
Elseworlds (Series 2: *Kingdom Come*)
DC Direct

RELEASE DATE: **2006**
SCALE: **6½ inches**
ARTICULATION: **9 points**
ACCESSORIES: **Display base**

JAKITA WAGNER
Planetary
DC Direct

RELEASE DATE: **2001**
SCALE: **6½ inches**
ARTICULATION: **3 points**
ACCESSORIES: **PLANETARY logo display base**
NOTE: **See also The Drummer and Elijah Snow.**

JASON TODD AS HUSH
Batman: Hush (Series 1)
DC Direct: ToyFare Exclusive

RELEASE DATE: **2004**
SCALE: **6½ inches**
ARTICULATION: **11 points**
ACCESSORIES: **Pistols molded to hands (2) and BATMAN logo display base**

> To date, this is the only action-figure likeness of Jason Todd, who fought beside Batman as Robin II before being killed by the Joker and later resurrected in one of Rā's al Ghūl's life-renewing Lazarus Pits.
>
> **FIRST APPEARANCE**
> *Batman* No. 357

JENNY SPARKS
The Authority
DC Direct

RELEASE DATE: **2006**
SCALE: **6½ inches**
ARTICULATION: **11 points**

JIMMY OLSEN
Pocket Super Heroes
(Superman Box Set)
DC Direct

RELEASE DATE: **2004**
SCALE: **3¼ inches**
ARTICULATION: **6 points**

JIMMY OLSEN
Silver Age Superman (Series 1)
DC Direct

RELEASE DATE: **2006**
SCALE: **6½ inches**
ARTICULATION: **11 points**
ACCESSORIES: **Camera**

> For times of trouble, Superman gave his best pal, Jimmy Olsen, a hypersonic signal-watch with which Jimmy could contact the Man of Steel.
>
> **FIRST APPEARANCE**
> *Superman* Vol. 1, No. 13

JOHN CONSTANTINE, HELLBLAZER
Mages, Mystics & Magicians
DC Direct

RELEASE DATE: **2000**
SCALE: **6½ inches**
ARTICULATION: **7 points**
ACCESSORIES: **Pint of beer**

> In his youth, "working-class warlock" John Constantine was a member of the British punk band Mucous Membrane. Their one-hit wonder was "Venus of the Hardsell."
>
> **FIRST APPEARANCE**
> *Saga of the Swamp Thing* No. 37

JOHNNY QUICK
Crime Syndicate
DC Direct

RELEASE DATE: **2002**
SCALE: **6½ inches**
ARTICULATION: **9 points**
ACCESSORIES: **CRIME SYNDICATE logo display base**

> The Clown Prince of Crime was once a failed comedian who became a costumed villain known as the Red Hood. During a robbery, he fell into a vat of chemicals that bleached his skin white, dyed his hair green, and turned his lips ruby red. Forever after, he would be known as the Joker.
>
> **FIRST APPEARANCE**
> *Batman* No. 1

THE JOKER
World's Greatest Super-Heroes!
Mego

RELEASE DATE: **1972–82**
SCALE: **3¾ inches**
ARTICULATION: **21 points**
ACCESSORIES: **Removable cloth costume and plastic shoes**
VEHICLE: **Joker Mobile**

THE JOKER
World's Greatest Super-Heroes!:
Fist Fighters
Mego

RELEASE DATE: **1975–76**
SCALE: **8 inches**
ARTICULATION: **21 points**
ACCESSORIES: **Removable cloth costume and plastic shoes**
ACTION FEATURE: **Power-fist fighting action**

THE JOKER
Comic Action Heroes
Mego

RELEASE DATE: **1975–78**
SCALE: **3¾ inches**
ARTICULATION: **5 points**
ACCESSORIES: **Cane and display base**

THE JOKER
Super Powers (Series 1)
Kenner

RELEASE DATE: **1984–86**
SCALE: **3¾ inches**
ARTICULATION: **7 points**
ACCESSORIES: **Mallet**
ACTION FEATURE: **Power-action madcap mallet**

THE JOKER
Batman
Toy Biz

RELEASE DATE: **1989**
SCALE: **3¾ inches**
ARTICULATION: **7 points**
ACCESSORIES: **Removable hat, cane, and water tube**
ACTION FEATURE: **Squirting orchid!**

KNOCKOUT JOKER
The Dark Knight Collection
Kenner

RELEASE DATE: **1990**
SCALE: **3¾ inches**
ARTICULATION: **5 points**
ACCESSORIES: **Bazooka and "POW"erful weapon**

SKY ESCAPE JOKER
The Dark Knight Collection
Kenner

RELEASE DATE: **1990**
SCALE: **3¾ inches**
ARTICULATION: **5 points**
ACCESSORIES: **Whirling copter pack, long gun**
ACTION FEATURE: **Face changes color in cold water**

THE JOKER
Batman: The Animated Series
Kenner

RELEASE DATE: **1992**
SCALE: **4¾ inches**
ARTICULATION: **5 points**
ACCESSORIES: **"Laughing gas" spray gun**
VARIANTS: **"White face" and "green face"**

JET PACK JOKER
Batman: Mask of the Phantasm
Kenner

RELEASE DATE: **1993**
SCALE: **4¾ inches**
ARTICULATION: **5 points**
ACCESSORIES: **Jetpack with capture nozzle**
VARIANT: **The Joker was produced with both a green face and a white face.**

THE JOKER
Legends of Batman
Kenner

RELEASE DATE: **1995**
SCALE: **5 inches**
ARTICULATION: **5 points**
ACCESSORIES: **BANG! prop pistol and biting gag teeth**

THE LAUGHING MAN JOKER
Legends of Batman
Kenner

RELEASE DATE: **1995**
SCALE: **5 inches**
ARTICULATION: **5 points**
ACCESSORIES: **Gatling gun (projectile launcher)**
ACTION FEATURE: **Powerful Gatling gun attack!**
VARIANT: **Redeco released as Warner Bros. Store Exclusive**

POGO STICK JOKER
The Adventures of Batman & Robin
Kenner

RELEASE DATE: **1997**
SCALE: **4¾ inches**
ARTICULATION: **5 points**
ACCESSORIES: **Power launcher**

The Joker's bag of tricks includes an acid-spurting boutonnière and a prop BANG! pistol that doubles as a spear gun.

LAUGHING GAS JOKER
Legends of the Dark Knight
Kenner

RELEASE DATE: **1997**
SCALE: **7 inches**
ARTICULATION: **3 points**
ACCESSORIES: **Exploding suit that reveals his true identity; pistol**

WILD CARD JOKER
The New Batman Adventures
Kenner

RELEASE DATE: **1998**
SCALE: **4¾ inches**
ARTICULATION: **5 points**
ACCESSORIES: **Calling card cannon and "funny" guns**
VARIANTS: **Arkham Assault Joker** *(Batman Beyond: ROTJ)*

THE JOKER
The New Batman Adventures
Kenner

RELEASE DATE: **1998**
SCALE: **12 inches**
ARTICULATION: **20 points**
ACCESSORIES: **Gag bazooka, satchel full of cash, and playing card**

HYDRO BLAST JOKER
The New Batman Adventures: Mission Masters 2
Hasbro

RELEASE DATE: **1998**
SCALE: **4¾ inches**
ARTICULATION: **5 points**
VARIANTS: **Redecoed from original Joker** *(Batman: TAS)*

THE JOKER
DC Super Heroes
Hasbro

RELEASE DATE: **1999**
SCALE: **7 inches**
ARTICULATION: **5 points**
ACCESSORIES: **Deck of cards and cane (each nonremovable)**
VARIANT: **Redecoed figure released in Batman/Joker Kay-Bee Toys exclusive two-pack**

VIRTUAL JOKER
Batman Beyond: Batlink
Hasbro

RELEASE DATE: **2000**
SCALE: **4¾ inches**
ARTICULATION: **3 points**
ACCESSORIES: **Virus-tech lashes and byte mouth**

PLASMA GLOW JOKER
World of Batman
Hasbro: Wal-Mart Exclusive

RELEASE DATE: **2000**
SCALE: **4¾ inches**
ARTICULATION: **5 points**
ACCESSORIES: **Chopper pack and Funny Gun**

ARKHAM ASSAULT JOKER
Batman Beyond: Return of the Joker
Hasbro

RELEASE DATE: **2001**
SCALE: **4¾ inches**
ARTICULATION: **5 points**
ACCESSORIES: **Secret image card launcher**

THE JOKER
Batman
Hasbro: Target Exclusive

RELEASE DATE: **2001**
SCALE: **9 inches**
ARTICULATION: **27 points**
ACCESSORIES: **Mallet**
ACTION FEATURE: **Cloth outfit, "surprise" package, cane, and gag pistol**

TERRORCAST JOKER
The New Batman Adventures: Mission Masters 4
Hasbro

RELEASE DATE: **2002**
SCALE: **4¾ inches**
ARTICULATION: **5 points**
ACCESSORIES: **Machine gun and dynamite bundle**

THE JOKER
*The Classic Silver Age
Batgirl and The Joker*
DC Direct

RELEASE DATE: **2003**
SCALE: **6½ inches**
ARTICULATION: **11 points**
ACCESSORIES: **Joker's cane and Interlocking Gotham City rooftop display base**

THE JOKER
Batman: Hush (Series 1)
DC Direct

RELEASE DATE: **2004**
SCALE: **6½ inches**
ARTICULATION: **15 points (including jaw)**
ACCESSORIES: **BANG! gun molded to hand; display base**

QUICK FIRE JOKER
Batman
Mattel

RELEASE DATE: **2003**
SCALE: **6 inches**
ARTICULATION: **9 points**
ACCESSORIES: **Joker cane and Quick Fire Gun**

In DC Comics' *Batman: The Killing Joke*, the Joker shot Barbara Gordon through her spine, crippling the former Batgirl, an act that led her to become the information broker known as Oracle.

THE JOKER
Batman: The Dark Knight Returns
(Series 1)
DC Direct

RELEASE DATE: **2004**
SCALE: **6½ inches**
ARTICULATION: **5 points**
ACCESSORIES: **Doll bomb and sidewalk display base**

CRAZY CUT-UP THE JOKER
The Batman
Mattel

RELEASE DATE: **2004**
SCALE: **5 inches**
ARTICULATION: **10 points**
ACCESSORIES: **Spinning star cutter**

HAMMER STRIKE THE JOKER
The Batman
Mattel

RELEASE DATE: **2004**
SCALE: **5 inches**
ARTICULATION: **5 points**
ACCESSORIES: **Hammer**

STRANGLE SLEEVES THE JOKER
The Batman
Mattel

RELEASE DATE: **2005**
SCALE: **5 inches**
ARTICULATION: **5 points**
NOTE: **Redeco of Hammer Strike The Joker**

THE JOKER
Batman: The Long Halloween (Series 1)
DC Direct

RELEASE DATE: **2006**
SCALE: **6½ inches**
ARTICULATION: **11 points**
ACCESSORIES: **Santa hat, bag of gifts, and calendar page**

THE JOKER
Justice (Series 3)
DC Direct

RELEASE DATE: **2006**
SCALE: **6½ inches**
ARTICULATION: **9 points**
ACCESSORIES: **Cane**

THE JOKERZ
Batman Beyond
Hasbro

RELEASE DATE: **1999**
SCALE: **4¾ inches**
ARTICULATION: **5 points**
ACCESSORIES: **Assault hover-cycle**

J'S GANG POWER THROW
Batman Beyond
Hasbro

RELEASE DATE: **1999**
SCALE: **4¾ inches**
ARTICULATION: **3 points**
ACCESSORIES: **Smirk (nonposeable) and spiked weapon**
ACTION FEATURE: **Happy tosses smirk!**

JOR-EL
Superman
Mego

RELEASE DATE: **1978–81**
SCALE: **12 inches**
ARTICULATION: **21 points**
ACCESSORIES: **Removable cloth costume, belt, and boots**

> Jor-El's costume may come from comics, but his likeness is based on actor Marlon Brando, who played Superman's father in *Superman: The Movie.*
>
> **FIRST APPEARANCE**
> *Action Comics* No. 1

JOR-EL
Pocket Super Heroes
Mego

RELEASE DATE: **1979–82**
SCALE: **3¾ inches**
ARTICULATION: **5 points**

"HOLOGRAPHIC" JOR-EL
Superman Returns
Mattel

RELEASE DATE: **2006**
SCALE: **5½ inches**
ARTICULATION: **13 points**

JOR-EL
Superman Returns
Mattel: Toys R Us Exclusive

RELEASE DATE: **2006**
SCALE: **5½ inches**
ARTICULATION: **10 points**

JUSTICE LORDS

Cartoon Network's popular *Justice League Unlimited* cartoon series paid homage to DC Comics' multiple-Earths plot contrivance by sending the stalwart super team to a parallel dimension populated by darker versions of themselves who ruled over their planet with super-powered fists. These Justice Lords were adapted by Mattel in 2005, with redecoed versions of Superman, Batman, and Wonder Woman released in a three-pack. Wonder Woman received a newly sculpted head, featuring the Amazing Amazon with a fashionably short coif. More Justice Lords followed, with the Flash, Green Lantern, and Martian Manhunter adapted in 2006, and J'onn J'onzz featuring a newly designed cape. The Superman and Batman three-pack was later re-released, replacing Wonder Woman with a Justice Lords version of Hawkgirl.

K

KALIBAK
Super Powers (Series 2)
Kenner

RELEASE DATE: **1985–86**
SCALE: **3¾ inches**
ARTICULATION: **5 points**
ACCESSORIES: **Beta club**
ACTION FEATURE: **Power-action beta-club wing**

KID FLASH
Teen Titans
Mego

RELEASE DATE: **1976**
SCALE: **7 inches**
ARTICULATION: **21 points**
ACCESSORIES: **Removable cloth costume, gloves, and boots**

KATMA TUI
(GREEN LANTERN CORPS)
*DC Super Heroes:
Justice League Unlimited*
Mattel

RELEASE DATE: **2006**
SCALE: **4¾ inches**
ARTICULATION: **5 points**

DC Comics' Katma Tui replaced fellow Korugarian and rogue Green Lantern Sinestro as GL of Space Sector 1417.

FIRST APPEARANCE
Green Lantern Vol. 1, No. 30

Kid Flash became the Flash III after super-speedster Barry Allen perished during DC Comics' *Crisis on Infinite Earths.*

FIRST APPEARANCE
The Flash Vol. 1, No. 110

KID FLASH
The New Teen Titans
DC Direct

RELEASE DATE: **1998**
SCALE: **6½ inches**
ARTICULATION: **9 points**
ACCESSORIES: **Flash insignia display base**

KID FLASH
The Silver Age Flash and Kid Flash
DC Direct

RELEASE DATE: **2001**
SCALE: **6½ inches**
ARTICULATION: **9 points**
ACCESSORIES: **Shares cosmic treadmill and full-size Flash signet ring w/ box set's Flash figure**

KID FLASH
Pocket Super Heroes (Series 2)
DC Direct

RELEASE DATE: **2003**
SCALE: **3¼ inches**
ARTICULATION: **6 points**
ACCESSORIES: **Display base**

KID FLASH II
Contemporary Teen Titans (Series 2)
DC Direct

RELEASE DATE: **2005**
SCALE: **6½ inches**
ARTICULATION: **11 points**
ACCESSORIES: **TEEN TITANS logo display base**

KID FLASH III
Kingdom Come (Series 2)
DC Direct

RELEASE DATE: **2003**
SCALE: **6½ inches**
ARTICULATION: **5 points**
ACCESSORIES: **Display base**

KILLER CROC
Batman: The Animated Series
Kenner

RELEASE DATE: **1994**
SCALE: **4¾ inches**
ARTICULATION: **5 points**
ACCESSORIES: **Pet crocodile**
ACTION FEATURE: **Power-punch arm**

TAILWHIP KILLER CROC
Batman: Knight Force Ninjas
Kenner

RELEASE DATE: **1998**
SCALE: **5 inches**
ARTICULATION: **10 points**
ACCESSORIES: **Removable claw gauntlet and chomping skull**
ACTION FEATURE: **Real whipping action!**

KILLER CROC
Batman
Mattel

RELEASE DATE: **2003**
SCALE: **6 inches**
ARTICULATION: **9 points**
ACCESSORIES: **Bendable attack tail and jaw crushin' action**
VARIANTS: **"Battle Damaged" redeco**

> Waylon Jones isn't really a crocodile, but instead suffers from a rare skin disease, which gives his flesh the appearance of a scaly reptile.
>
> **FIRST APPEARANCE**
> *Batman* No. 357

KILLER CROC
Batman
Mattel

RELEASE DATE: **2005**
SCALE: **6 inches**
ARTICULATION: **23 points**
ACCESSORIES: **Pipe weapon**

KILLER CROC
The Batman: EXP
Mattel

RELEASE DATE: **2006**
SCALE: **5 inches**
ARTICULATION: **6 points**
ACCESSORIES: **Thrashing tail**

KILLER CROC
Secret Files
(Series 1: *Batman Rogues Gallery*)
DC Direct

RELEASE DATE: **2005**
SCALE: **6½ inches**
ARTICULATION: **12 points**
ACCESSORIES: **Human skull and display base**

KILLER CROC
DC Super Heroes: Batman
Mattel

RELEASE DATE: **2005**
SCALE: **6 inches**
ARTICULATION: **11 points**
ACCESSORIES: **Pipe**
NOTE: **Body reused from previous Mattel release; new head sculpt**

KILOWOG
Green Lantern (Series 1)
DC Direct

RELEASE DATE: **2005**
SCALE: **6½ inches**
ARTICULATION: **13 points**
ACCESSORIES: **Power battery and Green Lantern insignia display base**

KILOWOG
*DC Super Heroes:
Justice League Unlimited*
Mattel

RELEASE DATE: **2005**
SCALE: **4¾ inches**
ARTICULATION: **5 points**

The Green Lantern of Space Sector 674, Kilowog, was called on to train many fellow Green Lantern Corps members, including Hal Jordan.

FIRST APPEARANCE
Green Lantern Corps No. 201

KING SHARK
DC Super Heroes
Hasbro

RELEASE DATE: **1996**
SCALE: **5 inches**
ARTICULATION: **5 points**

King Shark is the second of three shark-themed DC toys to date. Can you find the other two throughout these pages?

FIRST APPEARANCE
Superboy Vol. 2, No. 0

KRYPTO THE SUPERDOG
*The Classic Silver Age
Superboy and Supergirl*
DC Direct

RELEASE DATE: **2002**
SCALE: **6½ inches**
ARTICULATION: **5 points**

KRYPTO THE SUPERDOG
Krypto the Superdog
Fisher-Price

RELEASE DATE: **2005**
SCALE: **6 inches**
ARTICULATION: **4 points**
ACCESSORIES: **Color-change kryptonite and flying disc launcher food bowl**
ACTION FEATURE: **Pop-out cape and talking feature**

KRYPTO THE SUPERDOG
Krypto the Superdog
Fisher-Price

RELEASE DATE: **2005**
SCALE: **6 inches**
ARTICULATION: **5 points**
ACCESSORIES: **Kevin action figure**

Jor-El sent Kal-El's puppy dog, Krypto, off in a test rocket before sending his beloved baby son to Earth in a similar spacecraft.

FIRST APPEARANCE
Adventure Comics No. 210

KRYPTO THE SUPERDOG
Krypto the Superdog
Fisher-Price

RELEASE DATE: **2005**
SCALE: **6 inches**
ARTICULATION: **9 points**
ACCESSORIES: **Flying action**

Krypto possesses the same powers as his master, Superman, including super-strength, the ability to fly, and heat vision.

KRYPTO ROCKET

In addition to its line of action figures based on Krypto the Superdog's animated adventures, Fisher-Price also produced a scale replica of the rocket that carried Superman's canine pal from Krypton to Earth. Krypto's Rocket includes opening pods and windshield, a claw to scoop up dangerous kryptonite, an exclusive Dogbot figure, and sound features replicating take-off and landing effects, as well as character phrases from Krypto and friends.

LANA LANG
Smallville
DC Direct

RELEASE DATE: **2002**
SCALE: **6½ inches**
ARTICULATION: **9 points**
ACCESSORIES: **Pom-poms (2) and wearable 18-inch kryptonite necklace**

LEX LUTHOR
Superman
Mego

RELEASE DATE: **1978-81**
SCALE: **12 inches**
ARTICULATION: **14 points**
ACCESSORIES: **Removable cloth costume and plastic boots**

LEX LUTHOR
Pocket Super Heroes
Mego

RELEASE DATE: **1979-82**
SCALE: **3¾ inches**
ARTICULATION: **5 points**

Lana Lang was Clark Kent's first love, long before he met his future wife, Lois Lane.
FIRST APPEARANCE
Superboy No. 10

Though earning both a twelve-inch figure and a Pocket Super Hero from Mego, Lex Luthor was never produced in the company's long-running *World's Greatest Super-Heroes!* lineup.

LEX LUTHOR
Super Powers (Series 1)
Kenner

RELEASE DATE: **1984-86**
SCALE: **3¾ inches**
ARTICULATION: **7 points**
ACCESSORIES: **Removable armor**
ACTION FEATURE: **Power-action nuclear punch**

Ironically, Lex Luthor and Clark Kent were childhood friends in Smallville, Kansas.
FIRST APPEARANCE
Action Comics No. 23

LEX LUTHOR
DC Super Heroes
Toy Biz

RELEASE DATE: **1989**
SCALE: **3¾ inches**
ARTICULATION: **7 points**
ACCESSORIES: **Pistol and briefcase**
ACTION FEATURE: **Button-activated power punch**

LEX LUTHOR
Superman
Kenner

RELEASE DATE: **1998**
SCALE: **4¾ inches**
ARTICULATION: **6 points**
ACCESSORIES: **Kryptonite armor and launcher**
ACTION FEATURE: **Button-activated power punch**

LEX LUTHOR
Superman: Man of Steel
Kenner

RELEASE DATE: **1996**
SCALE: **5 inches**
ARTICULATION: **6 points**
ACCESSORIES: **Squirting hornet-attack backpack**

LEX LUTHOR
Super Friends!
DC Direct

RELEASE DATE: **2003**
SCALE: **6½ inches**
ARTICULATION: **11 points**
ACCESSORIES: **"Dream Machine" gun, chunk of green kryptonite, Hall of Doom miniature model, and SUPER FRIENDS! logo display base**

LEX LUTHOR
Pocket Super Heroes (Superman Box Set)
DC Direct

RELEASE DATE: **2004**
SCALE: **3¼ inches**
ARTICULATION: **6 points**

LEX LUTHOR
Justice League
Mattel

RELEASE DATE: **2003**
SCALE: **4¾ inches**
ARTICULATION: **5 points**
ACCESSORIES: **Removable assault armor (4 pieces)**

LEX LUTHOR
*DC Super Heroes:
Justice League Unlimited*
Mattel

RELEASE DATE: **2005**
SCALE: **4¾ inches**
ARTICULATION: **5 points**

LEX LUTHOR
Silver Age Superman (Series 1)
DC Direct

RELEASE DATE: **2006**
SCALE: **6½ inches**
ARTICULATION: **11 points**
ACCESSORIES: **Ray gun and headset**

LEX LUTHOR
Lex Luthor 1:6 Scale Deluxe Collector Figure
DC Direct

RELEASE DATE: **2006**
SCALE: **13 inches**
ARTICULATION: **26 points**
ACCESSORIES: **Interchangeable hands w/ fully poseable fingers, kryptonite gun w/ removable cartridge, and display base**

LEX LUTHOR
Crisis on Infinite Earths (Series 2)
DC Direct

RELEASE DATE: **2006**
SCALE: **6½ inches**
ARTICULATION: **11 points**
ACCESSORIES: **CRISIS logo display base**

LEX LUTHOR
Superman/Batman (Series 3)
DC Direct

RELEASE DATE: **2006**
SCALE: **6½ inches**
ARTICULATION: **17 points**
ACCESSORIES: **Display base**

LEX LUTHOR
DC Super Heroes: Superman
Mattel

RELEASE DATE: **2006**
SCALE: **6 inches**
ARTICULATION: **23 points**
ACCESSORIES: **Kryptonite weapon and kryptonite**

LEX LUTHOR
Justice (Series 5)
DC Direct

RELEASE DATE: **2007**
SCALE: **7 inches**
ARTICULATION: **9 points**
ACCESSORIES: **Display base**
NOTE: **See also SUPERMAN RETURNS.**

LEX LUTHOR
Smallville
DC Direct

RELEASE DATE: **2002**
SCALE: **6½ inches**
ARTICULATION: **7 points**
ACCESSORIES: **Laptop computer and LuthorCorp annual report**

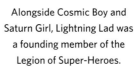

KRYPTONITE ARMOR LEX LUTHOR
Superman Returns
Mattel

RELEASE DATE: **2006**
SCALE: **5½ inches**
ARTICULATION: **9 points**
ACCESSORIES: **Kryptonite armor and kryptonite projectile launcher**

LEX LUTHOR
Superman Returns
Mattel

RELEASE DATE: **2006**
SCALE: **5½ inches**
ARTICULATION: **9 points**
ACCESSORIES: **Goggles, binoculars, missile launcher and missile w/ kryptonite warhead payload**

MISSILE LAUNCHING LEX LUTHOR
Superman Returns
Mattel

RELEASE DATE: **2006**
SCALE: **5½ inches**
ARTICULATION: **9 points**
ACCESSORIES: **Kryptonite missile and launcher**

LIGHTNING
Teen Titans
Bandai

RELEASE DATE: **2004**
SCALE: **3½ inches**
ARTICULATION: **9 points**

LIGHTNING LAD
Legion of Super-Heroes (Series 1)
DC Direct

RELEASE DATE: **2001**
SCALE: **6½ inches**
ARTICULATION: **10 points**
ACCESSORIES: **Interchangeable arms (2: human/robotic), removable flight belt, and one-size-fits-all Legion flight ring**

LIGHTNING LAD
Pocket Super Heroes (Series 1)
DC Direct

RELEASE DATE: **2002**
SCALE: **3¼ inches**
ARTICULATION: **6 points**
ACCESSORIES: **Removable cape and display base**

LIGHTRAY
DC Super Heroes: Justice League Unlimited
Mattel

RELEASE DATE: **2007**
SCALE: **4¾ inches**
ARTICULATION: **5 points**

Alongside Cosmic Boy and Saturn Girl, Lightning Lad was a founding member of the Legion of Super-Heroes.

FIRST APPEARANCE
Adventure Comics No. 247

LITTLE SURE SHOT
Sgt. Rock
Dreams & Visions

RELEASE DATE: **2002**
SCALE: **12 inches**
ARTICULATION: **21 points**
ACCESSORIES: **Removable uniform, dog tags, field jacket, helmet, and rifle w/ ammo clips (2)**

LOBO
DC Direct

RELEASE DATE: **2001**
SCALE: **6½ inches**
ARTICULATION: **12 points**
ACCESSORIES: **Cycle, removable hook and chain, interchangeable hands (2 sets), and Dawg figure (nonarticulated)**

LOBO
ReActivated (Series 1)
DC Direct

RELEASE DATE: **2006**
SCALE: **6½ inches**
ARTICULATION: **12 points**
ACCESSORIES: **Hook, chain, and REACTIVATED logo display base**
NOTE: **Same sculpt as previous DC Direct release w/ new head.**

Intergalactic bounty hunter Lobo is the last Czarnian, having killed every single person on his home planet with a horde of lethal insects, his own childhood science project.

FIRST APPEARANCE
Omega Men Vol. 1, No. 3

LOIS LANE
Superman: Battle for Metropolis
Hasbro

RELEASE DATE: **2001**
SCALE: **4¾ inches**
ARTICULATION: **3 points**
ACCESSORIES: **Clipboard and handheld computer**

LOIS LANE
The Classic Silver Age Superman and Lois Lane
DC Direct

RELEASE DATE: **2001**
SCALE: **6½ inches**
ARTICULATION: **7 points**
ACCESSORIES: **Interchangeable hands (2 sets), cloth skirt, and removable handbag**

LOIS LANE
Pocket Super Heroes (Series 2)
DC Direct

RELEASE DATE: **2003**
SCALE: **3¼ inches**
ARTICULATION: **6 points**
ACCESSORIES: **Purse, cloth skirt, and display base**

Lois Lane was the first reporter to use the name "Superman" to describe the flying hero who saved her and the crew of the space plane *Constitution* from a crash landing.

FIRST APPEARANCE
Action Comics No. 1

LOIS LANE AS SUPERWOMAN
Silver Age Superman (Series 1)
DC Direct

RELEASE DATE: **2006**
SCALE: **6½ inches**
ARTICULATION: **11 points**

M

MACHISTE
The Lost World of the Warlord
Remco

RELEASE DATE: **1982**
SCALE: **5¼ inches**
ARTICULATION: **6 points**
ACCESSORIES: **Axe and dagger**

> In the first run of *Warlord* comics, the former slave and gladiator Machiste was a friend and ally of Travis Morgan.
>
> **FIRST APPEARANCE**
> *Warlord* Vol. 1, No. 2

MAD HATTER
The New Batman Adventures
Kenner

RELEASE DATE: **1998**
SCALE: **4¾ inches**
ARTICULATION: **3 points**
ACCESSORIES: **Cane, robotic rabbit, and mind-control transmitter**
VARIANT: **Redecoed release in Kenner's *Spectrum of the Bat* collection**

TECHNOCAST JERVIS TETCH (MAD HATTER)
The New Batman Adventures: Mission Masters 4
Hasbro

RELEASE DATE: **2002**
SCALE: **4¾ inches**
ARTICULATION: **5 points**
ACCESSORIES: **Microphone cane and mind-controlling videocamera**

MADEMOISELLE MARIE
Sgt. Rock
Dreams & Visions

RELEASE DATE: **2002**
SCALE: **12 inches**
ARTICULATION: **21 points**
ACCESSORIES: **Removable clothing, disguises, and weapons**

MAGOG
Kingdom Come (Series 3)
DC Direct

RELEASE DATE: **2003**
SCALE: **6½ inches**
ARTICULATION: **7 points**
ACCESSORIES: **Power staff**

MAD HATTER
Batman: The Long Halloween (Series 1)
DC Direct

RELEASE DATE: **2005**
SCALE: **6½ inches**
ARTICULATION: **7 points**
ACCESSORIES: **Pistol, cracked teacup, calendar page, and display base**

> A master hypnotist, Jervis Tetch, a.k.a. the Mad Hatter, is obsessed with hats, using chapeaus to contain his mind-control devices.
>
> **FIRST APPEARANCE**
> *Batman* No. 49

MAN-BAT
Batman: The Animated Series
Kenner

RELEASE DATE: **1992**
SCALE: **4¾ inches**
ARTICULATION: **12 points**
ACCESSORIES: **Tow cable**
ACTION FEATURE: **Flapping wings**

MAN-BAT
Legends of the Dark Knight
Kenner

RELEASE DATE: **1997**
SCALE: **7 inches**
ARTICULATION: **9 points**

MAN-BAT
The Batman
Mattel

RELEASE DATE: **2005**
SCALE: **5 inches**
ARTICULATION: **15 points**
ACTION FEATURE: **Flapping wings**

Attempting to cure his own progressive deafness, zoologist Kirk Langstrom ingested a bat-extract serum that turned him into Man-Bat!

FIRST APPEARANCE
Detective Comics No. 400

MAN-BAT
Secret Files
(Series 1: *Batman Rogues Gallery*)
DC Direct

RELEASE DATE: **2005**
SCALE: **6½ inches**
ARTICULATION: **10 points**
ACCESSORIES: **Display base**

MAN-BAT
The Batman
Mattel: Target Exclusive

RELEASE DATE: **2006**
SCALE: **4¾ inches**
ARTICULATION: **11 points**
ACTION FEATURE: **Flapping wings**
NOTE: **Flocked deco version of Mattel's 2005 Man-Bat figure**

MANHUNTER ROBOT
Green Lantern (Series 2)
DC Direct

RELEASE DATE: **2006**
SCALE: **6½ inches**
ARTICULATION: **11 points**
ACCESSORIES: **Stun baton, opening faceplate, and Green Lantern insignia display base**

MANTID
Swamp Thing (Transducer Playset)
Kenner

RELEASE DATE: **1990**
SCALE: **5 inches**
ARTICULATION: **7 points**

> Created by the Guardians of the Universe, the Manhunters took their mission to extremes, believing that eradicating evil meant destroying all sentient life throughout the cosmos!
>
> **FIRST APPEARANCE**
> *Justice League of America* Vol. 1, No. 140

MANTIS
Super Powers (Series 2)
Kenner

RELEASE DATE: **1985–86**
SCALE: **3¾ inches**
ARTICULATION: **5 points**
ACTION FEATURE: **Power-action pincer thrust**

MARTIAN MANHUNTER
Super Powers (Series 2)
Kenner

RELEASE DATE: **1985–86**
SCALE: **3¾ inches**
ARTICULATION: **7 points**
ACCESSORIES: **Removable cloth cape**
ACTION FEATURE: **Power-action Martian punch**

> The sole surviving Martian, J'onn J'onzz's single weakness is fire. He is a founding member of the Justice League of America and a member of every JLA incarnation.
>
> **FIRST APPEARANCE**
> *Detective Comics* No. 225

MARTIAN MANHUNTER
JLA (Series 1)
Hasbro

RELEASE DATE: **1998**
SCALE: **5 inches**
ARTICULATION: **5 points**
ACCESSORIES: **Removable cape and JLA logo display base**

MARTIAN MANHUNTER
JLA
Hasbro: Kay-Bee Toys Exclusive

RELEASE DATE: **1999**
SCALE: **9 inches**
ARTICULATION: **27 points**
ACCESSORIES: **Removable cloth costume, chest harness, and cape**

MARTIAN MANHUNTER
Martian Manhunter
DC Direct

RELEASE DATE: **2001**
SCALE: **6½ inches**
ARTICULATION: **9 points**
VARIANT: **Redecoed MM included in** *First Appearance: JLA* (*The Brave and the Bold* No. 28) **gift set**

MARTIAN MANHUNTER
Pocket Super Heroes (Series 1)
DC Direct

RELEASE DATE: **2002**
SCALE: **3¼ inches**
ARTICULATION: **6 points**
ACCESSORIES: **Removable cape and JLA conference table and chairs (6)**

MARTIAN MANHUNTER
Justice League
Mattel

RELEASE DATE: **2003**
SCALE: **4¾ inches**
ARTICULATION: **5 points**
ACCESSORIES: **Display base**

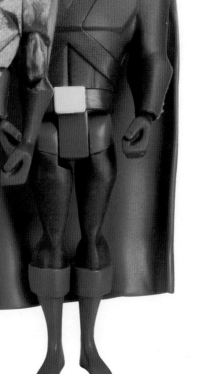

MARTIAN MANHUNTER
Justice League: Attack Armor
Mattel

RELEASE DATE: **2003**
SCALE: **4¾ inches**
ARTICULATION: **5 points**
ACCESSORIES: **Snap-on body**

This is the first rendering of the Martian Manhunter in his native Martian form.

MARTIAN MANHUNTER
Justice League
Mattel

RELEASE DATE: **2003**
SCALE: **10 inches**
ARTICULATION: **5 points**

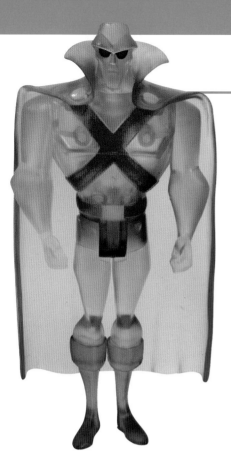

MARTIAN MANHUNTER
Justice League Unlimited
Mattel

RELEASE DATE: **2005**
SCALE: **4¾ inches**
ARTICULATION: **10 points**
VARIANTS: **"Invisible"** (single-carded) and **"Phasing"** (three-pack) redecos also released

MARTIAN MANHUNTER
Secret Files (Series 2: *Unmasked!*)
DC Direct

RELEASE DATE: **2003**
SCALE: **6½ inches**
ARTICULATION: **9 points**
ACCESSORIES: Interchangeable heads (2: standard/true Martian face) and UNMASKED! logo display base

MARTIAN MANHUNTER
JLA Classified (Series 1)
DC Direct

RELEASE DATE: **2006**
SCALE: **6½ inches**
ARTICULATION: **11 points**
ACCESSORIES: Display base

MARTIAN MANHUNTER
Justice (Series 5)
DC Direct

RELEASE DATE: **2007**
SCALE: **7 inches**
ARTICULATION: **9 points**
ACCESSORIES: Display base
VARIANT: **"Clear"** deco release

MARTIAN MANHUNTER
1:6 Scale Deluxe Collector Figure
DC Direct

RELEASE DATE: **2007**
SCALE: **13 inches**
ARTICULATION: **28 points**
ACCESSORIES: Interchangeable head

MAS
Teen Titans
Bandai

RELEASE DATE: **2005**
SCALE: **3½ inches**
ARTICULATION: **5 points**
NOTE: **See Menos.**

MASSACRE
Superman: Man of Steel
Kenner

RELEASE DATE: **1995**
SCALE: **5 inches**
ARTICULATION: **5 points**

MASTER OF GAMES
Teen Titans
Bandai

RELEASE DATE: **2005**
SCALE: **3½ inches**
ARTICULATION: **9 points**

MASTER OF GAMES
Teen Titans
Bandai

RELEASE DATE: **2005**
SCALE: **5 inches**
ARTICULATION: **7 points**
ACCESSORIES: Interchangeable heads (2), interchangeable gorilla arm, and arm cannon

MAX MERCURY
Max Mercury
DC Direct

RELEASE DATE: **2000**
SCALE: **6½ inches**
ARTICULATION: **11 points**
ACCESSORIES: **Flash insignia display base**

Speed guru Max Mercury has also gone by the super-aliases Lightning, Quicksilver, and Whip Whirlwind.

FIRST APPEARANCE
National Comics No. 5

MECHANIKAT
Krypto the Superdog
Fisher-Price

RELEASE DATE: **2006**
SCALE: **6 inches**
ARTICULATION: **7 points**
ACCESSORIES: **Interchangeable robot hands (2) and Snookie Wookums figure**
ACTION FEATURES: **Hook-launching action and belt push-button talking feature**

MENOS
Teen Titans
Bandai

RELEASE DATE: **2005**
SCALE: **3½ inches**
ARTICULATION: **5 points**
NOTE: **See Mas.**

MERA, QUEEN OF ATLANTIS
Super Queens
Ideal

RELEASE DATE: **1967**
SCALE: **11½ inches**
ARTICULATION: **5 points**
ACCESSORIES: **Cloth costume and trident**

METALHEAD
The Batman
Mattel

RELEASE DATE: **2006**
SCALE: **5 inches**
ARTICULATION: **5 points**
NOTE: **In the comics, this character is known as Gearhead.**

METALLO
Superman
Kenner: Diamond Comics Distributors Exclusive

RELEASE DATE: **1998**
SCALE: **4¾ inches**
ARTICULATION: **7 points (including chest plate)**
ACCESSORIES: **Hover attack vehicle**
ACTION FEATURE: **Kryptonite heart reveal**

METALLO
DC Super Heroes
Kenner

RELEASE DATE: **1999**
SCALE: **5 inches**
ARTICULATION: **8 points (including chest plate)**
ACCESSORIES: **Interchangeable hand accessories (2: fist and hammer)**
ACTION FEATURE: **Push-button claw hand**

METALLO
Superman/Batman
(Series 1: *Public Enemies*)
DC Direct

RELEASE DATE: **2005**
SCALE: **6½ inches**
ARTICULATION: **10 points**
ACCESSORIES: **Detachable human face, removable ribcage and kryptonite heart, and SUPERMAN/BATMAN logo display base**

His body crushed
in a car accident, John Corben
was rebuilt as Metallo,
a robot powered by a
kryptonite heart!

FIRST APPEARANCE
Action Comics No. 252

Exposure to the radioactive
Orb of Ra mutated soldier-
of-fortune Rex Mason into
Metamorpho the Element Man.

FIRST APPEARANCE
The Brave and the Bold No. 57

METAMORPHO
Metamorpho: The Element Man
DC Direct

RELEASE DATE: **2003**
SCALE: **6½ inches**
ARTICULATION: **11 points**
ACCESSORIES: **Interchangeable hands (2 sets: left, fist and blowtorch; right, open hand and hammer) and ice/water/steam base**

METAMORPHO
Justice League Unlimited
Mattel

RELEASE DATE: **2005–06**
SCALE: **4¾ inches**
ARTICULATION: **5 points**
ACCESSORIES: **Removable transforming arm accessory (single-carded only)**

MIDNIGHTER
The Authority
DC Direct

RELEASE DATE: **2002**
SCALE: **6½ inches**
ARTICULATION: **11 points**

MIKOLA
The Lost World of the Warlord
Remco

RELEASE DATE: **1982**
SCALE: **5¼ inches**
ARTICULATION: **6 points**
ACCESSORIES: **Staff and bow**

MINIMATES

In late 2006, DC Direct and Art Asylum launched a line of "Minimates" based on the latter toy design firm's popular mini figures. Previously, Art Asylum and Florida-based Play Along Toys had included DC Comics character Minimates in the short-lived C3 construction sets that allowed collectors to build their own Batmobile, Batwing, and other well-known DC vehicles. Those 'Mates remain fully compatible with the DC Direct two-packs featuring well-known super heroes pitted against their super-villain foes. Built on standard bodies easily equipped with unique character-centric accessories, the new Minimates line is poised to rival DC Direct's Pocket Super Heroes in sheer number.

2006 CONVENTION EXCLUSIVE

GREEN LANTERN: JOHN STEWART

WAVE ONE

CLASSIC SUPERMAN WITH
   ARMORED LEX LUTHOR
GREEN LANTERN WITH STAR SAPPHIRE
THE JOKER WITH HARLEY QUINN
MODERN BATMAN WITH OMAC
NOTE: Pictured at right

WAVE TWO

BATTLE-DAMAGE SUPERMAN WITH
   BRAINIAC 13
BOOSTER GOLD WITH BLUE BEETLE
POWER GIRL WITH DR. FATE
ROBIN WITH THE PENGUIN

WAVE THREE

AQUAMAN WITH OCEAN MASTER
BATTLE-DAMAGE BATMAN WITH
   KILLER CROC
GREEN ARROW WITH DEATHSTROKE
WONDER WOMAN WITH ARES

Play Along Toys' C3 line, including the following vehicles, were assembled from construction blocks compatible with other popular building toys, and featured at least one unique Minimate per package.

WAVE ONE

C3: BATMAN

BATCAVE WITH HEAVY ASSAULT
   BATMAN, BRUCE WAYNE (BATMAN
   ARMOR), AND THE JOKER
BATMOBILE WITH DARK KNIGHT
   BATMAN
BATGLIDER WITH STEALTH BATMAN
   AND CATWOMAN
BATWING WITH BATWING PILOT
   BATMAN
MINI-BATMOBILE WITH BATMAN
   AND ROBIN

C3: THE BATMAN

STEALTH BATMAN WITH BRUCE WAYNE
   AND STEALTH BATWING PILOT BATMAN
   (2004 CONVENTION EXCLUSIVE)

C3: JUSTICE LEAGUE

CHEMICAL WAREHOUSE BATTLE WITH
   BATMAN AND THE JOKER
THRONE ROOM BATTLE WITH
   SUPERMAN AND DARKSEID

WAVE TWO

C3: THE BATMAN

BATCYCLE WITH STREET JUSTICE
   BATMAN VS. MAN-BAT
BATCOPTER WITH TACTICAL BATMAN

C3: JUSTICE LEAGUE UNLIMITED

MINI JAVELIN WITH THE FLASH AND
   MARTIAN MANHUNTER

WAVE THREE

C3: BATMAN

BATGIRL MINI FLYER INCLUDING
   BATGIRL
BATMAN MINI FLYER INCLUDING
   BATMAN
NIGHTWING MINI FLYER INCLUDING
   NIGHTWING
THE RIDDLER MINI FLYER INCLUDING
   THE RIDDLER

C3: JUSTICE LEAGUE UNLIMITED

ALTERNATE SUPERMAN MINI FLYER
   INCLUDING ALTERNATE SUPERMAN
THE FLASH MINI FLYER INCLUDING
   THE FLASH

MIRROR MASTER
The Flash Rogues Gallery
DC Direct

RELEASE DATE: **2001**
SCALE: **6½ inches**
ARTICULATION: **11 points**
ACCESSORIES: **Mirror gun**

MIRROR MASTER
Pocket Super Heroes (Series 2)
DC Direct

RELEASE DATE: **2003**
SCALE: **3¼ inches**
ARTICULATION: **6 points**
ACCESSORIES: **Mirror gun and display base**

MIRROR MASTER
*DC Super Heroes:
Justice League Unlimited*
Mattel

RELEASE DATE: **2006**
SCALE: **4¾ inches**
ARTICULATION: **5 points**

Mirror Master's Mirror Gun
can create hyper-realistic
holograms and open reflective
portals to the so-called
"Mirror Dimension."

FIRST APPEARANCE
The Flash Vol. 1, No. 105

MISS FEAR
Blackhawk
Dreams & Visions

RELEASE DATE: **2002**
SCALE: **12 inches**
ARTICULATION: **21 points**
ACCESSORIES: **Removable clothing, disguises, and weapons**

MR. FREEZE
Super Powers (Series 3)
Kenner

RELEASE DATE: **1986**
SCALE: **3¾ inches**
ARTICULATION: **7 points**
ACTION FEATURE: **Power-action cold-blast punch**

Scientist Victor Fries was bathed in super-coolants while attempting to cure his frozen wife's mortal illness. Now he requires sub-zero temperatures in order to survive.

FIRST APPEARANCE
Batman No. 121

MR. FREEZE
DC Super Heroes
Toy Biz

RELEASE DATE: **1989**
SCALE: **3¾ inches**
ARTICULATION: **7 points**
ACCESSORIES: **Removable helmet**
ACTION FEATURE: **Changing colors!**

MR. FREEZE
Batman: The Animated Series
Kenner

RELEASE DATE: **1994**
SCALE: **4¾ inches**
ARTICULATION: **4 points**
ACCESSORIES: **Firing ice blaster**
VARIANTS: **Various redecoed versions in subsequent Hasbro series**

JET WING MR. FREEZE
Batman & Robin
Kenner

RELEASE DATE: **1997**
SCALE: **5 inches**
ARTICULATION: **5 points**
ACCESSORIES: **Glacier assault wing, ice blaster, and bonus Batman ring!**

ICEBLAST MR. FREEZE
Batman & Robin
Kenner

RELEASE DATE: **1997**
SCALE: **5 inches**
ARTICULATION: **5 points**
ACCESSORIES: **Ice-ray cannon and rocket thrusters**

MR. FREEZE
Batman & Robin
Kenner

RELEASE DATE: **1997**
SCALE: **5 inches**
ARTICULATION: **5 points**
ACCESSORIES: **Cryonic blast bazooka**

MR. FREEZE
(ULTIMATE ARMOR)
Batman & Robin
Kenner

RELEASE DATE: **1997**
SCALE: **5 inches**
ARTICULATION: **5 points**
ACCESSORIES: **Ultimate armor, Freeze-On missile, and bonus Batman ring!**

ICE TERROR MR. FREEZE
Batman & Robin
Kenner

RELEASE DATE: **1997**
SCALE: **5 inches**
ARTICULATION: **5 points**
ACCESSORIES: **Street chill dragster and ice crystal rocket**

COLD NIGHT IN GOTHAM CITY: BATMAN VS. MR. FREEZE TWO-PACK
Batman & Robin
Kenner

RELEASE DATE: **1997**
SCALE: **5 inches**
ARTICULATION: **5 points**
ACCESSORIES: **Ice-cryo blaster**

MR. FREEZE
Batman & Robin
Kenner

RELEASE DATE: **1997**
SCALE: **12 inches**
ARTICULATION: **9 points**
ACCESSORIES: **Cryo blaster**

INSECT BODY MR. FREEZE
The New Batman Adventures: Mission Masters
Kenner

RELEASE DATE: **1998**
SCALE: **4¾ inches**
ARTICULATION: **4 points (human body); 4 points (insect body)**
ACCESSORIES: **Insect robot body and ice master**

MR. FREEZE
Batman: Mission Masters 3
Hasbro

RELEASE DATE: **2001**
SCALE: **4¾ inches**
ARTICULATION: **4 points (ball-jointed legs)**
ACCESSORIES: **Arachnotech assault module**
NOTE: **This figure was designed for the *Batman Beyond Batlink* line, later released as a *Mission Masters* offering.**

ICE CANNON MR. FREEZE
Batman
Mattel

RELEASE DATE: **2003**
SCALE: **6 inches**
ARTICULATION: **12 points**
ACCESSORIES: **Ice cannon**
ACTION FEATURE: **Swivel head**
VARIANT: **Chase figure featured new head sculpt (w/o goggles)**

MR. FREEZE
The Batman
Mattel

RELEASE DATE: **2005**
SCALE: **5 inches**
ARTICULATION: **5 points**
ACCESSORIES: **Ice sword; ice blast hand**
VARIANT: **Mouth/no-mouth versions**

MR. FREEZE
Secret Files
(Series 1: *Batman Rogues Gallery*)
DC Direct

RELEASE DATE: **2003**
SCALE: **6½ inches**
ARTICULATION: **13 points**
ACCESSORIES: **Removable helmet, freeze gun, and display base**

MISTER MIRACLE
Super Powers (Series 3)
Kenner

RELEASE DATE: **1986**
SCALE: **3¾ inches**
ARTICULATION: **7 points**
ACCESSORIES: **Manacles and removable cloth cape**
ACTION FEATURE: **Power-action wrist-lock escape**

Escape artist Scott Free was forced to live on Apokolips as a child in order to secure a tentative peace treaty between Darkseid and Scott's native New Genesis.

FIRST APPEARANCE
Mister Miracle Vol. 1, No. 1

MISTER MIRACLE
Mister Miracle and Big Barda Box Set
DC Direct

RELEASE DATE: **2000**
SCALE: **6½ inches**
ARTICULATION: **11 points**
ACCESSORIES: **Removable cape**
NOTE: **Packaged with Big Barda and Oberon figures**

MR. MXYZPTLK
World's Greatest Super-Heroes!
Mego

RELEASE DATE: **1972–82**
SCALE: **8 inches**
ARTICULATION: **21 points**
ACCESSORIES: **Removable cloth costume**
VARIANT: **Mego released Mr. Mxyzptlk with two different head sculpts.**

Superman learned the hard way that the only way to return Mr. Mxyzptlk to the Fifth Dimension is to trick the imp into saying his name (pronunciation key: *Mix-yez-pittle-ick*) backward.

FIRST APPEARANCE
Superman Vol. 1, No. 30

MR. TERRIFIC
JSA (Series 1)
DC Direct

RELEASE DATE: **2006**
SCALE: **6½ inches**
ARTICULATION: **11 points**
ACCESSORIES: **T-spheres and JSA logo display base**

MON-EL
Legion of Super-Heroes (Series 2)
DC Direct

RELEASE DATE: **2002**
SCALE: **6½ inches**
ARTICULATION: **11 points**

MON-EL
Pocket Super Heroes (Series 1)
DC Direct

RELEASE DATE: **2000**
SCALE: **3¼ inches**
ARTICULATION: **6 points**
ACCESSORIES: **Removable cape and display base**

Born under a red sun on the planet Daxam, Mon-El gained the same powers as Superboy when exposed to a yellow sun. Mon-El's only vulnerability is exposure to lead.

FIRST APPEARANCE
Superman Vol. 1, No. 89

MONGUL
Infinite Crisis (Series 1)
DC Direct

RELEASE DATE: **2006**
SCALE: **6½ inches (actual size: 10 inches)**
ARTICULATION: **9 points**
ACCESSORIES: **Display base**
NOTE: **Mongul is the largest DC Direct figure to date released in the 6½ inch scale.**

MONITOR
Crisis on Infinite Earths (Series 1)
DC Direct

RELEASE DATE: **2005**
SCALE: **6½ inches**
ARTICULATION: **9 points**
ACCESSORIES: **CRISIS logo display base**

MORDRU
Legion of Super-Heroes (Series 2)
DC Direct

RELEASE DATE: **2002**
SCALE: **6½ inches**
ARTICULATION: **12 points**

NEMESIS
DC Super Heroes:
Justice League Unlimited
Mattel

RELEASE DATE: **2007**
SCALE: **4¾ inches**
ARTICULATION: **5 points**

NIGHTSTAR
Elseworlds (Series 3: Kingdom Come)
DC Direct

RELEASE DATE: **2007**
SCALE: **7 inches**
ARTICULATION: **9 points**
ACCESSORIES: **Display base**

NIGHTWING
Legends of Batman
Kenner

RELEASE DATE: **1995**
SCALE: **5 inches**
ARTICULATION: **5 points**
ACCESSORIES: **Super-strike rocket launcher**
VARIANT: **Redeco released as Warner Bros.
Store Exclusive**

CRIME SOLVER NIGHTWING
The New Batman Adventures
Kenner

RELEASE DATE: **1998**
SCALE: **5 inches**
ARTICULATION: **5 points**
ACCESSORIES: **Radar rocket and magnifying decoder**
VARIANTS: **Various other redecoed versions released
in store-exclusive multipacks**

NIGHTWING
The New Batman Adventures
Kenner

RELEASE DATE: **1998**
SCALE: **12 inches**
ARTICULATION: **16 points**
ACCESSORIES: **Night-vision goggles, Escrima
sticks (2), and Batarangs (3)**

Before taking up the role of
Nightwing, Dick Grayson battled
crime beside Batman as the first
Robin the Boy Wonder.

FIRST APPEARANCE
Tales of the Teen Titans No. 43

FORCE SHIELD NIGHTWING
The New Batman Adventures
Kenner

RELEASE DATE: **1998**
SCALE: **4¾ inches**
ARTICULATION: **5 points**
ACCESSORIES: **Decoder Shield Grappling Hook**

HYDROJET NIGHTWING
The New Batman Adventures
Kenner

RELEASE DATE: **1998**
SCALE: **4¾ inches**
ARTICULATION: **7 points**
ACCESSORIES: **Airborne water sled (a Jet Ski with
attachable wings) and two torpedo projectiles**
VARIANTS: **Turbo Force Nightwing** *(Batman:
Mission Masters 4)*

NIGHTWING
The New Batman Adventures
Kenner

RELEASE DATE: **1998**
SCALE: **12 inches**
ARTICULATION: **20 points**
ACCESSORIES: **Escrima sticks (2), night-vision
goggles, and nightarangs (3)**

NIGHTWING
Batman
Mattel

RELEASE DATE: **2004**
SCALE: **6 inches**
ARTICULATION: **9 points**
ACCESSORIES: **Harness and sling**

NIGHTWING
Batman
Mattel

RELEASE DATE: **2003**
SCALE: **6 inches**
ARTICULATION: **10 points**
ACCESSORIES: **Battle shield and fighting sticks (2)**
NOTE: **Packaged with Martial Arts Batman figure**

NIGHTWING
Batman: Hush
DC Direct

RELEASE DATE: **2004**
SCALE: **6½ inches**
ARTICULATION: **9 points**
ACCESSORIES: **Escrima sticks (2) and BATMAN logo display base**

NIGHTWING
First Appearance (Series 3)
DC Direct

RELEASE DATE: **2005**
SCALE: **6½ inches**
ARTICULATION: **11 points**
ACCESSORIES: **FIRST APPEARANCE logo display base**

NIGHTWING
Batman: Knightfall (Series 1)
DC Direct

RELEASE DATE: **2006**
SCALE: **6½ inches**
ARTICULATION: **9 points**
ACCESSORIES: **Throwing disc and KNIGHTFALL logo display base**

NIGHTWING
Superman/Batman
(Series 3: *Public Enemies*)
DC Direct

RELEASE DATE: **2007**
SCALE: **6½ inches**
ARTICULATION: **13 points**
ACCESSORIES: **Escrima sticks and display base**

NORMAN MCKAY
Elseworlds (Series 2: *Kingdom Come*)
DC Direct

RELEASE DATE: **2006**
SCALE: **6½ inches**
ARTICULATION: **3 points**
ACCESSORIES: **Display base**

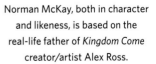

Norman McKay, both in character and likeness, is based on the real-life father of *Kingdom Come* creator/artist Alex Ross.

FIRST APPEARANCE
Kingdom Come No. 1

NUBIA
Wonder Woman
Mego

RELEASE DATE: **1977–80**
SCALE: **12 inches**
ARTICULATION: **5 points**
ACCESSORIES: **Removable costume/armor, sword w/ sheath, shield, and plastic stand**

133

OBERON
Mister Miracle and Big Barda Box Set
DC Direct

RELEASE DATE: **2000**
SCALE: **6½ inches**
ARTICULATION: **3 points**
NOTE: **Packaged with Big Barda and Mister Miracle figures**

OBSIDIAN
*DC Super Heroes:
Justice League Unlimited*
Mattel

RELEASE DATE: **2007**
SCALE: **4¾ inches**
ARTICULATION: **5 points**

OMAC
Infinite Crisis (Series 1)
DC Direct

RELEASE DATE: **2006**
SCALE: **6½ inches**
ARTICULATION: **11 points**
ACCESSORIES: **Interchangeable arm and display base w/ levitating post**

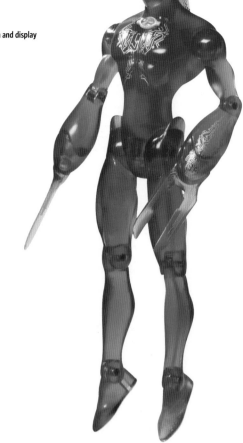

ORACLE
Birds of Prey
DC Direct

RELEASE DATE: **2003**
SCALE: **6½ inches**
ARTICULATION: **7 points**
ACCESSORIES: **Wheelchair w/ spinning wheels**

Oracle was once romantically linked to Nightwing, Batgirl II's former partner in crimefighting, Robin!

FIRST APPEARANCE
Detective Comics No. 359

ORION
Super Powers (Series 3)
Kenner

RELEASE DATE: **1986**
SCALE: **3¾ inches**
ARTICULATION: **7 points**
ACTION FEATURE: **Power-action Astro-Punch and changing face (calm/rage)**

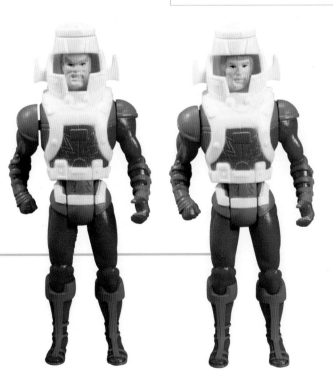

ORION
Orion and Darkseid Box Set
DC Direct

RELEASE DATE: **2001**
SCALE: **6½ inches**
ARTICULATION: **11 points**
ACCESSORIES: **Astro harness, removable helmet, and interchangeable heads (2: calm/rage)**

Although he is the biological son of Darkseid, Orion was raised on peaceful New Genesis by Highfather Izaya.

FIRST APPEARANCE
New Gods Vol. 1. No. 1

ORION
Justice League Unlimited
Mattel

RELEASE DATE: **2005-06**
SCALE: **5 inches**
ARTICULATION: **5 points**
ACCESSORIES: **Astro harness (single-carded only)**

OWLMAN
Crime Syndicate
DC Direct

RELEASE DATE: **2002**
SCALE: **6½ inches**
ARTICULATION: **9 points**
ACCESSORIES: **CRIME SYNDICATE Logo display base**

PARADEMON
Super Powers (Series 2)
Kenner

RELEASE DATE: **1985–86**
SCALE: **3¾ inches**
ARTICULATION: **7 points**
ACCESSORIES: **Gun**
ACTION FEATURE: **Power-action battle flight**

PARALLAX
Pocket Super Heroes
(Green Lantern Box Set)
DC Direct

RELEASE DATE: **1985–86**
SCALE: **3¼ inches**
ARTICULATION: **6 points**
ACCESSORIES: **Removable cape**

> As Parallax, Hal Jordan
> absorbed the Central Power
> Battery of Oa and wielded
> the energies of every single
> Green Lantern.
>
> **FIRST APPEARANCE**
> *Green Lantern* Vol. 2, No. 50

PARALLAX
Total Justice (Series 3)
Kenner

RELEASE DATE: **1996**
SCALE: **5 inches**
ARTICULATION: **5 points**
ACCESSORIES: **Removable cape**

PARALLAX
Green Lantern (Series 1)
DC Direct

RELEASE DATE: **2005**
SCALE: **6½ inches**
ARTICULATION: **11 points**
ACCESSORIES: **Green Lantern insignia display base**

PARASITE
Justice (Series 2)
DC Direct

RELEASE DATE: **2005**
SCALE: **7 inches**
ARTICULATION: **9 points**
ACCESSORIES: **Display base**

PARASITE
*DC Super Heroes:
Justice League Unlimited*
Mattel

RELEASE DATE: **2007**
SCALE: **4¾ inches**
ARTICULATION: **5 points**

PARASITE
DC Super Heroes: Superman
Mattel

RELEASE DATE: **2007**
SCALE: **6 inches**
ARTICULATION: **23 points**

> One of Superman's
> deadliest foes, the Parasite
> absorbs the life energy of
> anyone or anything he touches.
>
> **FIRST APPEARANCE**
> *Action Comics* No. 240

THE PENGUIN
World's Greatest Super-Heroes!
Mego

RELEASE DATE: **1972–82**
SCALE: **8 inches**
ARTICULATION: **21 points**

THE PENGUIN
Pocket Super Heroes
Mego

RELEASE DATE: **1979–82**
SCALE: **3¾ inches**
ARTICULATION: **5 points**

THE PENGUIN
DC Super Heroes
Toy Biz

RELEASE DATE: **1989**
SCALE: **3¾ inches**
ARTICULATION: **7 points**
ACCESSORIES: **Missile-firing umbrella**

THE PENGUIN
Batman: The Animated Series
Kenner

RELEASE DATE: **1991**
SCALE: **4¾ inches**
ARTICULATION: **5 points**
ACCESSORIES: **Removable cloth overcoat and launching "Hypno-Spin" umbrella**

THE PENGUIN
Batman Returns
Kenner

RELEASE DATE: **1992**
SCALE: **4¾ inches**
ARTICULATION: **5 points**
ACCESSORIES: **Blast-off umbrella launcher**

THE PENGUIN
Legends of the Dark Knight
Kenner

RELEASE DATE: **1997**
SCALE: **7 inches**
ARTICULATION: **4 points**
ACCESSORIES: **Spinning attack umbrella**

THE PENGUIN
Batman: Revenge of the Penguin Box Set
Hasbro

RELEASE DATE: **2002**
SCALE: **4¾ inches**
ARTICULATION: **5 points**
ACCESSORIES: **Umbrella**

THE PENGUIN
Comic Action Heroes
Mego

RELEASE DATE: **1975–1978**
SCALE: **3¾ inches**
ARTICULATION: **5 points**
ACCESSORIES: **Umbrella and display base**

THE PENGUIN
Super Powers (Series 1)
Kenner

RELEASE DATE: **1984**
SCALE: **3¾ inches**
ARTICULATION: **7 points**
ACCESSORIES: **Umbrella w/ retractable blade**
ACTION FEATURE: **Power-action umbrella arm**

Forced to carry an umbrella by his hypochondriac mother even on sunny days, Oswald Cobblepot now arms himself with umbrella-themed weapons as the Penguin.

FIRST APPEARANCE
Detective Comics No. 58

THE PENGUIN
Batman: Gotham City Villains
Hasbro: Target Exclusive

RELEASE DATE: **2002**
SCALE: **9 inches**
ARTICULATION: **27 points**
ACCESSORIES: **Cloth outfit, squirting umbrella, emperor penguins (2)**

THE PENGUIN
The Classic Silver Age
Catwoman and The Penguin Box Set
DC Direct

RELEASE DATE: **2004**
SCALE: **6½ inches**
ARTICULATION: **9 points**
ACCESSORIES: **Umbrella and interlocking Gotham City rooftop display base**

THE PENGUIN
The Batman
Mattel

RELEASE DATE: **2004**
SCALE: **5 inches**
ARTICULATION: **7 points**
ACCESSORIES: **Removable top hat, umbrella, and Mace**
VARIANT: **Tuxedo redecos**

THE PENGUIN
Batman: Dark Victory (Series 1)
DC Direct

RELEASE DATE: **2006**
SCALE: **6½ inches**
ARTICULATION: **7 points**
ACCESSORIES: **Umbrella gun and display base**

THE PENGUIN
Secret Files
(Series 1: *Batman Rogues Gallery*)
DC Direct

RELEASE DATE: **2005**
SCALE: **6½ inches**
ARTICULATION: **7 points**
ACCESSORIES: **Top hat, umbrella, and display base**

PENGUIN COMMANDOS
Batman Returns
Kenner

RELEASE DATE: **1992**
SCALE: **4¾ inches**
ARTICULATION: **5 points**
ACCESSORIES: **Mind-control gear and firing missile**

PERRY WHITE
Silver Age Superman (Series 1)
DC Direct

RELEASE DATE: **2006**
SCALE: **6½ inches**
ARTICULATION: **9 points**
ACCESSORIES: **Daily Planet Building and rolled-up newspaper**

PHANTASM
Batman: Mask of the Phantasm
Kenner

RELEASE DATE: **1993**
SCALE: **4¾ inches**
ARTICULATION: **4 points**
ACCESSORIES: **Removable cowl, laser weapon, and scythe gauntlet**
ACTION FEATURE: **Chopping arm action!**

PHANTOM GIRL
Pocket Super Heroes (Series 2)
DC Direct

RELEASE DATE: **2003**
SCALE: **3¼ inches**
ARTICULATION: **6 points**
ACCESSORIES: **Removable cape**

Legion of Super-Heroes heroine Phantom Girl hails from the planet Bgtzl, a world whose inhabitants can become intangible at will.

FIRST APPEARANCE
Action Comics No. 276

PHANTOM LADY
Classic Heroes
DC Direct

RELEASE DATE: **2002**
SCALE: **6½ inches**
ARTICULATION: **9 points**
ACCESSORIES: **Display base**

THE PHANTOM STRANGER
The Phantom Stranger
DC Direct

RELEASE DATE: **2002**
SCALE: **6½ inches**
ARTICULATION: **11 points**

The Phantom Stranger was once offered membership in the Justice League of America, but disappeared instead of joining.

FIRST APPEARANCE
The Phantom Stranger No. 1

PLASTIC MAN
Super Powers (Series 3)
Kenner

RELEASE DATE: **1986**
SCALE: **3¾ inches**
ARTICULATION: **8 points**
ACTION FEATURE: **Power-action stretching neck**

PLASTIC MAN
JLA (Series 2)
Hasbro

RELEASE DATE: **1999**
SCALE: **5 inches**
ARTICULATION: **5 points**
ACCESSORIES: **JLA logo display base**
ACTION FEATURE: **Bendable arms**

ELASTIC PLASTIC MAN

While the *Super Powers* Plastic Man enjoys the distinction of being the debut Plastic Man action figure, the premiere Plas toy was a Mego Corporation offering first released in 1979. The *Elastic Super Heroes* Plastic Man featured a cloth costume over a super-stretchable body. "So you can bend 'em, twist 'em, and stretch 'em any way you like," as Mego's *ESH* ads touted. Obviously, this play pattern was a natural fit for DC Comics' pliable hero, the rarest and most valuable toy in the short-lived line. Of course, Plas wasn't alone in the *ESH* collection, which also included stretchable Batman and Superman toys.

PLASTIC MAN
Justice (Series 4)
DC Direct

RELEASE DATE: **2006**
SCALE: **7 inches**
ARTICULATION: **7 points**
ACCESSORIES: **Display base**
ACTION FEATURE: **Bendy arms and "spring" legs**

PLASTIC MAN
Plastic Man
DC Direct

RELEASE DATE: **1999**
SCALE: **6½ inches**
ARTICULATION: **7 points**
ACCESSORIES: **Removable goggles**
ACTION FEATURE: **Stretchable arms**
VARIANT: **Alternate release with hammer and pliers for hands**

Before falling into a vat of acid and becoming the pliable Plastic Man, Eel O'Brian was a lowlife gangster.

FIRST APPEARANCE
Police Comics No. 1

PNEUMAN
Tom Strong Box Set
DC Direct

RELEASE DATE: **2000**
SCALE: **6½ inches**
ARTICULATION: **6 points, plus working wheels**

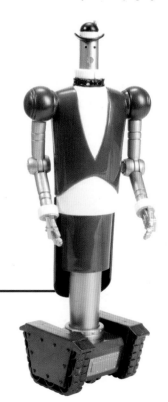

POCKET PLASTIC

Picking up where *Comic Action Heroes* left off, Mego's *Pocket Super Heroes* added hip articulation to its line of 3¾-inch action figures, as well as standing rather than crouched poses. Featuring just a handful (or pocketful) of DC Comics characters, the collection was notable for several Bat-themed items, including a Batmobile that fit both Batman and Robin, as well as a plastic Batcave playset featuring a Batmobile entrance, a working jail cell, a crime laboratory, and a Batpole! Toward the line's end, Mego released the Bat Machine, a computerized battery-operated vehicle that would drive the Dynamic Duo through a variety of programmable maneuvers.

POCKET SUPER HEROES REDUX

DC Direct dusted off the *Pocket Super Heroes* name in 2002 with an innovative line of 3¼-inch action figures that (at least initially) intended to adapt every hero in the DC Universe. Using a set of standard bodies with six points of articulation, DC Direct's *PSH* added tampo-imprinted decos, unique hairstyles, capes, and other accessories to create a collection that ultimately included twenty-six figures in two series and subsequent character-specific box sets. While these mini figures didn't catch on enough to warrant a third assortment, some collectors still hope to supplement their collections with future *Pocket Super Heroes* releases.

POISON IVY
Batman: The Animated Series
Kenner

RELEASE DATE: **1994**
SCALE: **4¾ inches**
ARTICULATION: **5 points**
ACCESSORIES: **Snapping Venus flytrap and poison dart crossbow**
VARIANTS: **Various redecos released in subsequent collections**

NIGHT HUNTER ROBIN VS. EVIL ENTRAPMENT POISON IVY TWO-PACK
Batman & Robin
Kenner

RELEASE DATE: **1997**
SCALE: **5 inches**
ARTICULATION: **5 points**
ACCESSORIES: **Chomping plant**

JUNGLE VENOM POISON IVY
Batman & Robin
Kenner

RELEASE DATE: **1997**
SCALE: **5 inches**
ARTICULATION: **5 points**
ACCESSORIES: **Venom-spray cannon and entanglement vines**

BATMAN VS. POISON IVY TWO-PACK
Batman & Robin
Kenner

RELEASE DATE: **1997**
SCALE: **12 inches**
ARTICULATION: **9 points each**
ACCESSORIES: **Heat ray**

Botanist Pamela Lillian Isley is now a human/plant hybrid and uses her knowledge of flora to further her eco-terrorist agenda as Poison Ivy.

FIRST APPEARANCE
Batman No. 181

POISON IVY
Batman: Frozen Assets
Hasbro: Toys R Us Exclusive

RELEASE DATE: **2002**
SCALE: **4¾ inches**
ARTICULATION: **5 points**
ACCESSORIES: **Venus flytrap and crossbow**
VARIANT: **Also included in *Batman: Girls of Gotham City* TRU Exclusive four-pack**

POISON IVY
Batman: Hush (Series 1)
DC Direct

RELEASE DATE: **2004**
SCALE: **6½ inches**
ARTICULATION: **9 points**
ACCESSORIES: **Lianas vine and BATMAN logo display base**

POISON IVY
Justice (Series 4)
DC Direct

RELEASE DATE: **2006**
SCALE: **7 inches**
ARTICULATION: **9 points**
ACCESSORIES: **Display base**

POISON IVY
The Batman
Mattel

RELEASE DATE: **2006**
SCALE: **5 inches**
ARTICULATION: **5 points**
ACCESSORIES: **Display base**

Power Girl has been a member
of the Justice Society,
Justice League, and Infinity Inc.

FIRST APPEARANCE
All-Star Comics No. 58

POWER GIRL
Justice Society of America (Series 3)
DC Direct

RELEASE DATE: **2001**
SCALE: **6½ inches**
ARTICULATION: **7 points**

POWER GIRL
Infinite Crisis (Series 1)
DC Direct

RELEASE DATE: **2006**
SCALE: **6½ inches**
ARTICULATION: **9 points**
ACCESSORIES: **INFINITE CRISIS logo display base**

POWER RING
Crime Syndicate
DC Direct

RELEASE DATE: **2002**
SCALE: **6½ inches**
ARTICULATION: **9 points**
ACCESSORIES: **Power battery, one-size-fits-all power ring, and CRIME SYNDICATE logo display base**

PREACHER
Preacher
DC Direct

RELEASE DATE: **1999**
SCALE: **6½ inches**
ARTICULATION: **9 points**
ACCESSORIES: **Removable eye-patch**
ACTION FEATURE: **Battery-operated light-up eyes**
VARIANT: **Alternate release with Jesse Custer in white suit**

PROFESSOR ZOOM
Total Justice
Kenner: ToyFare Exclusive

RELEASE DATE: **1997**
SCALE: **5 inches**
ARTICULATION: **5 points**

PROFESSOR ZOOM
Pocket Super Heroes (Series 2)
DC Direct

RELEASE DATE: **2003**
SCALE: **3¼ inches**
ARTICULATION: **6 points**
ACCESSORIES: **Display base**

Also known as the Reverse-Flash,
evil speed-demon Professor Zoom
hails from the twenty-fifth century.

FIRST APPEARANCE
The Flash Vol. 1, No. 139

PROMETHEA
Promethea and Sophie
DC Direct

RELEASE DATE: **2002**
SCALE: **6½ inches**
ARTICULATION: **9 points**
ACCESSORIES: **Staff and display base**

PSYCHO-PIRATE
Crisis on Infinite Earths (Series 1)
DC Direct

RELEASE DATE: **2005**
SCALE: **6½ inches**
ARTICULATION: **13 points**
ACCESSORIES: **Removable Medusa mask
and CRISIS logo display base**

With his Medusa mask,
Roger Hayden could force
his victims to experience any
emotion he expressed as the
Psycho-Pirate.

FIRST APPEARANCE
Showcase No. 56

PUPPET KING
Teen Titans
Bandai

RELEASE DATE: **2005**
SCALE: **3½ inches**
ARTICULATION: **6 points**

QUEEN HIPPOLYTE [SIC]
Wonder Woman
Mego

RELEASE DATE: **1977–80**
SCALE: **12 inches**
ARTICULATION: **5 points**
ACCESSORIES: **Removable cloth robes and scroll**

THE QUESTION
Classic Heroes
DC Direct

RELEASE DATE: **2002**
SCALE: **6½ inches**
ARTICULATION: **11 points**
ACCESSORIES: **Removable hat and mask**

Queen Hippolyta molded
daughter Diana out of clay.
The statue was then brought
to life by the Greek goddesses of
Mount Olympus.

FIRST APPEARANCE
All-Star Comics No. 8

The Question's face mask can
be removed only with a special
chemical spray.

FIRST APPEARANCE
Blue Beetle No. 1

R

RĀ'S AL GHŪL
The Adventures of Batman & Robin
Kenner

RELEASE DATE: **1995**
SCALE: **4¾ inches**
ARTICULATION: **5 points**
ACCESSORIES: **Strike shooter, combat sword, and mask**

RĀ'S AL GHŪL
Batman: Shadows of Gotham City Box Set
Hasbro

RELEASE DATE: **2001**
SCALE: **4¾ inches**
ARTICULATION: **5 points**
ACCESSORIES: **Firing projectile launcher and removable cloak**

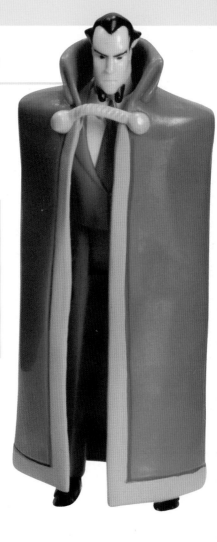

Hasbro's second stab at the immortal rogue Rā's al Ghūl featured him as he first appeared in June 1971. The company's first Rā's figure was clad in battle armor.

FIRST APPEARANCE
Batman No. 232

RĀ'S AL GHŪL
Batman: Hush (Series 3)
DC Direct

RELEASE DATE: **2005**
SCALE: **6½ inches**
ARTICULATION: **9 points**
ACCESSORIES: **Sword and BATMAN logo display base**

RĀ'S AL GHŪL
Batman Begins
Mattel

RELEASE DATE: **2005**
SCALE: **5½ inches**
ARTICULATION: **6 points**
ACCESSORIES: **Cape, staff weapon, and spring-loaded projectile sword**

RĀ'S AL GHŪL
Batman Begins
Mattel: Toys R Us Exclusive

RELEASE DATE: **2005**
SCALE: **5½ inches**
ARTICULATION: **10 points**
ACCESSORIES: **Gauntlet sword**

RĀ'S AL GHŪL
Batman Begins
Mattel

RELEASE DATE: **2005**
SCALE: **5 inches**
ARTICULATION: **10 points**
ACCESSORIES: **Nunchaku and scabbard launcher**
VARIANT: **Orange dragon tunic deco**

RĀ'S AL GHŪL
Batman Begins
Mattel

RELEASE DATE: **2005**
SCALE: **7 inches**
ARTICULATION: **10 points**
ACCESSORIES: **Gauntlet blade**

RAVAGER II
Contemporary Teen Titans (Series 2)
DC Direct

RELEASE DATE: **2005**
SCALE: **6½ inches**
ARTICULATION: **9 points**
ACCESSORIES: **Sword and TEEN TITANS logo display base**

Rose Wilson, a.k.a. the Ravager, is the daughter of Slade Wilson, better known as Deathstroke the Terminator. Rose assumed the identity of her brother, the first Ravager.

FIRST APPEARANCE
Deathstroke the Terminator No. 15

RAVEN
The New Teen Titans (Series 2)
DC Direct

RELEASE DATE: **2001**
SCALE: **6½ inches**
ARTICULATION: **5 points**
ACCESSORIES: **Smoke cloud display base**
VARIANT: **Released in white costume with** *The Classic New Teen Titans* **gift set**

RAVEN
Teen Titans
Bandai

RELEASE DATE: **2004**
SCALE: **3½ inches**
ARTICULATION: **7 points**
ACCESSORIES: **Weapon**

The empath known as Raven is the daughter of Trigon, a near-omnipotent demon from another dimension.

FIRST APPEARANCE
DC Comics Presents No. 26

RAVEN
Teen Titans
Bandai

RELEASE DATE: **2004**
SCALE: **3½ inches**
ARTICULATION: **7 points**
ACCESSORIES: **Weapon**
VARIANT: **Raven in white costume**

RAVEN
Teen Titans
Bandai

RELEASE DATE: **2005**
SCALE: **3½ inches**
ARTICULATION: **7 points**

THE RAY II
DC Super Heroes: Justice League Unlimited Comic Convention Exclusive
Mattel

RELEASE DATE: **2007**
SCALE: **4¾ inches**
ARTICULATION: **5 points**
NOTE: **Convention exclusive three-pack also included new "unmasked" Hawkgirl (Shayera Hol) and Green Lantern (John Stewart) re-release.**

RED ARROW
Kingdom Come (Series 2)
DC Direct: ToyFare Exclusive

RELEASE DATE: **2004**
SCALE: **6½ inches**
ARTICULATION: **11 points**
ACCESSORIES: **Bow**

In the possible future of DC Comics' *Kingdom Come*, Red Arrow is actually Roy Harper, a.k.a. Speedy, all grown up and filling the role of his former mentor, Green Arrow.

FIRST APPEARANCE
Kingdom Come No. 2

The current light-empowered Ray is the son of the original Ray, "Happy" Terrill, a founding member of Uncle Sam's first team of Freedom Fighters.

FIRST APPEARANCE
The Ray Vol. 2, No. 1

THE RED HOOD
Secret Files (Series 2: *Unmasked!*)
DC Direct

RELEASE DATE: **2005**
SCALE: **6½ inches**
ARTICULATION: **10 points**
ACCESSORIES: **Interchangeable Joker head/helmet and UNMASKED! logo display base**

RED ROBIN
Kingdom Come (Series 2)
DC Direct

RELEASE DATE: **2003**
SCALE: **6½ inches**
ARTICULATION: **5 points**

RED TORNADO
Super Powers (Series 2)
Kenner

RELEASE DATE: **1985-86**
SCALE: **3¾ inches**
ARTICULATION: **7 points**
ACCESSORIES: **Removable cloth cape**
ACTION FEATURE: **Power-action tornado twist**

RED TORNADO
JLA (Series 4)
Hasbro

RELEASE DATE: **1999**
SCALE: **5 inches**
ARTICULATION: **5 points**
ACCESSORIES: **Removable plastic cape and JLA logo display base**

RED TORNADO
Red Tornado
DC Direct

RELEASE DATE: **2001**
SCALE: **6½ inches**
ARTICULATION: **9 points**

RED TORNADO
Pocket Super Heroes (Series 1)
DC Direct

RELEASE DATE: **2002**
SCALE: **3¼ inches**
ARTICULATION: **6 points**
ACCESSORIES: **Removable cape and display base**

RED TORNADO
Justice (Series 5)
DC Direct

RELEASE DATE: **2007**
SCALE: **7 inches**
ARTICULATION: **9 points**
ACCESSORIES: **Display base**

> Red Tornado's android body was built by mad scientist T. O. Morrow to destroy the JLA. Morrow later helped to construct Tomorrow Woman with Professor Ivo, creator of Amazo.
>
> **FIRST APPEARANCE**
> *Justice League of America* Vol. 1, No. 17

RED TORNADO
Justice League Unlimited
Mattel

RELEASE DATE: **2004**
SCALE: **4¾ inches**
ARTICULATION: **5 points**
ACCESSORIES: **Mini-cyclone (single-carded only)**
VARIANT: **Filled-in "V" logo**

RIDDLE ME THIS!

DC Comics' conundrum-crazed villain the Riddler never made it into Kenner's *Super Powers* collection, like a few of his other fellow Bat-Rogues—at least north of the border. Strangely, Batman's enigma-obsessed enemy (his real name was Edward Nygma, after all) was fortunate enough to be included in Pacipa's *Super Amigos* collection released in Mexico and South America. Since Super Amigos used existing Super Powers sculpts, the Riddler (or el Acertijo) was just a redecoed Green Lantern figure! If you look hard enough, you'll find the telltale marks of Green Lantern's signature power ring on the Riddler's right hand. *¡Ay caramba, Bat-Hombre!*

RESEALED FOR FRESHNESS

In 2002, DC Direct offered an alternative to collectors who routinely purchased two of the same action figure, one to keep "mint in package," the other to open for play or display. For three assortments only—*Crime Syndicate, Green Lantern,* and *Legion of Super Heroes* (Series 3)—DC Comics' direct-only toy division created special "resealable packaging" that allowed collectors to release an action figure from its plastic snap-fitted clamshell blister and then return the toy later to its custom-fitted tray for safekeeping if so desired. Gone were the glued-on cardboard card backs, with identifying logos and such inserted inside the clamshell. At purchase time, the resealable packaging remained sealed with tiny circular DC Direct logo stickers lining the edges of the clamshell, each of which could be easily peeled away. Unfortunately, this unique packaging innovation didn't catch on with collectors, and DC Direct returned to standard blister-carded packaging soon after.

THE RIDDLER
World's Greatest Super-Heroes!
Mego

RELEASE DATE: **1972-82**
SCALE: **8 inches**
ARTICULATION: **21 points**
ACCESSORIES: **Removable plastic belt**

THE RIDDLER
World's Greatest Super-Heroes!: Fist Fighters
Mego

RELEASE DATE: **1975-76**
SCALE: **8 inches**
ARTICULATION: **21 points**
ACCESSORIES: **Removable plastic belt**
ACTION FEATURE: **Power-fist fighting action**

THE RIDDLER
DC Super Heroes
Toy Biz

RELEASE DATE: **1989**
SCALE: **4¾ inches**
ARTICULATION: **5 points**
ACCESSORIES: **Pre-printed riddles and clues**

Obsessed with puzzles, conundrums, and brain-teasers, the Riddler is compelled to commit crimes, preceded by riddles for Batman to solve.

FIRST APPEARANCE
Detective Comics No. 140

THE RIDDLER
Batman: The Animated Series
Kenner

RELEASE DATE: **1992**
SCALE: **4¾ inches**
ARTICULATION: **5 points**
ACCESSORIES: **Cane and question-mark launcher**
VARIANT: **Redecoed** *Batman: D.U.O. Force*
collection figure in 1997, released with Roto Chopper vehicle/accessory

THE RIDDLER
Legends of Batman
Kenner

RELEASE DATE: **1995**
SCALE: **5 inches**
ARTICULATION: **5 points**
ACCESSORIES: **Mace**
ACTION FEATURE: **Question-mark projectile launcher**
VARIANT: **Redeco released as Warner Bros. Store Exclusive**

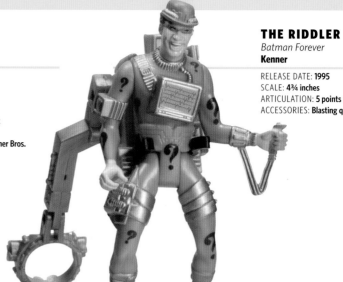

THE RIDDLER
Batman Forever
Kenner

RELEASE DATE: **1995**
SCALE: **4¾ inches**
ARTICULATION: **5 points**
ACCESSORIES: **Blasting question-mark bazooka**

THE RIDDLER
Batman Forever
Kenner

RELEASE DATE: **1995**
SCALE: **4¾ inches**
ARTICULATION: **5 points**
ACCESSORIES: **Trapping brain-drain helmet**
VARIANT: **Target Exclusive redeco**

THE TALKING RIDDLER
Batman Forever
Kenner

RELEASE DATE: **1995**
SCALE: **4¾ inches**
ARTICULATION: **5 points**
ACCESSORIES: **Question-mark cane, backpack**
ACTION FEATURE: **Three real movie phrases**

THE RIDDLER & TWO-FACE TWO-PACK
Batman Forever
Kenner

RELEASE DATE: **1995**
SCALE: **4¾ inches**
ARTICULATION: **5 points**
ACCESSORIES: **Cane**

TORNADO BLADE RIDDLER
Batman: Knight Force Ninjas
Kenner

RELEASE DATE: **1998**
SCALE: **6 inches**
ARTICULATION: **11 points**
ACCESSORIES: **Question-mark tornado blade weapons**
ACTION FEATURE: **Cyclone whirl attack**

During DC Comics' "Hush" storyline in the pages of *Batman*, the Riddler revealed to the Dark Knight that he had correctly figured out his secret identity.

THE RIDDLER
The New Batman Adventures: Mission Masters
Kenner

RELEASE DATE: **1998**
SCALE: **4¾ inches**
ARTICULATION: **5 points**
ACCESSORIES: **Question mobile and quiz missile**
ACTION FEATURE: **Cyclone whirl attack**
NOTE: **Listed on card as Rumble Ready Riddler**

THE RIDDLER
Super Friends!
DC Direct

RELEASE DATE: **2003**
SCALE: **6½ inches**
ARTICULATION: **9 points**
ACCESSORIES: **Remote-control "mind device" and SUPER FRIENDS! logo display base**

THE RIDDLER
Batman: Hush (Series 2)
DC Direct

RELEASE DATE: **2004**
SCALE: **6½ inches**
ARTICULATION: **9 points**
ACCESSORIES: **Removable bowler hat, cane, and BATMAN logo display base**

THE RIDDLER
First Appearance (Series 3)
DC Direct

RELEASE DATE: **2005**
SCALE: **6½ inches**
ARTICULATION: **9 points**
ACCESSORIES: **Mini comic and FIRST APPEARANCE logo display base**

THE RIDDLER
The Batman
Mattel

RELEASE DATE: **2005**
SCALE: **5 inches**
ARTICULATION: **5 points**
ACCESSORIES: **Question-mark scythe**

ROBIN
Action Boy (Captain Action)
Ideal

RELEASE DATE: **1966**
SCALE: **9 inches**
ARTICULATION: **14 points**
ACCESSORIES: **Utility Belt, mask, cloth costume, gloves, boots, cape, suction grips for climbing (2), Batarang launcher, Batarang, and Bat-Grenades (2)**

ROBIN
World's Greatest Super-Heroes!
Mego

RELEASE DATE: **1972–82**
SCALE: **8 inches**
ARTICULATION: **21 points**
ACCESSORIES: **Removable cloth costume, plastic pixie boots and belt, and vinyl gloves**
VARIANT: **Early release included removable domino mask**

> When circus aerialist Dick Grayson's parents were murdered by "Boss" Zucco, Batman offered Dick the opportunity to fight by his side and uphold justice as Robin the Boy Wonder.
>
> **FIRST APPEARANCE**
> *Detective Comics* No. 38

ROBIN
World's Greatest Super-Heroes!: Fist Fighters
Mego

RELEASE DATE: **1975–76**
SCALE: **8 inches**
ARTICULATION: **21 points**
ACCESSORIES: **Removable cloth costume, plastic pixie boots and belt, and vinyl gloves**
ACTION FEATURE: **Power-fist fighting action**

ROBIN
Comic Action Heroes
Mego

RELEASE DATE: **1975–78**
SCALE: **3¾ inches**
ARTICULATION: **5 points**
ACCESSORIES: **Batrope with Batarang and display base**

ROBIN
World's Greatest Super-Heroes!
Mego

RELEASE DATE: **1978–80**
SCALE: **9½ inches**
ARTICULATION: **21 points**
ACCESSORIES: **Removable cloth costume, plastic pixie boots and belt, and vinyl gloves**

ROBIN
World's Greatest Super-Heroes!
Mego

RELEASE DATE: **1978–80**
SCALE: **12 inches**
ARTICULATION: **21 points**
ACCESSORIES: **Removable cloth costume, plastic pixie boots and belt, and vinyl gloves**

ROBIN
World's Greatest Super-Heroes!
Mego

RELEASE DATE: **1978–80**
SCALE: **12¼ inches**
ARTICULATION: **21 points**
ACCESSORIES: **Removable cloth costume and plastic belt**
ACTION FEATURE: **Magnetic hands and feet; fly-away action**

ROBIN
Pocket Super Heroes
Mego

RELEASE DATE: **1979–82**
SCALE: **3¾ inches**
ARTICULATION: **5 points**

ROBIN
Super Powers (Series 1)
Kenner

RELEASE DATE: **1984**
SCALE: **3¾ inches**
ARTICULATION: **7 points**
ACTION FEATURE: **Power-action karate chop**

ROBIN
DC Super Heroes
Toy Biz

RELEASE DATE: **1979–82**
SCALE: **3¾ inches**
ARTICULATION: **7 points**
ACCESSORIES: **Grappling hook and line; Batarang**
ACTION FEATURE: **Karate chop!**

GLIDER ROBIN
Batman: The Animated Series
Kenner

RELEASE DATE: **1992**
SCALE: **4¾ inches**
ARTICULATION: **5 points**
ACCESSORIES: **Winged jetpack and firing claw**

NINJA ROBIN
Batman: The Animated Series
Kenner

RELEASE DATE: **1992**
SCALE: **4¾ inches**
ARTICULATION: **5 points**
ACCESSORIES: **Chopping arm action and ninja weapon**

ROBIN
Batman: The Animated Series
Kenner

RELEASE DATE: **1992**
SCALE: **4¾ inches**
ARTICULATION: **5 points**
ACCESSORIES: **Turbo Glider and drop missiles**

SKI BLAST ROBIN
Batman: The Animated Series:
Crime Squad
Kenner

RELEASE DATE: **1992**
SCALE: **4¾ inches**
ARTICULATION: **5 points**
ACCESSORIES: **Techno-Ski backpack**

FIRST MATE ROBIN
Legends of Batman
Kenner

RELEASE DATE: **1995**
SCALE: **5 inches**
ARTICULATION: **5 points**
ACCESSORIES: **Blasting cannon and cutlass sword**
VARIANT: **Redeco released as Warner Bros. Store**
Exclusive

CRUSADER ROBIN
Legends of Batman
Kenner

RELEASE DATE: **1995**
SCALE: **5 inches**
ARTICULATION: **5 points**
ACCESSORIES: **Helmet, firing crossbow,**
and battle shield
VARIANT: **Redeco released as Warner Bros.**
Store Exclusive

HYDRO CLAW ROBIN
Batman Forever
Kenner

RELEASE DATE: **1995**
SCALE: **4¾ inches**
ARTICULATION: **5 points**
ACCESSORIES: **Aqua-attack launcher and diving gear**

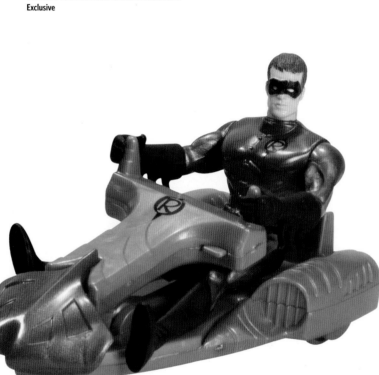

SKYBOARD ROBIN
Batman Forever
Kenner

RELEASE DATE: **1995**
SCALE: **4¾ inches**
ARTICULATION: **5 points**
ACCESSORIES: **Missile-blasting pursuit vehicle**

STREET BIKER ROBIN
Batman Forever
Kenner

RELEASE DATE: **1995**
SCALE: **4¾ inches**
ARTICULATION: **5 points**
ACCESSORIES: **Launching grappling hooks and**
battle staff

TIDE RACER ROBIN
Batman Forever
Kenner: Target Exclusive

RELEASE DATE: **1995**
SCALE: **4¾ inches**
ARTICULATION: **5 points**
ACCESSORIES: **Deep-dive gear and sea claw launcher**
NOTE: **This is a redeco of Hydro Claw Robin.**

TRIPLE STRIKE ROBIN
Batman Forever
Kenner

RELEASE DATE: **1995**
SCALE: **4¾ inches**
ARTICULATION: **5 points**
ACCESSORIES: **Multi-cannon slinger**

MARTIAL ARTS ROBIN
Batman Forever
Kenner

RELEASE DATE: **1995**
SCALE: **4¾ inches**
ARTICULATION: **8 points**
ACCESSORIES: **Ninja kicking action and battle**
weapons

GUARDIANS OF GOTHAM CITY TWO-PACK (BATMAN & ROBIN)
Batman Forever
Kenner

RELEASE DATE: **1995**
SCALE: **4¾ inches**
ARTICULATION: **5 points**
ACCESSORIES: **Grapple gun**

BOLA TRAP ROBIN
The Adventures of Batman & Robin
Kenner

RELEASE DATE: **1997**
SCALE: **4¾ inches**
ARTICULATION: **5 points**
ACCESSORIES: **Whirling battle blades**

AIR STRIKE ROBIN
The Adventures of Batman & Robin: D.U.O. Force
Kenner

RELEASE DATE: **1997**
SCALE: **4¾ inches**
ARTICULATION: **5 points**
ACCESSORIES: **Air glider**

HYDRO STORM ROBIN
The Adventures of Batman & Robin: D.U.O. Force
Kenner

RELEASE DATE: **1997**
SCALE: **4¾ inches**
ARTICULATION: **5 points**
ACCESSORIES: **Deep dive and sea skiff modes**

DIVE CLAW ROBIN
Legends of the Dark Knight
Kenner

RELEASE DATE: **1997**
SCALE: **7 inches**
ARTICULATION: **5 points**
ACCESSORIES: **Blast attack missile and powerglide wings**

JUNGLE RAGE ROBIN
Legends of the Dark Knight
Kenner

RELEASE DATE: **1997**
SCALE: **7 inches**
ARTICULATION: **5 points**
ACCESSORIES: **Battle staff and utility gauntlet**

ATTACK WING ROBIN
Batman & Robin
Kenner

RELEASE DATE: **1997**
SCALE: **5 inches**
ARTICULATION: **5 points**
ACCESSORIES: **Vertical assault cape and bonus Batman ring!**
VARIANT: **W/o bonus Batman ring**

BLADE BLAST ROBIN
Batman & Robin
Kenner

RELEASE DATE: **1997**
SCALE: **5 inches**
ARTICULATION: **5 points**
ACCESSORIES: **Rapid-deploy vine slicers and blasting battle spear**

ICE BOARD ROBIN
Batman & Robin
Kenner

RELEASE DATE: **1997**
SCALE: **5 inches**
ARTICULATION: **5 points**
ACCESSORIES: **Laser launcher and spinning attack staff**

RAZOR SKATE ROBIN
Batman & Robin
Kenner

RELEASE DATE: **1997**
SCALE: **5 inches**
ARTICULATION: **5 points**
ACCESSORIES: **Chopping blade launcher and ice battle armor**

TALON STRIKE ROBIN
Batman & Robin
Kenner

RELEASE DATE: **1997**
SCALE: **5 inches**
ARTICULATION: **5 points**
ACCESSORIES: **Twin capture claws, roto blade, bonus Batman ring**
VARIANT: **W/o bonus Batman ring**

TRIPLE STRIKE ROBIN
Batman & Robin
Kenner

RELEASE DATE: **1997**
SCALE: **5 inches**
ARTICULATION: **5 points**
ACCESSORIES: **Multi-cannon slinger**

GLACIER BATTLE ROBIN
Batman & Robin
Kenner

RELEASE DATE: **1997**
SCALE: **5 inches**
ARTICULATION: **5 points**
ACCESSORIES: **Tandem assault snow-skiff and stinger missile**

WING BLAST ROBIN
Batman & Robin
Kenner

RELEASE DATE: **1997**
SCALE: **5 inches**
ARTICULATION: **5 points**
ACCESSORIES: **Deployable wings**
ACTION FEATURE: **Blast-open battle cape and anti-freeze rocket**

CHALLENGERS OF THE NIGHT: BATMAN & ROBIN TWO-PACK
Batman & Robin
Kenner

RELEASE DATE: **1997**
SCALE: **5 inches**
ARTICULATION: **5 points**
ACCESSORIES: **Net**

GUARDIANS OF GOTHAM CITY: BATMAN & ROBIN TWO-PACK
Batman & Robin
Kenner

RELEASE DATE: **1997**
SCALE: **5 inches**
ARTICULATION: **5 points**
ACCESSORIES: **Birdarang launcher**

NIGHT HUNTER ROBIN VS. EVIL ENTRAPMENT POISON IVY TWO-PACK
Batman & Robin
Kenner

RELEASE DATE: **1997**
SCALE: **5 inches**
ARTICULATION: **5 points**
ACCESSORIES: **Birdarang weapon**

ROBIN
Batman & Robin
Kenner

RELEASE DATE: **1997**
SCALE: **12 inches**
ARTICULATION: **16 points**
ACCESSORIES: **Birdarang**

ULTIMATE ROBIN
Batman & Robin
Kenner

RELEASE DATE: **1997**
SCALE: **15 inches**
ARTICULATION: **5 points**
ACCESSORIES: **Bo staff and Bat-Symbol display base**

ROBIN
DC Super Heroes
(Golden Age Batman & Robin)
Hasbro

RELEASE DATE: **1998**
SCALE: **9 inches**
ARTICULATION: **27 points**

ARCTIC AMBUSH ROBIN
The New Batman Adventures: Mission Masters 2
Hasbro

RELEASE DATE: **1998**
SCALE: **4¾ inches**
ARTICULATION: **5 points**
ACCESSORIES: **Tundrablast sled pack**

FIREWALL ROBIN
Batman Beyond: Batlink
Hasbro

RELEASE DATE: **2000**
SCALE: **4¾ inches**
ARTICULATION: **5 points**
ACCESSORIES: **Anti-virus blaster**

RAPID ATTACK ROBIN
World of Batman
Hasbro: Wal-Mart Exclusive

RELEASE DATE: **2000**
SCALE: **4¾ inches**
ARTICULATION: **5 points**
ACCESSORIES: **Claw Shooter**

SUB-PULSE DETONATOR ROBIN
The New Batman Adventures: Mission Masters 4
Hasbro

RELEASE DATE: **2002**
SCALE: **3¾ inches**
ARTICULATION: **5 points**
ACCESSORIES: **Grappling hook and launcher**

X-RAY ASSAILANT ROBIN
The New Batman Adventures: Mission Masters 4
Hasbro

RELEASE DATE: **2002**
SCALE: **3¾ inches**
ARTICULATION: **5 points**
ACCESSORIES: **Glider w/ detachable bombs**

ROBIN
The Classic Silver Age Batman and Robin
DC Direct

RELEASE DATE: **2003**
SCALE: **6½ inches**
ARTICULATION: **11 points**
ACCESSORIES: **Batarang and interlocking Gotham City rooftop display base**

ROBIN
Super Friends!
DC Direct

RELEASE DATE: **2003**
SCALE: **6½ inches**
ARTICULATION: **9 points**
ACCESSORIES: **Batmobile miniature and SUPER FRIENDS! logo display base**

ROBIN
Pocket Super Heroes (Batman Box Set)
DC Direct

RELEASE DATE: **2004**
SCALE: **3¾ inches**
ARTICULATION: **6 points**
ACCESSORIES: **Removable cape**

ROBIN
First Appearance (Series 2)
DC Direct

RELEASE DATE: **2004**
SCALE: **6½ inches**
ARTICULATION: **9 points**
ACCESSORIES: **Cloth cape, mini comic, and FIRST APPEARANCE logo display base**

ROBIN
Batman: Dark Victory (Series 1)
DC Direct

RELEASE DATE: **1979–82**
SCALE: **6½ inches**
ARTICULATION: **7 points**
ACCESSORIES: **Bo staff and display base**

SIDE STRIKE ROBIN
Batman: Knight Force Ninjas
Kenner

RELEASE DATE: **1998**
SCALE: **6 inches**
ARTICULATION: **10 points**
ACCESSORIES: **Ninja combat weaponry**
ACTION FEATURE: **Real striking action!**

HYPER CRUSH ROBIN
Batman: Knight Force Ninjas
Kenner

RELEASE DATE: **1998**
SCALE: **6 inches**
ARTICULATION: **12 points**
ACCESSORIES: **Ninja combat weaponry**
ACTION FEATURE: **Karate-chop action!**

ROBIN III
Batman Returns
Kenner

RELEASE DATE: **1992**
SCALE: **4¾ inches**
ARTICULATION: **5 points**
ACCESSORIES: **Launching grappling hook**
NOTE: **This version of Robin did not actually appear in the movie *Batman Returns*.**

CRIME FIGHTER ROBIN
The New Batman Adventures
Kenner

RELEASE DATE: **1998**
SCALE: **4¾ inches**
ARTICULATION: **5 points**
ACCESSORIES: **Redwing Skyfighter, Mirror Image Decoder, black cape w/ yellow lining**
VARIANTS: **Arctic Blast Robin *(Batman: Mission Masters 1)***

ROBIN III
Total Justice (Series 1)
Kenner

RELEASE DATE: **1996**
SCALE: **5 inches**
ARTICULATION: **5 points**
ACCESSORIES: **Fractal Techgear armor, spinning razor disc and battle staff, and removable cape**
VARIANT: **Redecoed figure released in Hasbro's JLA collection**

> A natural detective, Tim Drake deduced the secret identities of Batman and Nightwing before he became the third Boy Wonder.
>
> **FIRST APPEARANCE**
> *Batman No. 436*

ROBIN III
The New Batman Adventures
Kenner

RELEASE DATE: **1998**
SCALE: **12 inches**
ARTICULATION: **10 points**
ACCESSORIES: **Utility Belt radios, grapnel gun, and Batarangs (3)**

ROBIN III
The New Batman Adventures: Mission Masters
Kenner

RELEASE DATE: **1998**
SCALE: **4¾ inches**
ARTICULATION: **5 points**
ACCESSORIES: **Jetblade sled**

ROBIN III
Batman
Mattel

RELEASE DATE: **2003**
SCALE: **6 inches**
ARTICULATION: **9 points**
ACCESSORIES: **Battleboard w/ launching disc**
VARIANT: **Redecoed in 2004 w/ green costume. Re-released in 2006 as part of Mattel's DC Super Heroes lineup.**

ROBIN III
The Contemporary Teen Titans (Series 1)
DC Direct

RELEASE DATE: **2004**
SCALE: **6½ inches**
ARTICULATION: **11 points**
ACCESSORIES: **Bo staff and TEEN TITANS logo display base**

ROBIN III
DC Super Heroes: Batman
Mattel

RELEASE DATE: **2006**
SCALE: **6 inches**
ARTICULATION: **12 points**

ROBIN (CARRIE KELLY)
Batman: The Dark Knight Returns (Series 1)
DC Direct

RELEASE DATE: **2004**
SCALE: **6½ inches**
ARTICULATION: **5 points**
ACCESSORIES: **Slingshot and Gotham glow-in-the-dark streetlight display base**

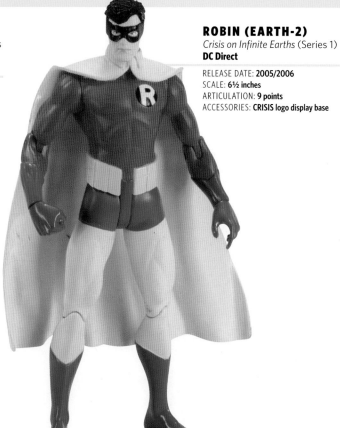

ROBIN (EARTH-2)
Crisis on Infinite Earths (Series 1)
DC Direct

RELEASE DATE: **2005/2006**
SCALE: **6½ inches**
ARTICULATION: **9 points**
ACCESSORIES: **CRISIS logo display base**

ROBIN (TEEN TITANS)
Teen Titans
Bandai

RELEASE DATE: **2004**
SCALE: **3½ inches**
ARTICULATION: **7 points**
ACCESSORIES: **Weapon**

ROBIN (TEEN TITANS)
Teen Titans
Bandai

RELEASE DATE: **2005**
SCALE: **3½ inches**
ARTICULATION: **7 points**

ROBIN (W/ HELMET)
Teen Titans
Bandai

RELEASE DATE: **2004**
SCALE: **3½ inches**
ARTICULATION: **9 points**
ACCESSORIES: **Weapon**

RED X ROBIN
Teen Titans
Bandai

RELEASE DATE: **2005**
SCALE: **3½ inches**
ARTICULATION: **9 points**
ACCESSORIES: **Throwing X**

RED X ROBIN
Teen Titans
Bandai

RELEASE DATE: **2005**
SCALE: **5 inches**
ARTICULATION: **10 points**
ACCESSORIES: **Skull mask and Red X missile launcher**

ROCKET RED
DC Super Heroes: Justice League Unlimited
Mattel

RELEASE DATE: **2006**
SCALE: **4¾ inches**
ARTICULATION: **5 points**
ACCESSORIES: **Shoulder-mounted cannon and mini rocket**

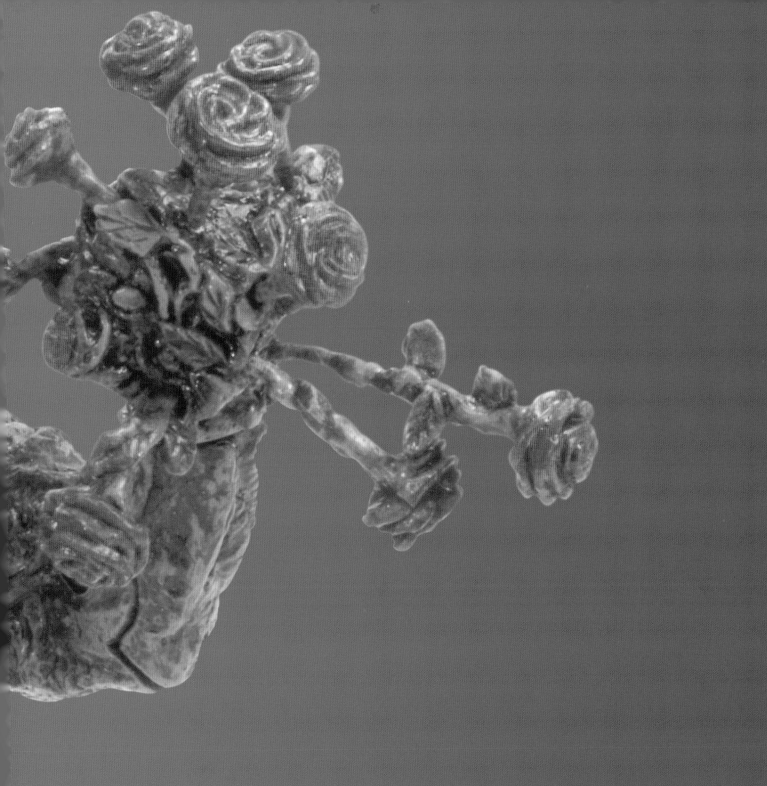

S

THE SAINT OF KILLERS
Preacher
DC Direct

RELEASE DATE: **2000**
SCALE: **6½ inches**
ARTICULATION: **10 points**
ACCESSORIES: **Removable cowboy hat, six-shooter, and Winchester rifle**

SALAKK
Green Lantern (Series 2)
DC Direct

RELEASE DATE: **2006**
SCALE: **6½ inches**
ARTICULATION: **13 points**
ACCESSORIES: **Green Lantern insignia display base**

> While Katma Tui was training John Stewart, Green Lantern Salakk policed Katma's Space Sector 1417 in addition to his own Space Sector 1418.
>
> **FIRST APPEARANCE**
> *Green Lantern* Vol. 1, No. 149

SAMURAI
Super Powers (Series 3)
Kenner

RELEASE DATE: **1986**
SCALE: **3¾ inches**
ARTICULATION: **7 points**
ACCESSORIES: **Lightning sword and removable cloth kimono top**
ACTION FEATURE: **Power-action gale-force spin**

SAND
DC Super Heroes: Justice League Unlimited
Mattel

RELEASE DATE: **2007**
SCALE: **4¾ inches**
ARTICULATION: **5 points**

> Sand was formerly known as Sandy the Golden Boy, partner of the Golden Age Sandman.
>
> **FIRST APPEARANCE**
> *Adventure Comics* No. 69

> Like fellow heroes Apache Chief and El Dorado, Samurai was created for the *Super Friends!* animated series.

THE SANDMAN I
The Sandman
DC Direct

RELEASE DATE: **1999**
SCALE: **6½ inches**
ARTICULATION: **11 points**
ACCESSORIES: **Removable hat, gas mask, and gas gun**
VARIANT: **Redecoed version w/ alternate Golden Age gas mask (far right)**

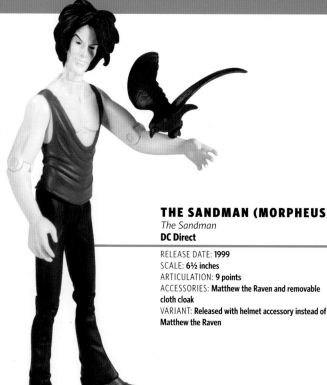

THE SANDMAN (MORPHEUS)
The Sandman
DC Direct

RELEASE DATE: 1999
SCALE: 6½ inches
ARTICULATION: 9 points
ACCESSORIES: **Matthew the Raven and removable cloth cloak**
VARIANT: **Released with helmet accessory instead of Matthew the Raven**

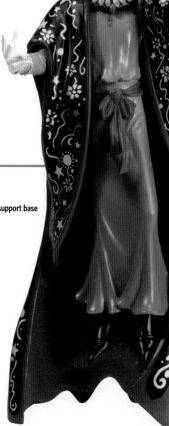

"ARABIAN KNIGHTS" SANDMAN
The Sandman: Incarnations
DC Direct

RELEASE DATE: **2000**
SCALE: **6½ inches**
ARTICULATION: **5 points**
ACCESSORIES: **Crystal ball and floating support base**

"DREAM HUNTERS" SANDMAN
The Sandman: Incarnations
DC Direct

RELEASE DATE: **2000**
SCALE: **6½ inches**
ARTICULATION: **7 points**
ACCESSORIES: **Baku**

SATURN GIRL
Legion of Super-Heroes (Series 1)
DC Direct

RELEASE DATE: **2001**
SCALE: **6½ inches**
ARTICULATION: **8 points**
ACCESSORIES: **Removable flight belt, one-size-fits-all Legion flight ring, and Saturn Girl emblem display base**

SATURN GIRL
Pocket Super Heroes (Series 1)
DC Direct

RELEASE DATE: **2002**
SCALE: **3¼ inches**
ARTICULATION: **6 points**
ACCESSORIES: **Display base**

SCARECROW
Batman: The Animated Series
Kenner

RELEASE DATE: **1993**
SCALE: **4¾ inches**
ARTICULATION: **6 points**
ACCESSORIES: **Sickle and crow**
ACTION FEATURES: **Thrashing sickle and light-pipe eyes**

TWISTER STRIKE SCARECROW
Legends of the Dark Knight
Kenner

RELEASE DATE: **1997**
SCALE: **7 inches**
ARTICULATION: **6 points**
ACCESSORIES: **Scythe**
ACTION FEATURES: **Scythe slash attack and nightmare glow eyes**

SCARECROW
Super Friends!
DC Direct

RELEASE DATE: **2003**
SCALE: **6½ inches**
ARTICULATION: **9 points**
ACCESSORIES: **Belt magnet ray and SUPER FRIENDS! logo display base**

SCARECROW
Batman: Hush
DC Direct

RELEASE DATE: **2005**
SCALE: **6½ inches**
ARTICULATION: **11 points**
ACCESSORIES: **BATMAN logo display base**

SCARECROW
Batman Begins
Mattel

RELEASE DATE: **2005**
SCALE: **5 inches**
ARTICULATION: **10 points**
ACCESSORIES: **Fear gun**
VARIANT: **"Blood" deco**

SKULL STRIKE SCARECROW
Batman Begins
Mattel

RELEASE DATE: **2005**
SCALE: **5 inches**
ARTICULATION: **10 points**
ACCESSORIES: **Missile launcher**
VARIANT: **Green "poison" deco**

SCARECROW
DC Super Heroes: Batman
Mattel

RELEASE DATE: **2005**
SCALE: **6 inches**
ARTICULATION: **18 points**
ACCESSORIES: **Scythe/pitchfork and fear-gas sprayer**

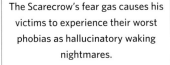

> The Scarecrow's fear gas causes his victims to experience their worst phobias as hallucinatory waking nightmares.
>
> **FIRST APPEARANCE**
> *World's Finest Comics* No. 3

SCARECROW
Batman: Dark Victory (Series 1)
DC Direct

RELEASE DATE: **2006**
SCALE: **6½ inches**
ARTICULATION: **9 points**
ACCESSORIES: **Rag doll and display base**

SENTINEL
Pocket Super Heroes
(Green Lantern Box Set)
DC Direct

RELEASE DATE: **2004**
SCALE: **3¼ inches**
ARTICULATION: **6 points**
ACCESSORIES: **Removable cape**

> Sentinel is a costumed identity briefly adopted by a "de-aged" Alan Scott, Earth's first Green Lantern.
>
> **FIRST APPEARANCE**
> *Showcase '95* No. 1

> Many believe that Sgt. Frank Rock was killed by the last enemy bullet fired before the end of hostilities in World War II.
>
> **FIRST APPEARANCE**
> *Our Army at War* No. 81

SGT. ROCK
Sgt. Rock and His Tough Action Soldiers
Remco

RELEASE DATE: **1981**
SCALE: **3¾ inches**
ARTICULATION: **9 points**
ACCESSORIES: **M-16 rifle, bayonet, and wearable dog tags w/ unique serial number**
NOTE: **Pictured (left to right) are Raider, Sgt. Rock, and Ranger.**

ROCK IN THE FREE WORLD

Fans of DC Comics' Sgt. Rock know that the stoic soldier's exploits took place during the biggest battles of World War II. But when Remco adapted Frank Rock to toy form in 1981, his BAR rifle was replaced with an M-16. Easy Company's familiar grunts were nowhere to be found in the ranks of *Sgt. Rock and His Tough Action Soldiers,* which included the generic Ranger, Marine, Green Beret, Commando, Infantry, and Gunner. In addition, Rock's Nazi nemeses and Axis adversaries now included the equally nondescript Aggressor, Raider, and Guerilla, while all playsets and vehicles featured modern military equipment and accessories.

SGT. ROCK
Our Fighting Forces
DC Direct

RELEASE DATE: **2002**
SCALE: **6½ inches**
ARTICULATION: **9 points**
ACCESSORIES: **Removable helmet, Thompson machine gun, and grenades (2)**

SGT. ROCK
Sgt. Rock
Dreams & Visions

RELEASE DATE: **2002**
SCALE: **12 inches**
ARTICULATION: **21 points**
ACCESSORIES: **Fatigues, rifle, U.S. Army uniform (Ike jacket, EM service trousers, EM service shirt w/ tie, EM overseas garrison cap, EM service belt, and Corcoran boots), winter combat gear (U.S. Army M43 fatigue jacket w/ scarf, M1 combat helmet, M1 Garland rifle, grenades, web belt w/ grommets, canteen w/ cover, 45 caliber pistol w/ leather holster, and M1 bayonet w/ scabbard bandolier), and giant 80-page comic book *Sgt. Rock's Prize Battle Tales***

EASY COMPANY

Dreams & Visions' *Sgt. Rock* collection was a match made in heaven, pairing Hasbro's classic G.I. Joe body with newly sculpted heads and individualized uniforms. The end result was Sgt. Rock and Easy Company realized as twelve-inch fully articulated action figures that could stand shoulder to shoulder with Joe and take advantage of his many vehicles and accessories. In addition to Rock, the line included recognizable Easy Company grunts Bulldozer, Jackie Johnson, and Little Sure Shot. Later, Dreams & Visions expanded its offerings to spotlight fellow DC Comics war characters Blackhawk, Mlle. Marie, Miss Fear, and the Unknown Soldier. (See individual listings.)

THE SHADE
Justice Society of America Villains
DC Direct

RELEASE DATE: **2002**
SCALE: **6½ inches**
ARTICULATION: **9 points**
ACCESSORIES: **Cane**

THE SHADE
Pocket Super Heroes (Series 1)
DC Direct

RELEASE DATE: **2005**
SCALE: **3¾ inches**
ARTICULATION: **11 points**
ACCESSORIES: **Display base**

THE SHADE
*DC Super Heroes:
Justice League Unlimited*
Mattel

RELEASE DATE: **2007**
SCALE: **4¾ inches**
ARTICULATION: **5 points**
ACCESSORIES: **Cane**

THE SHARK
Green Lantern (Series 2)
DC Direct

RELEASE DATE: **2006**
SCALE: **6½ inches**
ARTICULATION: **13 points**
ACCESSORIES: **Green Lantern insignia display base**

SHAZAM!
World's Greatest Super-Heroes!
Mego

RELEASE DATE: **1972–82**
SCALE: **8 inches**
ARTICULATION: **14 points**
ACCESSORIES: **Removable cloth costume and plastic boots**

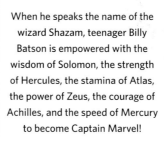

SHAZAM!
Comic Action Heroes
Mego

RELEASE DATE: **1975–78**
SCALE: **3¾ inches**
ARTICULATION: **5 points**
ACCESSORIES: **Display base**

SHAZAM!
Pocket Super Heroes
Mego

RELEASE DATE: **1979–82**
SCALE: **3¾ inches**
ARTICULATION: **5 points**

When he speaks the name of the wizard Shazam, teenager Billy Batson is empowered with the wisdom of Solomon, the strength of Hercules, the stamina of Atlas, the power of Zeus, the courage of Achilles, and the speed of Mercury to become Captain Marvel!

FIRST APPEARANCE
Whiz Comics No. 1

SHAZAM!
Super Powers (Series 3)
Kenner

RELEASE DATE: **1986**
SCALE: **3¾ inches**
ARTICULATION: **7 points**
ACCESSORIES: **Removable cloth cape**
ACTION FEATURE: **Power-action thunder punch**

SHAZAM!
DC Super Heroes
Hasbro

RELEASE DATE: **1999**
SCALE: **7 inches**
ARTICULATION: **10 points**
ACCESSORIES: **Removable cape, comic book cover art, and display base**

SHAZAM!
Shazam!
DC Direct

RELEASE DATE: **2000**
SCALE: **6½ inches**
ARTICULATION: **9 points**
ACCESSORIES: **Transformation stand
and Rock of Eternity/WHIZ Radio diorama
(w/ built-in "thunderclap" sound chip)**

SHAZAM!
Shazam!
DC Direct

RELEASE DATE: **2002**
SCALE: **6½ inches**
ARTICULATION: **9 points**
ACCESSORIES: **Mr. Mind mini figure**

SHAZAM!
Pocket Super Heroes (Series 2)
DC Direct

RELEASE DATE: **2003**
SCALE: **3¼ inches**
ARTICULATION: **6 points**
ACCESSORIES: **Removable cape and display base**

MARVEL FAMILY

Before DC Direct ended production of its *Pocket Super Heroes* line, plans were in place to release the Marvel Family—including the wizard Shazam, Captain Marvel Jr., and Mary Marvel—in a series of two-packs with Captain Marvel himself, or as a box set. Only two sets of the Marvel Family exist, including the one pictured, owned by one very lucky collector.

SHAZAM!
Kingdom Come (Series 2)
DC Direct

RELEASE DATE: **2003**
SCALE: **6½ inches**
ARTICULATION: **7 points**

SHAZAM!
First Appearance (Series 1)
DC Direct

RELEASE DATE: **2004**
SCALE: **6½ inches**
ARTICULATION: **9 points**
ACCESSORIES: **Cloth cape, mini comic, and
FIRST APPEARANCE logo display base**

SHAZAM!
Superman/Batman
(Series 1: *Public Enemies*)
DC Direct

RELEASE DATE: **2005**
SCALE: **6½ inches**
ARTICULATION: **11 points**
ACCESSORIES: **SUPERMAN/BATMAN logo
display base**
NOTE: **See also Superman as Shazam!**

SHAZAM!
Justice (Series 4)
DC Direct

RELEASE DATE: **2006**
SCALE: **7 inches**
ARTICULATION: **11 points**
ACCESSORIES: **Display base**

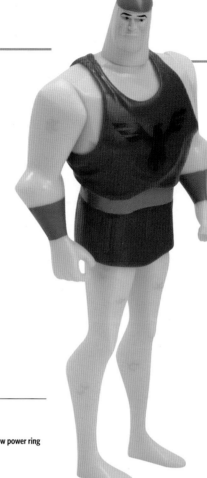

SHINING KNIGHT
*DC Super Heroes:
Justice League Unlimited*
Mattel

RELEASE DATE: **2006**
SCALE: **4¾ inches**
ARTICULATION: **5 points**
ACCESSORIES: **Sword (single-carded only)**

> Sir Justin, the Shining Knight, was a knight of King Arthur's Round Table brought to the future to battle twentieth-century evils.
> **FIRST APPEARANCE**
> *Adventure Comics* No. 66

SINESTRO
Green Lantern
DC Direct

RELEASE DATE: **2001**
SCALE: **6½ inches**
ARTICULATION: **7 points**
ACCESSORIES: **One-size-fits-all yellow power ring**

SINESTRO
Pocket Super Heroes (Series 1)
DC Direct

RELEASE DATE: **2002**
SCALE: **3¼ inches**
ARTICULATION: **6 points**
ACCESSORIES: **Display base**

SINESTRO
Super Friends!
DC Direct

RELEASE DATE: **2003**
SCALE: **6½ inches**
ARTICULATION: **9 points**
ACCESSORIES: **One-size-fits-all yellow power ring
and SUPER FRIENDS! logo display base**

SINESTRO
Justice League Unlimited
Mattel

RELEASE DATE: **2004/2007**
SCALE: **4¾ inches**
ARTICULATION: **5 points**
ACCESSORIES: **Yellow energy spiked mace (single-carded only)**

SINESTRO
Justice (Series 1)
DC Direct

RELEASE DATE: **2005**
SCALE: **6½ inches**
ARTICULATION: **11 points**
ACCESSORIES: **Mega-rod and display base**

SINESTRO
Green Lantern (Series 2)
DC Direct

RELEASE DATE: **2006**
SCALE: **6½ inches**
ARTICULATION: **9 points**
ACCESSORIES: **Green Lantern insignia display base**

> Formerly Green Lantern of Space Sector 1417, Sinestro betrayed the Guardians of the Universe and was ousted from the GL Corps. After forging an alliance with the Weaponers of Qward, Sinestro procured a yellow power ring to wreak havoc and have his revenge.
> **FIRST APPEARANCE**
> *Green Lantern* Vol. 1, No. 7

> Evil genius Thaddeus Bodog Sivana is the archenemy of Captain Marvel and the Marvel Family.
> **FIRST APPEARANCE**
> *Whiz Comics* No. 2

SIVANA
Pocket Super Heroes (Series 2)
DC Direct

RELEASE DATE: **2003**
SCALE: **3¼ inches**
ARTICULATION: **6 points**
ACCESSORIES: **Ray gun and display base**
NOTE: **This character is commonly known as "Dr. Sivana."**

SKINMAN
Swamp Thing
Kenner

RELEASE DATE: **1990**
SCALE: **5 inches**
ARTICULATION: **5 points**
ACCESSORIES: **Glow-in-the-dark Fangbat bio-mask and pickax**

SLADE
Teen Titans
Bandai

RELEASE DATE: **2005**
SCALE: **3½ inches**
ARTICULATION: **10 points**
VARIANT: **Re-released with S-scar on forehead**
NOTE: **Slade is commonly known as Deathstroke the Terminator in the DC Comics Universe.**

SLADE
Teen Titans
Bandai

RELEASE DATE: **2005**
SCALE: **5 inches**
ARTICULATION: **9 points**
ACCESSORIES: **Maces (2), flaming gauntlets (2), and clawed gauntlet**

A man murdered in Gotham City's Slaughter Swamp, the so-called Solomon Grundy (whose name comes from an old nursery rhyme) qualifies as DC Comics' only zombie action figure—so far.

FIRST APPEARANCE
All-American Comics No. 61

SOLOMON GRUNDY
Justice Society of America (Series 3)
DC Direct

RELEASE DATE: **2004**
SCALE: **6½ inches**
ARTICULATION: **9 points**
ACCESSORIES: **Tree branch club**
NOTE: **Box packaging included free promotional** *Pocket Super Heroes* **Golden Age Wonder Woman**

SOLOMON GRUNDY
Pocket Super Heroes (Series 1)
DC Direct

RELEASE DATE: **2002**
SCALE: **3¼ inches**
ARTICULATION: **6 points**
ACCESSORIES: **Display base**

SOLOMON GRUNDY
Justice (Series 4)
DC Direct

RELEASE DATE: **2006**
SCALE: **7 inches**
ARTICULATION: **6 points**
ACCESSORIES: **Display base**

SOLOMON GRUNDY
DC Super Heroes:
Justice League Unlimited
Mattel: 2006 Convention Exclusive

RELEASE DATE: **2006**
SCALE: **5 inches**
ARTICULATION: **5 points**
VARIANT: **Rare "Green Slime" deco chase figure w/ cloth tattered jacket**

SOPHIE
Promethea and Sophie
DC Direct

RELEASE DATE: **2002**
SCALE: **6½ inches**
ARTICULATION: **5 points**
ACCESSORIES: **Removable backpack and display base**

THE SPECTRE
Mages, Mystics & Magicians
DC Direct

RELEASE DATE: **2000**
SCALE: **6½ inches**
ARTICULATION: **9 points**
ACCESSORIES: **Spear of Destiny and floating cape**

THE SPECTRE
Pocket Super Heroes (Series 1)
DC Direct

RELEASE DATE: **2002**
SCALE: **3¼ inches**
ARTICULATION: **6 points**
ACCESSORIES: **Removable hood/cape and display base**

God's Spirit of Vengeance, the Spectre was first bound to the soul of murdered police detective Jim Corrigan.

FIRST APPEARANCE
More Fun Comics No. 52

THE SPECTRE
Elseworlds (Series 2: Kingdom Come)
DC Direct

RELEASE DATE: **2006**
SCALE: **6½ inches**
ARTICULATION: **5 points**
ACCESSORIES: **Display base**

THE SPECTRE II (HAL JORDAN)
Other Worlds
DC Direct

RELEASE DATE: **2004**
SCALE: **6½ inches**
ARTICULATION: **9 points**
ACCESSORIES: **Poseable and removable cloth cape**
ACTION FEATURE: **Glow-in-the-dark deco**

SPEEDY
Teen Titans
Mego

RELEASE DATE: **1976**
SCALE: **7 inches**
ARTICULATION: **21 points**
ACCESSORIES: **Removable cloth costume and plastic cap, gloves, and boots; bow and quiver**

SPEEDY (SILVER AGE)
The Silver Age Green Arrow and Speedy
DC Direct

RELEASE DATE: **2001**
SCALE: **6½ inches**
ARTICULATION: **9 points**
ACCESSORIES: **Bow and trick arrows**

As a boy, Speedy targeted criminals alongside his mentor, Oliver Queen, a.k.a. Green Arrow.

FIRST APPEARANCE
More Fun Comics No. 73

SPEEDY (SILVER AGE)
Pocket Super Heroes (Series 2)
DC Direct

RELEASE DATE: **2003**
SCALE: **3¼ inches**
ARTICULATION: **6 points**
ACCESSORIES: **Bow, removable quiver, and display base**

SPEEDY
Teen Titans
Bandai

RELEASE DATE: **2004**
SCALE: **3½ inches**
ARTICULATION: **5 points**
ACCESSORIES: **Bow and arrows**

SPEEDY
Teen Titans
Bandai

RELEASE DATE: **2006**
SCALE: **5 inches**
ARTICULATION: **9 points**
ACCESSORIES: **Bow and arrows**

SPIDER JERUSALEM
Transmetropolitan
DC Direct

RELEASE DATE: **1999**
SCALE: **6½ inches**
ARTICULATION: **9 points**
ACCESSORIES: **Laptop computer and two-headed cat**
VARIANT: **Figure also released with Bowel Disruptor Gun accessory (instead of laptop computer) and alternate hand**

STAR BOY
Legion of Super-Heroes (Series 3)
DC Direct

RELEASE DATE: **2004**
SCALE: **6½ inches**
ARTICULATION: **11 points**

STARFIRE
The New Teen Titans (Series 1)
DC Direct

RELEASE DATE: **2004**
SCALE: **6½ inches**
ARTICULATION: **8 points**
ACCESSORIES: **Flying hair display base**
ACTION FEATURE: **Light-up eyes and hair**
VARIANT: **Redecoed figure included in the *Classic Teen Titans* gift set.**

STARFIRE
Teen Titans
Bandai

RELEASE DATE: **2004**
SCALE: **3½ inches**
ARTICULATION: **7 points**
ACCESSORIES: **Weapon**

STARFIRE
Teen Titans
Bandai

RELEASE DATE: **2005**
SCALE: **3½ inches**
ARTICULATION: **7 points**

> Tamaranean Princess Koriand'r, a.k.a. Starfire, was on the run from Gordanian slavers when the New Teen Titans rescued her and made her a member of the reconstituted super-team.
>
> **FIRST APPEARANCE**
> *DC Comics Presents* No. 26

STARMAN
Justice Society of America (Series 1)
DC Direct

RELEASE DATE: **2000**
SCALE: **6½ inches**
ARTICULATION: **8 points**
ACCESSORIES: **Battery-powered light-up gravity rod**

STARMAN
Pocket Super Heroes (Series 1)
DC Direct

RELEASE DATE: **2002**
SCALE: **3¼ inches**
ARTICULATION: **6 points**
ACCESSORIES: **Gravity rod, removable cape, and display base**

> Starman's gravity rod harnesses cosmic energy and allows its wielder to defy gravity and fire energy bolts.
>
> **FIRST APPEARANCE**
> *Adventure Comics* No. 61

STARMAN II
Justice League Unlimited
Mattel

RELEASE DATE: **2005**
SCALE: **4¾ inches**
ARTICULATION: **5 points**
ACCESSORIES: **Staff (single-carded only)**

Starman II is really Prince Gavyn, of the planet known to him as Throneworld.

FIRST APPEARANCE
Adventure Comics No. 467

STARMAN III
DC Direct

RELEASE DATE: **1999**
SCALE: **6½ inches**
ARTICULATION: **9 points**
ACCESSORIES: **Removable goggles and battery-powered light-up gravity rod**
VARIANT: **Redecoed figure featuring Jack Knight with a goatee, released in 2001**

STAR SAPPHIRE
Green Lantern
DC Direct

RELEASE DATE: **2001**
SCALE: **6½ inches**
ARTICULATION: **7 points**
ACCESSORIES: **Star Sapphire gem display base**

STAR SAPPHIRE
*DC Super Heroes:
Justice League Unlimited*
Mattel

RELEASE DATE: **2007**
SCALE: **4¾ inches**
ARTICULATION: **5 points**

STAR-SPANGLED KID II
*DC Super Heroes:
Justice League Unlimited*
Mattel

RELEASE DATE: **2007**
SCALE: **4¾ inches**
ARTICULATION: **5 points**

When she first appeared, Green Lantern Hal Jordan's fetching foe, Star Sapphire, was actually Jordan's Ferris Aircraft boss and girlfriend, Carol Ferris.

FIRST APPEARANCE
Green Lantern Vol. 1, No. 16

BLAST HAMMER STEEL
Superman: Man of Steel
Kenner

RELEASE DATE: **1995**
SCALE: **5 inches**
ARTICULATION: **5 points**
ACCESSORIES: **Shield and firing hammers**
ACTION FEATURE: **Rivet ratchet sounds**

STEEL: THE MOVIE

John Henry Irons made it to the big screen in 1997, when *Steel* hit theaters with basketball superstar Shaquille O'Neal playing the armored DC Comics hero. Joining Shaq on screen, as well as in Kenner's movie-based *Steel* action-figure assortments, were Annabeth Gish as the wheelchair-bound Lt. Sparks and Judd Nelson taking a villainous turn as Nathaniel Burke. Though faithful to the essence of the comic book character, Steel's inspiration, Superman, was nowhere in sight. Kenner's action figures—although well-sculpted and sporting nifty action features—remained on toy shelves only briefly.

ARMOR-UP STEEL
ARTICULATION: **5 points**
ACCESSORIES: **"Sonic Flash" stun gun and full body shield.**

LT. SPARKS
ARTICULATION: **7 points**
ACCESSORIES: **Mobile defense power chair**

POWER GAUNTLET STEEL
ARTICULATION: **5 points**
ACCESSORIES: **Turbo grappling claw**

SHELL SHOCK BURKE
ARTICULATION: **5 points**
ACCESSORIES: **Triple fire rotoblaster**

Shaq performed many of his own stunts in *Steel* due to a lack of 7'1" stuntmen who could double for the NBA all-star.

Steel's armor in the 1997 film was molded from rubber, not steel.

STEEL A.K.A. JOHN HENRY IRONS
ARTICULATION: **5 points**
ACCESSORIES: **"Hardened Steel" armor suit**

VAPOR TRAIL STEEL
ARTICULATION: **5 points**
ACCESSORIES: **Battle flight armor and boost blaster gauntlets**

DELUXE FIGURES

ELECTROMAGNETIC STEEL
ARTICULATION: **5 points**
ACCESSORIES: **Recoil action capture snare**

MOBILE BARRIER STEEL
ARTICULATION: **5 points**
ACCESSORIES: **Rapid fire assault sled**

VEHICLES

STEEL ASSAULT CYCLE
ACTION FEATURE: **Power launch hammer blaster**
ACCESSORIES: **Exclusive Blast Hammer Steel figure helmet**

STEEL III (A.K.A. JOHN HENRY IRONS)
Superman: Man of Steel
Kenner

RELEASE DATE: **1995**
SCALE: **5 inches**
ARTICULATION: **5 points**
ACCESSORIES: **Sledgehammer and removable cape**
ACTION FEATURE: **Pounding hammer blows**

STEEL III
JLA (Series 4)
Kenner

RELEASE DATE: **1998**
SCALE: **5 inches**
ARTICULATION: **5 points**
ACCESSORIES: **Sledgehammer, removable cape, and JLA logo display base**

STEEL III
The Return of Superman (Series 1)
DC Direct

RELEASE DATE: **2004**
SCALE: **6½ inches**
ARTICULATION: **13 points**
ACCESSORIES: **Sledgehammer and Superman S-shield insignia display base**

The death of Superman inspired John Henry Irons— whose life was once saved by the Man of Steel—to adopt the armor and guise of Steel, to carry on in Superman's stead.

FIRST APPEARANCE
Adventures of Superman No. 500

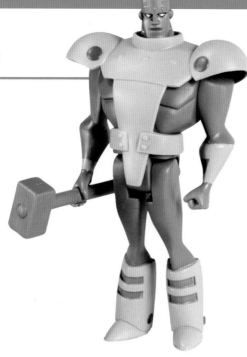

STEEL III
DC Super Heroes:
Justice League Unlimited
Mattel

RELEASE DATE: **2005**
SCALE: **4¾ inches**
ARTICULATION: **5 points**
ACCESSORIES: **Sledgehammer**

STEEL IV
Superman/Batman
(Series 3: *Public Enemies*)
DC Direct

RELEASE DATE: **2007**
SCALE: **6½ inches**
ARTICULATION: **11 points**
ACCESSORIES: **Hammer, removable mask,**
and display base

STEPPENWOLF
Super Powers (Series 2)
Kenner

RELEASE DATE: **1985–86**
SCALE: **3¾ inches**
ARTICULATION: **7 points**
ACCESSORIES: **Electro-Axe (tethered to**
nonremovable backpack)
ACTION FEATURE: **Power-action Electro-Axe chop**

STEVE TREVOR
Wonder Woman
Mego

RELEASE DATE: **1977–80**
SCALE: **12 inches**
ARTICULATION: **20 points**
ACCESSORIES: **Removable cloth Air Force uniform**
and hat

STREAKY THE SUPERCAT
The Classic Silver Age
Superboy and Supergirl
DC Direct

RELEASE DATE: **2002**
SCALE: **6½ inches**
ARTICULATION: **5 points**

> Streaky the Supercat belonged
> to the Legion of Super-Pets,
> alongside Krypto the Superdog,
> Beppo the Supermonkey, Comet
> the Superhorse, and the shape-
> changing Proty II.

STREAKY THE SUPERCAT
Krypto the Superdog
Fisher-Price

RELEASE DATE: **2006**
SCALE: **6 inches**
ARTICULATION: **5 points**
ACCESSORIES: **Jimmy the Rat, garbage pail, and**
pizza slice
ACTION FEATURE: **Push-button talking feature and**
blinking light

SUN BOY
Legion of Super-Heroes (Series 3)
DC Direct

RELEASE DATE: **2003**
SCALE: **6½ inches**
ARTICULATION: **11 points**

SUPERBOY
Action Boy (Captain Action)
Ideal

RELEASE DATE: **1966**
SCALE: **9 inches**
ARTICULATION: **14 points**
ACCESSORIES: **Super-uniform (w/ belt, boots, and cape); telepathic scrambler, interspace language translator, and chemistry lab**

SUPERBOY
The Classic Silver Age Superboy and Supergirl
DC Direct

RELEASE DATE: **2002**
SCALE: **6½ inches**
ARTICULATION: **15 points**
ACCESSORIES: **Famous Smallville billboard**

SUPERBOY II
Superman: Man of Steel
Kenner

RELEASE DATE: **1995**
SCALE: **5 inches**
ARTICULATION: **5 points**
ACCESSORIES: **Mammoth claw and taser missiles**
VEHICLE: **Superboy VTOL cycle**
NOTE: **Released in *Superboy vs. King Shark* box set.**

SUPERBOY II
DC Super Heroes
Hasbro

RELEASE DATE: **1999**
SCALE: **5 inches**
ARTICULATION: **5 points**
ACCESSORIES: **Surfboard**

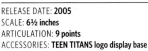

> With DNA modeled on Superman's, Superboy learned to his horror that his human side came from Lex Luthor's genetic material.
>
> **FIRST APPEARANCE**
> *Adventures of Superman* No. 500

SUPERBOY II
JLA (Series 2)
Kenner

RELEASE DATE: **1999**
SCALE: **5 inches**
ARTICULATION: **5 points**
ACCESSORIES: **JLA logo display base**

SUPERBOY II
The Return of Superman (Series 1)
DC Direct

RELEASE DATE: **1995**
SCALE: **6½ inches**
ARTICULATION: **11 points**
ACCESSORIES: **Removable sunglasses and Superman S-shield insignia display base**

SUPERBOY II
The Contemporary Teen Titans (Series 2)
DC Direct

RELEASE DATE: **2005**
SCALE: **6½ inches**
ARTICULATION: **9 points**
ACCESSORIES: **TEEN TITANS logo display base**

> Superboy died in battle with the Earth-Prime Superboy during DC Comics' *Infinite Crisis* in 2006.

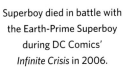

SUPERBOY (EARTH-PRIME)
Infinite Crisis (Series 1)
DC Direct

RELEASE DATE: **2006**
SCALE: **6½ inches**
ARTICULATION: **9 points**
ACCESSORIES: **Display base**

SUPERBOY (EARTH-PRIME)
Crisis on Infinite Earths (Series 3)
DC Direct

RELEASE DATE: **2006**
SCALE: **6½ inches**
ARTICULATION: **15 points**
ACCESSORIES: **CRISIS logo display base**

SUPERGIRL
Super Queens
Ideal

RELEASE DATE: **1967**
SCALE: **11½ inches**
ARTICULATION: **5 points**
ACCESSORIES: **Cloth costume and Krypto the Superdog**

SUPERGIRL
World's Greatest Super-Heroes!
Mego

RELEASE DATE: **1972-82**
SCALE: **8 inches**
ARTICULATION: **21 points**
ACCESSORIES: **Removable cloth costume**
VARIANT: **Screen-printed boots, later replaced with removable plastic boots**

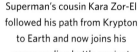

SUPERGIRL
*The Classic Silver Age
Superboy and Supergirl*
DC Direct

RELEASE DATE: **2002**
SCALE: **6½ inches**
ARTICULATION: **13 points**
ACCESSORIES: **Orphanage/Smallville billboard**

SUPERGIRL
Pocket Super Heroes (Series 2)
DC Direct

RELEASE DATE: **2003**
SCALE: **3¼ inches**
ARTICULATION: **6 points**
ACCESSORIES: **Removable cape, cloth skirt, and display base**

SUPERGIRL
Crisis on Infinite Earths (Series 1)
DC Direct

RELEASE DATE: **2005/2006**
SCALE: **6½ inches**
ARTICULATION: **9 points**
ACCESSORIES: **CRISIS logo display base**

SUPERGIRL (MODERN)
Superman
Kenner: Diamond Comics Distributor Exclusive

RELEASE DATE: **1995**
SCALE: **4¾ inches**
ARTICULATION: **6 points**
ACCESSORIES: **Aerial assault armor**

> Superman's cousin Kara Zor-El followed his path from Krypton to Earth and now joins his never-ending battle against evil as Supergirl.
>
> **FIRST APPEARANCE**
> *Action Comics* No. 252

SUPERGIRL (MODERN)
Superman
Hasbro

RELEASE DATE: **2001**
SCALE: **12 inches**
ARTICULATION: **10 points**
ACCESSORIES: **Cloth costume**

SUPERGIRL (MODERN)
Superman (Series 1)
DC Direct

RELEASE DATE: **2003**
SCALE: **6½ inches**
ARTICULATION: **11 points**
ACCESSORIES: **Superman S-shield display base**

SUPERGIRL (MODERN)
*DC Super Heroes:
Justice League Unlimited*
Mattel

RELEASE DATE: **2005**
SCALE: **4¾ inches**
ARTICULATION: **5 points**
ACCESSORIES: **Purse**

SUPERGIRL (MODERN)
DC Super Heroes: Superman
Mattel

RELEASE DATE: **2006**
SCALE: **6 inches**
ARTICULATION: **17 points**

> Supergirl donned this revealing costume during the *Superman/Batman* storyline in which she was abducted to Apokolips, where the evil Darkseid attempted to corrupt her to do his bidding.

SUPERGIRL (MODERN)
Superman/Batman
(Series 2: *The Return of Supergirl*)
DC Direct

RELEASE DATE: **2006**
SCALE: **6½ inches**
ARTICULATION: **9 points**
ACCESSORIES: **SUPERMAN/BATMAN logo display base**

CORRUPTED SUPERGIRL
Superman/Batman
(Series 2: *The Return of Supergirl*)
DC Direct

RELEASE DATE: **2006**
SCALE: **6½ inches**
ARTICULATION: **9 points**
ACCESSORIES: **SUPERMAN/BATMAN logo display base**

SUPERGIRL
Elseworlds (Series 3: Elseworlds Finest)
DC Direct

RELEASE DATE: **2007**
SCALE: **6½ inches**
ARTICULATION: **9 points**
ACCESSORIES: **Display base**

SUPERMAN
Captain Action
Ideal

RELEASE DATE: **1967**
SCALE: **12 inches**
ARTICULATION: **18 points**
ACCESSORIES: **Removable cloth costume and Superman face mask, belt, flying cape, boots, arm shackles, block of green kryptonite, and Superman's dog, Krypto**

> Rocketed to Earth from the doomed planet Krypton, infant Kal-El gained miraculous powers under Earth's yellow sun and lighter gravity to become his adopted world's greatest champion, Superman.
>
> **FIRST APPEARANCE**
> *Action Comics* No. 1

SUPERMAN
World's Greatest Super-Heroes!
Mego

RELEASE DATE: **1972-82**
SCALE: **8 inches**
ARTICULATION: **21 points**
ACCESSORIES: **Removable cloth costume and plastic boots**

SUPERMAN
Comic Action Heroes
Mego

RELEASE DATE: **1975-78**
SCALE: **3¾ inches**
ARTICULATION: **6 points**
ACCESSORIES: **Display base**
VEHICLE/PLAYSET: **Fortress of Solitude playset**

SUPERMAN
Superman (Diecast Metal)
Mego

RELEASE DATE: **1978-80**
SCALE: **12 inches**
ARTICULATION: **14 points**
ACCESSORIES: **Removable cloth costume and plastic boots**

SUPERMAN
World's Greatest Super-Heroes!
Mego

RELEASE DATE: **1978-81**
SCALE: **5½ inches**
ARTICULATION: **12 points**

SUPERMAN
Superman
Mego

RELEASE DATE: **1978-81**
SCALE: **12 inches**
ARTICULATION: **14 points**
ACCESSORIES: **Removable cloth costume and plastic boots**

SUPERMAN
Pocket Super Heroes
Mego

RELEASE DATE: **1979-82**
SCALE: **3¾ inches**
ARTICULATION: **5 points**

SUPERMAN
Super Powers (Series 1)
Kenner

RELEASE DATE: **1984**
SCALE: **3¾ inches**
ARTICULATION: **7 points**
ACCESSORIES: **Removable cloth cape**
ACTION FEATURE: **Power-action punch**

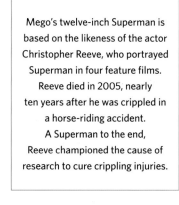

> Mego's twelve-inch Superman is based on the likeness of the actor Christopher Reeve, who portrayed Superman in four feature films. Reeve died in 2005, nearly ten years after he was crippled in a horse-riding accident. A Superman to the end, Reeve championed the cause of research to cure crippling injuries.

SUPERMAN
DC Super Heroes
Toy Biz

RELEASE DATE: **1989**
SCALE: **3¾ inches**
ARTICULATION: **7 points**
ACCESSORIES: **Removable cloth cape and kryptonite ring**
ACTION FEATURE: **Magnet in ring repels and knocks over Superman**

SUPERMAN
Superman: Man of Steel
Kenner

RELEASE DATE: **1995**
SCALE: **5 inches**
ARTICULATION: **5 points**
ACCESSORIES: **Chains and removable cape**
ACTION FEATURE: **Take-Off Force arm action**

SUPERMAN
Total Justice (Series 2)
Kenner

RELEASE DATE: **1996**
SCALE: **5 inches**
ARTICULATION: **5 points**
ACCESSORIES: **Fractal techgear kryptonite ray emitter and removable cape**

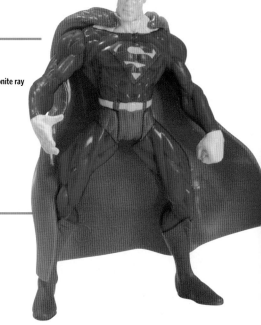

SUPERMAN
JLA (Series 1)
Hasbro

RELEASE DATE: **1998**
SCALE: **5 inches**
ARTICULATION: **5 points**
ACCESSORIES: **JLA logo display base**

SUPERMAN
JLA (Series 4)
Hasbro

RELEASE DATE: **1998**
SCALE: **5 inches**
ARTICULATION: **5 points**
ACCESSORIES: **JLA logo display base**

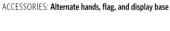

SUPERMAN
DC Super Heroes
Kenner

RELEASE DATE: **1999**
SCALE: **7 inches**
ARTICULATION: **12 points**
ACCESSORIES: **Removable cape and display base**
VARIANT: **Cloth-cape version featured in Toys R Us exclusive four-pack**

SUPERMAN
DC Super Heroes
Hasbro: Target Exclusive

RELEASE DATE: **1999**
SCALE: **9 inches**
ARTICULATION: **27 points**
ACCESSORIES: **DC Comics BULLET logo display base**

SUPERMAN
The Classic Silver Age Superman and Lois Lane
DC Direct

RELEASE DATE: **2001**
SCALE: **6½ inches**
ARTICULATION: **15 points**
ACCESSORIES: **Alternate hands, flag, and display base**

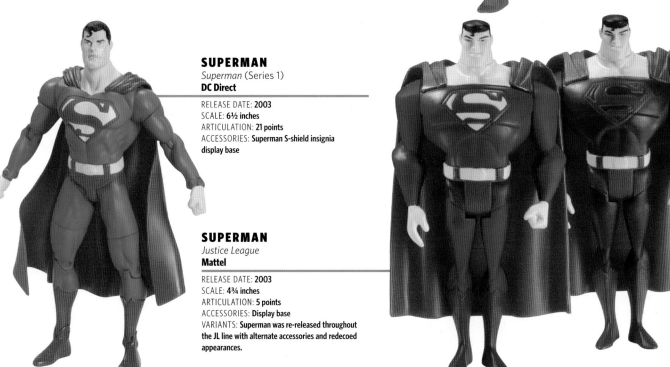

SUPERMAN
Superman (Series 1)
DC Direct

RELEASE DATE: **2003**
SCALE: **6½ inches**
ARTICULATION: **21 points**
ACCESSORIES: **Superman S-shield insignia display base**

SUPERMAN
Justice League
Mattel

RELEASE DATE: **2003**
SCALE: **4¾ inches**
ARTICULATION: **5 points**
ACCESSORIES: **Display base**
VARIANTS: **Superman was re-released throughout the JL line with alternate accessories and redecoed appearances.**

SUPERMAN
Justice League
Mattel

RELEASE DATE: **2003**
SCALE: **10 inches**
ARTICULATION: **5 points**

SUPERMAN
JLA (Series 1)
DC Direct

RELEASE DATE: **2003**
SCALE: **6½ inches**
ARTICULATION: **21 points**
ACCESSORIES: **American flag and JLA logo display base (w/ foot pegs)**

SUPERMAN
Pocket Super Heroes (Series 2)
DC Direct

RELEASE DATE: **2003**
SCALE: **3¼ inches**
ARTICULATION: **6 points**
ACCESSORIES: **Removable cape, kryptonite meteor, and display base**

SUPERMAN
Pocket Super Heroes (JLA Box Set)
DC Direct

RELEASE DATE: **2003**
SCALE: **3¼ inches**
ARTICULATION: **6 points**
ACCESSORIES: **Removable cape**

SUPERMAN
Super Friends!
DC Direct

RELEASE DATE: **2003**
SCALE: **6½ inches**
ARTICULATION: **11 points**
ACCESSORIES: **Interchangeable hands (2 sets: fists/open palms) and SUPER FRIENDS! logo display base**

SUPERMAN
Kingdom Come (Series 1)
DC Direct

RELEASE DATE: **2003**
SCALE: **6½ inches**
ARTICULATION: **5 points**

SUPERMAN IN RECOVERY SUIT
The Return of Superman (Series 1)
DC Direct

RELEASE DATE: **2004**
SCALE: **6½ inches**
ARTICULATION: **11 points**
ACCESSORIES: **Superman S-shield insignia display base**

SUPERMAN
Batman Two-Pack
Mattel

RELEASE DATE: **2004**
SCALE: **6 inches**
ARTICULATION: **22 points**
ACCESSORIES: **Combat communicator**

SUPERMAN
Batman: The Dark Knight Returns
(Series 1)
DC Direct

RELEASE DATE: **2004**
SCALE: **6½ inches**
ARTICULATION: **9 points**
ACCESSORIES: **Crushed Batman armor helmet, kryptonite armor, and display base**

SUPERMAN
Justice League: Mission Vision
Mattel

RELEASE DATE: **2004**
SCALE: **4¾ inches**
ARTICULATION: **10 points**
ACCESSORIES: **Shield, missile launcher, and armor with goggles**
VARIANT: **Subterranean heat sensor with shield**

SUPERMAN
First Appearance (Series 2)
DC Direct

RELEASE DATE: **2004**
SCALE: **6½ inches**
ARTICULATION: **9 points**
ACCESSORIES: **Cloth cape, mini comic, and FIRST APPEARANCE logo display base**

SUPERMAN
Batman: Hush (Series 2)
DC Direct

RELEASE DATE: **2004**
SCALE: **6½ inches**
ARTICULATION: **11 points**
ACCESSORIES: **BATMAN logo display base/flying stand**

CYBER-DEFENDER SUPERMAN
Justice League Unlimited
Mattel

RELEASE DATE: **2005**
SCALE: **4¾ inches**
ARTICULATION: **10 points**
ACCESSORIES: **Virtual-reality gear**

SUPERMAN
Justice (Series 1)
DC Direct

RELEASE DATE: **2005**
SCALE: **7 inches**
ARTICULATION: **11 points**
ACCESSORIES: **Display base**

SUPERMAN
Justice (Series 1) (variant)
DC Direct: Retailer Exclusive

RELEASE DATE: **2005**
SCALE: **7 inches**
ARTICULATION: **11 points**
ACCESSORIES: **Display base**

SUPERMAN
JLA Gift Set
DC Direct

RELEASE DATE: **2005**
SCALE: **7 inches**
ARTICULATION: **21 points**
ACCESSORIES: **JLA logo display base**

SUPERMAN
Superman/Batman
(Series 1: *Public Enemies*)
DC Direct

RELEASE DATE: **2005**
SCALE: **6½ inches**
ARTICULATION: **13 points**
ACCESSORIES: **SUPERMAN/BATMAN logo display base**

SUPERMAN
Elseworlds (Series 1: *Red Son*)
DC Direct

RELEASE DATE: **2005**
SCALE: **6½ inches**
ARTICULATION: **11 points**
ACCESSORIES: **Communist flag**

SUPERMAN
DC Super Heroes: Superman
Mattel

RELEASE DATE: **2006**
SCALE: **6 inches**
ARTICULATION: **23 points**

SUPERMAN
Superman/Batman
(Series 2: *The Return of Supergirl*)
DC Direct

RELEASE DATE: **2006**
SCALE: **6½ inches**
ARTICULATION: **15 points**
ACCESSORIES: **SUPERMAN/BATMAN logo display base**

SUPERMAN
DC: The New Frontier (Series 1)
DC Direct

RELEASE DATE: **2006**
SCALE: **6½ inches**
ARTICULATION: **11 points**
ACCESSORIES: **Movie camera and display base**

GOLDEN AGE SUPERMAN
Superman Through the Ages Gift Set
DC Direct

RELEASE DATE: **2006**
SCALE: **6½ inches**
ARTICULATION: **9 points**
ACCESSORIES: **Display base**

JIM LEE SUPERMAN
Superman Through the Ages Gift Set
DC Direct

RELEASE DATE: **2006**
SCALE: **6½ inches**
ARTICULATION: **11 points**
ACCESSORIES: **Display base**

1980S SUPERMAN
Superman Through the Ages Gift Set
DC Direct

RELEASE DATE: **2006**
SCALE: **6½ inches**
ARTICULATION: **11 points**
ACCESSORIES: **Display base**

ROBOT SUPERMAN
Superman Through the Ages Gift Set
DC Direct

RELEASE DATE: **2006**
SCALE: **6½ inches**
ARTICULATION: **13 points**
ACCESSORIES: **Display base**

SUPERMAN
Elseworlds (Series 2: *Red Son*)
DC Direct

RELEASE DATE: **2006**
SCALE: **6½ inches**
ARTICULATION: **9 points**
ACCESSORIES: **Brainiac head and display base**

SUPERMAN
ReActivated (Series 1)
DC Direct

RELEASE DATE: **2006**
SCALE: **6½ inches**
ARTICULATION: **21 points**
ACCESSORIES: **REACTIVATED logo display base**

SUPERMAN
DC Super Heroes: Superman
Mattel

RELEASE DATE: **2006**
SCALE: **6 inches**
ARTICULATION: **23 points**

Superman wore this electrically inspired costume when he lost his original superpowers and gained new energy-based abilities, after Earth's yellow sun was snuffed by the extraterrestrial Sun-Eater.

SUPERMAN AS SHAZAM!
Superman/Batman
(Series 1: *Public Enemies*)
DC Direct: ToyFare Exclusive

RELEASE DATE: **2005**
SCALE: **6½ inches**
ARTICULATION: **13 points**
ACCESSORIES: **SUPERMAN/BATMAN logo display base**

SUPERMAN BLUE
JLA (Series 1)
Hasbro

RELEASE DATE: **1998**
SCALE: **5 inches**
ARTICULATION: **5 points**
ACCESSORIES: **JLA logo display base**

SUPERMAN RED
JLA (Series 1)
Hasbro

RELEASE DATE: **1998**
SCALE: **5 inches**
ARTICULATION: **5 points**
ACCESSORIES: **JLA logo display base**

SUPERMAN
JLA
Hasbro: Kay-Bee Toys Exclusive

RELEASE DATE: **1999**
SCALE: **9 inches**
ARTICULATION: **27 points**

SUPERMAN
DC Super Heroes
Hasbro

RELEASE DATE: **1999**
SCALE: **6 inches**
ARTICULATION: **12 points**
ACCESSORIES: **Display base**

SUPERMAN
DC Super Heroes
Hasbro: Toys R Us Exclusive

RELEASE DATE: **1999**
SCALE: **6 inches**
ARTICULATION: **12 points**
ACCESSORIES: **Display base**

SUPERMAN (EARTH-2)
Crisis on Infinite Earths (Series 2)
DC Direct

RELEASE DATE: **2006**
SCALE: **6½ inches**
ARTICULATION: **11 points**
ACCESSORIES: **CRISIS logo display base**

FUTURE SUPERMAN
Superman/Batman
(Series 3: *Public Enemies*)
DC Direct

RELEASE DATE: **2007**
SCALE: **6½ inches**
ARTICULATION: **13 points**
ACCESSORIES: **Display base**

SUPERMAN ROBOT
Silver Age Superman (Series 1)
DC Direct

RELEASE DATE: **2006**
SCALE: **6½ inches**
ARTICULATION: **16 points**
ACCESSORIES: **Superman robot and Beppo**

SUPERMAN (KENNER)

Kenner no doubt counted on the fact that its success with *Batman: The Animated Series* and subsequent lines would translate to the Man of Steel's 1996 cartoon-based collection. *Superman: The Animated Series,* however, ended after just two seasons on television, while Kenner's *Superman* lineup endured just as long. Diamond Comics Distributors saved the day by soliciting several line-ending toys, including the first Bizarro action figure, extending the collection's life into 1998. And Toys R Us gave collectors the very first Lois Lane action figure. After all, what is Superman without his eternal love interest?

ANTI-KRYPTONITE SUPERMAN
ARTICULATION: **6 points**
ACCESSORIES: **Kryptonite disposal claw, kryptonite, and helmet**

CAPTURE CLAW SUPERMAN
ARTICULATION: **6 points**
ACCESSORIES: **Villain snare launcher**

CAPTURE NET SUPERMAN
ARTICULATION: **6 points**
ACCESSORIES: **S-shield snare shooter**

SUPERMAN (KENNER)

DEEP DIVE SUPERMAN
ARTICULATION: **6 points**
ACCESSORIES: **Underwater rocket blaster**

ELECTRO ENERGY SUPERMAN
ARTICULATION: **6 points**
ACCESSORIES: **Energy-burst unit and capture cape**

FORTRESS OF SOLITUDE SUPERMAN
ARTICULATION: **6 points**
ACCESSORIES: **Turbo-spin crystal cannon**

NEUTRON STAR SUPERMAN
ARTICULATION: **6 points**
ACCESSORIES: **Galactic armor and rockets**

QUICK CHANGE SUPERMAN
ARTICULATION: **6 points**
ACCESSORIES: **Clark Kent disguise**
ACTION FEATURE: **Instant-reveal action**

CITY CAMO SUPERMAN (DELUXE)
ARTICULATION: **6 points**
ACCESSORIES: **Urban camouflage flightpack and tracking launcher**

FLYING SUPERMAN (DELUXE)
ARTICULATION: **1 point**
ACCESSORIES: **S-shield base/launcher**
ACTION FEATURE: **Soars over 25 feet!**

VISION BLAST SUPERMAN (DELUXE)
ARTICULATION: **6 points**
ACCESSORIES: **Light-up S-shield**
ACTION FEATURE: **Power-glow eyes**

STRONG-ARM SUPERMAN
ARTICULATION: **6 points**
ACCESSORIES: **Truck bumper and broken wall**
ACTION FEATURE: **Power-Throw Action and Double-Uppercut Punch**

POWER SWING SUPERMAN (DIAMOND COMICS DISTRIBUTORS EXCLUSIVE)
ARTICULATION: **6 points**
ACCESSORIES: **Blast-apart robot and pipe**

TORNADO FORCE SUPERMAN (DIAMOND COMICS DISTRIBUTORS EXCLUSIVE)
ARTICULATION: **8 points**
ACCESSORIES: **Manacles (2)**
ACTION FEATURE: **Whirlwind-escape action**

QUICK CHANGE SUPERMAN (MISSION MASTERS)
ARTICULATION: **6 points**
ACCESSORIES: **Clark Kent disguise**
ACTION FEATURE: **Instant-reveal action**

FOUR-PACKS

SUPERMAN: BATTLE FOR METROPOLIS (TOYS R US EXCLUSIVE)
NOTE: **Includes Superman, Lois Lane, Lex Luthor, and Brainiac. Exclusive Lois Lane figure w/ clipboard and handheld computer unavailable elsewhere. See individual listing.**

SUPER-HEROES VS. SUPER-VILLAINS (TOYS R US EXCLUSIVE)
NOTE: **Includes Superman, Supergirl, Metallo, and Bizarro**

VEHICLES

KRYPTONIAN BATTLE SUIT
NOTE: **Armored suit and robotic tank all in one!**

SUPERMAN CONVERSION COUPE (W/ CLARK KENT FIGURE)
ARTICULATION: **6 points**
ACTION FEATURE: **Sports car converts to space jet!**

SUPERMAN: MAN OF STEEL

Hot on the heels of Superman's much-publicized death and resurrection in his various DC Comics publications, Kenner's 1995 *Superman: Man of Steel* collection focused heavily on that particular storyline and its various supporting characters, including the first-ever toy likenesses of replacement Supermen like Steel, Super-boy, and the Eradicator (see individual listings). Of course, the monster that slew Superman was also rendered in plastic, with the debut Doomsday action figure. The entire line lasted little more than a year. For collectors, however, Man of Steel offerings stand nicely with Kenner's *JLA* and *Total Justice* action figures to create a formidable DC Comics character lineup.

LASER SUPERMAN
ARTICULATION: **6 points**
ACCESSORIES: **Super-charged "laser" cannon**

POWER FLIGHT SUPERMAN
ARTICULATION: **6 points**
ACCESSORIES: **Breakaway chains**
ACTION FEATURE: **Take-off force arm action**

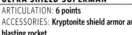

SOLAR SUIT SUPERMAN
ARTICULATION: **6 points**
ACCESSORIES: **Space probe launcher backpack**

STREET GUARDIAN SUPERMAN
ARTICULATION: **6 points**
ACCESSORIES: **Swinging battle chain and armor shield**

ULTRA SHIELD SUPERMAN
ARTICULATION: **6 points**
ACCESSORIES: **Kryptonite shield armor and blasting rocket**

SUPERMAN: MAN OF STEEL

ULTRA HEAT VISION SUPERMAN (DELUXE)
ARTICULATION: **5 points**
ACCESSORIES: **Electronic light & sound backpack and metallic chest plate**

TWO-PACKS

HUNTER-PREY SUPERMAN VS. DOOMSDAY
ARTICULATION: **6 points**

FULL ASSAULT SUPERMAN VS. MASSACRE
ARTICULATION: **6 points**

CYBER-LINK SUPERMAN AND CYBER-LINK BATMAN (DIAMOND COMICS DISTRIBUTORS EXCLUSIVE)
ARTICULATION: **5 points each**

VEHICLES

KRYPTONIAN BATTLE SUIT
NOTE: **Matrix conversion coupe (w/ Clark Kent figure)**

SUPERBOY V.T.O.L. CYCLE

SUPERMAN RETURNS

Mattel's 2006 *Superman Returns* toys were released ahead of the summer blockbuster, the first motion picture for the Man of Steel in more than two decades. A thematic sequel to *Superman II, Superman Returns* chronicled the Last Son of Krypton returning to Earth after a sojourn through space and once more engaging his arch-enemy Lex Luthor in battle while attempting to rekindle a romance with Lois Lane, now mother to a five-year-old son! Mattel's action figures focused on Superman's superpowers and featured spot-on likenesses of new Man of Steel Brandon Routh, as well as Kevin Spacey's diabolical Lex Luthor. All figures are 5½" scale unless otherwise noted.

BULLETPROOF SUPERMAN
ARTICULATION: **9 points**
ACCESSORIES: **Missile and launcher**

CLARK-TO-SUPERMAN
ARTICULATION: **12 points**
ACCESSORIES: **Glasses, wig, and Clark Kent clothing**

FAST ATTACK SUPERMAN
ARTICULATION: **11 points**
ACTION FEATURE: **Rolling fast attack flying feature**

FLIGHT FORCE SUPERMAN (ULTRA-FIGURE)
SCALE: **7 inches**
ARTICULATION: **13 points**
ACCESSORIES: **Vibrating "billowing" cape**

HEAT VISION SUPERMAN
ARTICULATION: **12 points**
ACCESSORIES: **Heat rays and kryptonite asteroid**

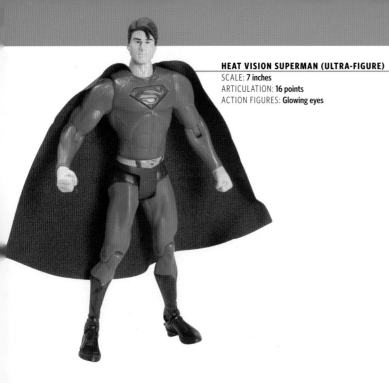

HEAT VISION SUPERMAN (ULTRA-FIGURE)
SCALE: **7 inches**
ARTICULATION: **16 points**
ACTION FIGURES: **Glowing eyes**

HYPERPOSEABLE SUPERMAN (TOYS R US EXCLUSIVE)
SCALE: **13 inches**
ARTICULATION: **35 points**

KRYPTONITE ESCAPE SUPERMAN
ARTICULATION: **11 points**
ACCESSORIES: **Breakaway kryptonite cocoon**

KRYPTONITE SMASH SUPERMAN
ARTICULATION: **15 points**
ACCESSORIES: **Breakaway kryptonite column and base**

MACH SPEED SUPERMAN (WAL-MART EXCLUSIVE)
ARTICULATION: **11 points**
ACTION FEATURE: **Mach speed sonic boom sound**

MEGA-PUNCH SUPERMAN (ULTRA-FIGURE)
SCALE: **7 inches**
ARTICULATION: **8 points**

SOLAR FORCE SUPERMAN
ARTICULATION: **6 points**
ACCESSORIES: **Friction fireball**

SPEED PUNCH SUPERMAN (ULTRA-FIGURE)
SCALE: **7 inches**
ARTICULATION: **7 points**
ACTION FEATURE: **Speed punching action**

SUPER BREATH SUPERMAN
ARTICULATION: **11 points**
ACCESSORIES: **Lex Luthor blow-down cut-out**

WALL BUSTING SUPERMAN
ARTICULATION: **11 points**
ACCESSORIES: **Breakable wall**

X-RAY ALERT SUPERMAN
ARTICULATION: **15 points**
ACCESSORIES: **Break-open safe and kryptonite bomb**

SUPERMAN
Superman Returns 1:6 Scale Deluxe Collector Figure
DC Direct

RELEASE DATE: **2006**
SCALE: **13 inches**
ARTICULATION: **26 points**
ACCESSORIES: **Interchangeable head and display base**

SUPERNOVA
52 (Series 1)
DC Direct

RELEASE DATE: **2007**
SCALE: **6½ inches**
ARTICULATION: **9 points**
ACCESSORIES: **Display base**

SUPER POWERS
Prior to Mattel's ongoing *Justice League/Justice League Unlimited* lines, Kenner's *Super Powers* collection boasted the most expansive collection of DC heroes and villains to date based on animated renderings of the characters. *Super Powers* is also notable for producing more than a few dynamic vehicles and accessories, including the unproduced Tower of Darkness (see sidebar, page 70) and All-Terrain Trapper. The following toys expanded the play-pattern for *Super Powers* collectors during the line's 1984–86 duration.

BATCOPTER

BATMOBILE

DARKSEID DESTROYER

DELTA PROBE ONE

HALL OF JUSTICE

JUSTICE JOGGER

KALIBAK BOULDER BOMBER

LEX-SOAR 7

SUPERMOBILE

SUPERWOMAN
Crime Syndicate
DC Direct

RELEASE DATE: **2002**
SCALE: **6½ inches**
ARTICULATION: **9 points**
ACCESSORIES: **Golden Lasso and CRIME SYNDICATE logo display base**

> Superwoman is actually the Wonder Woman of Earth-3, a parallel planet ruled by the sinister Crime Syndicate.
>
> **FIRST APPEARANCE**
> *Justice League of America* Vol. 1, No. 29

SUPERWOMAN
Superman/Batman (Series 4)
DC Direct

RELEASE DATE: **2007**
SCALE: **6½ inches**
ARTICULATION: **9 points**
ACCESSORIES: **Display base**

SWAMP THING

Kenner's 1990 *Swamp Thing* collection grew out of the short-lived animated series featuring DC Comics' cult-favorite muck-encrusted monster. Aided by Vietnam vet Bayou Jack and Native American Tomahawk, the five-inch-scale Swamp Thing sprouted specialized plant-based action features to battle arch-foe Anton Arcane and his army of Evil Un-Men Villains (see individual listings). Lasting a mere year, *Swamp Thing* included three vehicles—the Bayou Blaster, Bog Rover, and Marsh Buggy—as well as a pair of playsets: the fantastically foliated Swamp Trap and the Transducer, which allowed Arcane to transform a hapless minion into the monstrous Mantid action figure.

BIO-GLOW SWAMP THING
ARTICULATION: **4 points**
ACCESSORIES: **Action-arm swing axe and mace**
ACTION FEATURE: **Swinging action arm; glows in the dark**

CAMOUFLAGE SWAMP THING
ARTICULATION: **8 points**
ACCESSORIES: **Vine snare**
ACTION FEATURE: **Changes color to blend with surroundings**
VARIANT: **Two versions: green arms/brown arms**

CAPTURE SWAMP THING
ARTICULATION: **5 points**
ACCESSORIES: **Organic net and cypress club**
ACTION FEATURE: **Retractable hand captures foes in net**

CLIMBING SWAMP THING
ARTICULATION: **4 points**
ACCESSORIES: **Bayou staff and shield of reeds**
ACTION FEATURE: **Grappling hook slides through figure for climbing**

SNAP UP SWAMP THING
ARTICULATION: **8 points**
ACCESSORIES: **Log bazooka**
ACTION FEATURE: **Push-button feature changes pile of loose branches into Swamp Thing**

SNARE ARM SWAMP THING
ARTICULATION: **8 points**
ACCESSORIES: **Vine-winch arm and monster trap**
ACTION FEATURE: **Push-button feature pulls in villains with vine-winch arm**

VEHICLES/PLAYSETS

BAYOU BLASTER
ACTION FEATURE: **Firing torpedo and thrashing blades**

BOG ROVER
ACTION FEATURE: **Launching grappling missile**

MARSH BUGGY
ACTION FEATURE: **Giant grabbing claws**

SWAMP TRAP
ACTION FEATURE: **Vine snare and giant Venus flytrap**

TRANSDUCER
ACCESSORIES: **Mutated insect (Mantid) figure**
ACTION FEATURE: **Bio-mutator changes men into monsters**

SWAMP THING
Swamp Thing
DC Direct

RELEASE DATE: **1999**
SCALE: **6½ inches**
ARTICULATION: **10 points**
ACCESSORIES: **Interchangeable hands (2 sets: standard/blooming roses)**
VARIANT: **Redecoed glow-in-the-dark version**

> There have been many plant elementals since Earth's creation. The latest Swamp Thing grew from the remains of scientist Alec Holland, who was bathed in his bio-restorative formula after an explosion destroyed his bayou laboratory.
>
> **FIRST APPEARANCE**
> *House of Secrets* No. 92

T

TAIL TERRIER
Krypto the Superdog
Fisher-Price

RELEASE DATE: **2006**
SCALE: **6 inches**
ARTICULATION: **6 points**
ACTION FEATURE: **Spinning tail**

TALIA
Batman: Shadows of Gotham City
Hasbro: Toys R Us Exclusive

RELEASE DATE: **2001**
SCALE: **4¾ inches**
ARTICULATION: **4 points**
ACCESSORIES: **Pistols (2)**

TEMBLOR
The Batman
Mattel

RELEASE DATE: **2006**
SCALE: **5 inches**
ARTICULATION: **6 points**
ACCESSORIES: **Seismic gauntlets (2)**
ACTION FEATURE: **Figure vibrates when wound up**

TEEN TITANS

In 1976, DC Comics' *Teen Titans* title was facing cancellation, but that didn't stop the Mego Corporation from capitalizing on the appeal of the young heroes by spinning the Titans off from its best-selling *World's Greatest Super-Heroes!* collection. The *Teen Titans* line featured a new logo and card art, not to mention a retooled seven-inch body for boy heroes Aqualad, Kid Flash, and Speedy, in addition to a similarly scaled Wonder Girl. Missing from the roster was team leader Robin, although collectors could still pick up the Boy Wonder in Mego's *World's Greatest Super-Heroes!* assortment. However, at eight inches, Robin towered over his teammates.

The daughter of Rā's al Ghūl, Talia Head once served as CEO of LexCorp while Lex Luthor held the office of President of the United States!

FIRST APPEARANCE
Detective Comics No. 411

TITANS, GO!

Bandai's anime-flavored *Teen Titans* action figure collection, based on the popular Cartoon Network animated series, made its debut in 2004. *Teen Titans* toys run the gamut from 1½-inch PVC miniatures to 10-inch large-size figures, with 3½- and 5-inch Titans in between. As well, the *TT* line has included a wealth of mini vehicles that link together to form mega vehicles fit for the entire team of 3½-inch Titans. In 2006, Bandai planned to add heroes of the Doom Patrol and villains from the Brotherhood of Evil to its *Teen Titans* assortments, both supergroups rendered as titanic toys for the first time. However, the *TT* animated series was canceled, and Bandai pulled the plug on the line.

The Vietnamese hero Thunder and his super-charged brother, Lightning, are fraternal twins.

FIRST APPEARANCE
The New Teen Titans Vol. 1, No. 32

TERRA
Teen Titans
Bandai

RELEASE DATE: **2004**
SCALE: **3½ inches**
ARTICULATION: **7 points**

TERRA
Teen Titans
Bandai

RELEASE DATE: **2005**
SCALE: **3½ inches**
ARTICULATION: **5 points**
ACCESSORIES: **Earth-blast hand attachment**

THUNDER
Teen Titans
Bandai

RELEASE DATE: **2005**
SCALE: **3½ inches**
ARTICULATION: **7 points**

TIMBER WOLF
Legion of Super-Heroes (Series 4)
DC Direct

RELEASE DATE: **2004**
SCALE: **6½ inches**
ARTICULATION: **11 points**

TOMAHAWK
Swamp Thing
Kenner

RELEASE DATE: **1990**
SCALE: **5 inches**
ARTICULATION: **5 points**
ACCESSORIES: **Swift-shot crossbow**

TIM HUNTER
Books of Magic
DC Direct

RELEASE DATE: **2002**
SCALE: **6½ inches**
ARTICULATION: **7 points**
ACCESSORIES: **Enchanted owl Yo-Yo, which
magnetically attaches to Tim's shoulder**

TOMAR-RE
Green Lantern Corps
DC Direct

RELEASE DATE: **2002**
SCALE: **6½ inches**
ARTICULATION: **9 points**
ACCESSORIES: **Power battery and one-size-fits-all
power ring**

TOMAR-RE
*DC Super Heroes:
Justice League Unlimited*
Mattel

RELEASE DATE: **2006**
SCALE: **4¾ inches**
ARTICULATION: **5 points**

Tomorrow Woman was created by
T.O. Morrow—who also built the
android Amazo—and fellow mad
scientist Professor Ivo. She overrode
her evil programming to save her
JLA teammates from destruction.

FIRST APPEARANCE
JLA No. 5

TOMORROW WOMAN
JLA: Amazing Androids
DC Direct

RELEASE DATE: **2000**
SCALE: **6½ inches**
ARTICULATION: **7 points**

TOM STRONG
Tom Strong Box Set
DC Direct

RELEASE DATE: **2000**
SCALE: **6½ inches**
ARTICULATION: **7 points**
ACCESSORIES: **Helicopter backpack w/ manually spinning blades, goggles, pistol, and knife**

TULIP
Preacher
DC Direct

RELEASE DATE: **2000**
SCALE: **6½ inches**
ARTICULATION: **8 points**
ACCESSORIES: **Pistol and Uzi machine gun**

TRIDENT
Teen Titans (Launch Tower Playset)
Bandai

RELEASE DATE: **2004**
SCALE: **3½ inches**
ARTICULATION: **9 points**
ACCESSORIES: **Trident**

TOTAL JUSTICE

AND JUSTICE FOR ALL

Kenner's *Total Justice* collection in 1996 was the first line in a decade to focus on DC Comics' Justice League of America and its super-powerful members. Unlike the company's *Super Powers* collection, featuring characters standing at attention with built-in action features, the *TJ* figures initially came with snap-on "Fractal Techgear" armor and accessories, each sculpted with muscles rippling in near-exaggerated poses. Kenner products soon folded into parent company Hasbro's masthead, *Total Justice* becoming *JLA*, Hasbro's attempt to capitalize on the popular DC Comics title with redecoed Justice League heroes complemented by new characters, including the first-ever *Young Justice* figures.

TWO-FACE
DC Super Heroes
Toy Biz

RELEASE DATE: **1990**
SCALE: **3¾ inches**
ARTICULATION: **8 points**
ACCESSORIES: **Two-headed silver dollar (nonremovable)**
ACTION FEATURE: **Coin-flipping action!**

TWO-FACE
Batman: The Animated Series
Kenner

RELEASE DATE: **1992**
SCALE: **4¾ inches**
ARTICULATION: **5 points**
ACCESSORIES: **Firing roulette wheel gun**

PIRATE TWO-FACE
Legends of Batman
Kenner

RELEASE DATE: **1995**
SCALE: **5 inches**
ARTICULATION: **6 points**

TWO-FACE
Batman Forever
Kenner

RELEASE DATE: **1995**
SCALE: **4¾ inches**
ARTICULATION: **5 points**
ACCESSORIES: **Turbo-charge cannon and good/evil coin; pistol molded to hand**

TWO-FACE
The New Batman Adventures
Kenner

RELEASE DATE: **1999**
SCALE: **4¾ inches**
ARTICULATION: **5 points**
ACCESSORIES: **Pistol and machine gun**

TWO-FACE
Batman
Mattel

RELEASE DATE: **2002**
SCALE: **4¾ inches**
ARTICULATION: **5 points**
VARIANT: **Redecoed single-carded release**

TWO-FACE
Pocket Super Heroes (Batman Box Set)
DC Direct

RELEASE DATE: **2004**
SCALE: **3¼ inches**
ARTICULATION: **6 points**

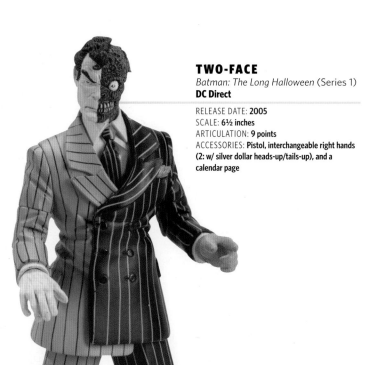

TWO-FACE
Batman: The Long Halloween (Series 1)
DC Direct

RELEASE DATE: **2005**
SCALE: **6½ inches**
ARTICULATION: **9 points**
ACCESSORIES: **Pistol, interchangeable right hands (2: w/ silver dollar heads-up/tails-up), and a calendar page**

TWO-FACE
Two-Face 1:6 Scale Deluxe Collector Figure
DC Direct

RELEASE DATE: **2006**
SCALE: **13 inches**
ARTICULATION: **26 points**
ACCESSORIES: **Guns (2), shoulder holsters, and metal coin**

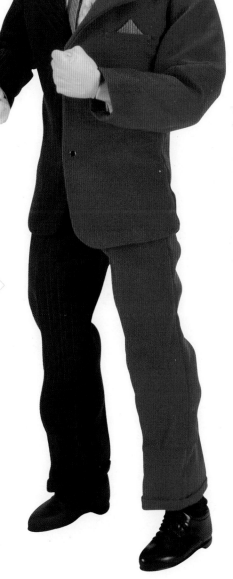

> Harvey Dent's obsessive compulsion over his two-headed silver dollar forces him to act according to whatever side lands faceup: unscarred for good, scarred for evil!
>
> **FIRST APPEARANCE**
> *Detective Comics* No. 66

TYR
Super Powers (Series 3)
Kenner

RELEASE DATE: **1986**
SCALE: **3¾ inches**
ARTICULATION: **7 points**
ACCESSORIES: **Power-action rocket launch**

> Before becoming a *Super Powers* fixture, the alien warlord Tyr menaced DC Comics' Legion of Super-Heroes.
>
> **FIRST APPEARANCE**
> *Superboy and the Legion of Super-Heroes* No. 197

U&V

ULTRA BOY
Legion of Super-Heroes (Series 3)
DC Direct

RELEASE DATE: **2003**
SCALE: **6½ inches**
ARTICULATION: **11 points**

ULTRA BOY
Pocket Super Heroes (Series 2)
DC Direct

RELEASE DATE: **2003**
SCALE: **3¼ inches**
ARTICULATION: **6 points**
ACCESSORIES: **Display base**

ULTRAMAN
Crime Syndicate
DC Direct

RELEASE DATE: **2002**
SCALE: **6½ inches**
ARTICULATION: **9 points**
ACCESSORIES: **CRIME SYNDICATE logo display base**

ULTRA-HUMANITE
Justice League: Morph Gear
Mattel

RELEASE DATE: **2004**
SCALE: **4¾ inches**
ARTICULATION: **9 points**
ACCESSORIES: **2-in-1 blaster/hoverboard**

Superman's evil doppelganger from Earth-3, Ultraman gains a new ability each time he is exposed to green kryptonite.

FIRST APPEARANCE
Justice League of America Vol. 1, No. 29

UNCLE SAM
Classic Heroes
DC Direct

RELEASE DATE: **2002**
SCALE: **6½ inches**
ARTICULATION: **11 points**
ACCESSORIES: **Removable top hat**

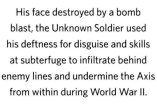

His face destroyed by a bomb blast, the Unknown Soldier used his deftness for disguise and skills at subterfuge to infiltrate behind enemy lines and undermine the Axis from within during World War II.

FIRST APPEARANCE
Star-Spangled War Stories No. 151

UNKNOWN SOLDIER
Unknown Soldier
Dreams & Visions

RELEASE DATE: **2004**
SCALE: **12 inches**
ARTICULATION: **21 points**
ACCESSORIES: **Removable mask, clothing, and alternate heads (2: scarred/bandaged)**
VARIANT: **Figure released with both dark and tan trenchcoats**

VANDAL SAVAGE
Justice Society of America Villains
DC Direct

RELEASE DATE: **2002**
SCALE: **6½ inches**
ARTICULATION: **9 points**
ACCESSORIES: **Sword**

Ventriloquist Arnold Wesker's wooden puppet, Scarface, was carved from lumber used in the hangman's gallows at Gotham City's Blackgate Penitentiary.

FIRST APPEARANCE
Detective Comics No. 583

VENTRILOQUIST WITH SCARFACE
Batman: Puppets of Crime Box Set
Hasbro: Toys R Us Exclusive

RELEASE DATE: **2002**
SCALE: **4¾ inches**
ARTICULATION: **Ventriloquist: 3 points; Scarface: 1 point**
ACCESSORIES: **Scarface's tommy gun (nonremovable)**

VENTRILOQUIST WITH SCARFACE
The Batman Box Set
Mattel: Target Exclusive

RELEASE DATE: **2006**
SCALE: **4¾ inches**
ARTICULATION: **10 points**
ACCESSORIES: **Scarface puppet**
VARIANT: **Chase figure featured "Snoots" puppet instead of Scarface**

VIXEN
DC Super Heroes:
Justice League Unlimited
Mattel

RELEASE DATE: **2006**
SCALE: **4¾ inches**
ARTICULATION: **5 points**
ACCESSORIES: **Snap-on claws (single-carded only)**

Before gaining superpowers from the animal kingdom from her magical Tantu Totem, Mari McCabe was a supermodel.

FIRST APPEARANCE
Action Comics No. 521

VIGILANTE
DC Super Heroes:
Justice League Unlimited
Mattel

RELEASE DATE: **2006**
SCALE: **4¾ inches**
ARTICULATION: **5 points**
ACCESSORIES: **Pistol and lariat**

VOLCANA
DC Super Heroes:
Justice League Unlimited
Mattel

RELEASE DATE: **2007**
SCALE: **4¾ inches**
ARTICULATION: **5 points**

WARLORD
The Lost World of the Warlord
Remco

RELEASE DATE: **1982**
SCALE: **5¼ inches**
ARTICULATION: **6 points**
ACCESSORIES: **Sword and removable cloak**

WARLORD
First Appearance (Series 4)
DC Direct

RELEASE DATE: **2007**
SCALE: **6½ inches**
ARTICULATION: **10 points**
ACCESSORIES: **Helmet, sword, spear, and display base**

ENTER THE LOST WORLD

Remco's short-lived *The Lost World of Warlord* collection combined several of DC Comics' sword-and-sorcery properties under the banner of writer/artist Mike Grell's popular *Warlord* comic book series, starring Lt. Col. Travis Morgan, an ace Air Force pilot trapped in the savage realm of Skartaris, as its newest Warlord. Warrior Machiste and werewolf Mikola were the Warlord's allies, while Deimos was his arch foe. Native American Arak and demigod Hercules hailed from DC's *Arak, Son of Thunder,* and *Hercules Unbound* comics, respectively. All figures and vehicles were designed for play with Remco's similarly sized lines, including *The Warrior Beasts,* properties not owned by DC.

> Air Force Lt. Col. Travis Morgan was on a spy mission over Russia when he discovered the hidden world of savage Skartaris.
>
> **FIRST APPEARANCE**
> *First Issue Special* No. 8

WAVERIDER
Justice League Unlimited
Mattel

RELEASE DATE: **2005-06**
SCALE: **4¾ inches**
ARTICULATION: **5 points**
ACCESSORIES: **Energy blast (single-carded only)**

WEAPONER OF QWARD
Crisis on Infinite Earths (Series 3)
DC Direct

RELEASE DATE: **2006**
SCALE: **6½ inches**
ARTICULATION: **9 points**
ACCESSORIES: **Thunderbolt, quivers (2), shield, and CRISIS logo display base**

> The Weaponers of the antimatter universe of Qward constructed Sinestro's yellow power ring.
>
> **FIRST APPEARANCE**
> *Green Lantern* No. 2

WEED KILLER
Swamp Thing
Kenner

RELEASE DATE: **1990**
SCALE: **5 inches**
ARTICULATION: **5 points**
ACCESSORIES: **Glow-in-the-dark bogsucker bio-mask and defoliant spray gun**

WILDCAT
Justice Society of America (Series 3)
DC Direct

RELEASE DATE: **2006**
SCALE: **6½ inches**
ARTICULATION: **12 points**

WILDCAT
Justice League Unlimited
Hasbro

RELEASE DATE: **2005-06**
SCALE: **4¾ inches**
ARTICULATION: **5 points**
ACCESSORIES: **Protective headgear and Cat-Gloves (single-carded only)**

WILDEBEEST
Teen Titans
Bandai

RELEASE DATE: **2005**
SCALE: **3½ inches**
ARTICULATION: **4 points**
ACCESSORIES: **Club**

WILD MAN
Sgt. Rock
Dreams & Visions

RELEASE DATE: **2004**
SCALE: **12 inches**
ARTICULATION: **21 points**
ACCESSORIES: **Field jacket, helmet, and rifle**

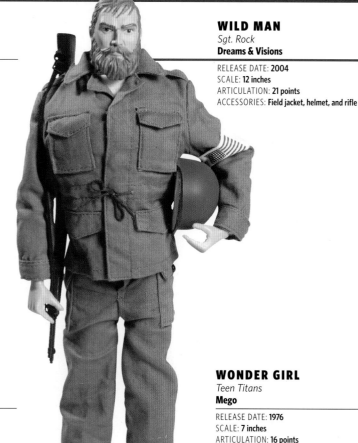

Wonder Girl has gone through many super-heroine identities since giving up her Golden Lasso. To date, she has also been Troia and Darkstar, and is presently Harbinger II.

FIRST APPEARANCE
The Brave and the Bold No. 60

WONDER GIRL
Pocket Super Heroes (Series 2)
DC Direct

RELEASE DATE: **2003**
SCALE: **3¾ inches**
ARTICULATION: **6 points**
ACCESSORIES: **Golden Lasso and display base**

WONDER GIRL
The Silver Age
Wonder Woman and Wonder Girl
DC Direct

RELEASE DATE: **2001**
SCALE: **6½ inches**
ARTICULATION: **5 points**
ACCESSORIES: **Golden Lasso, toga, interchangeable hands, and display base (for both figures)**

WONDER GIRL
Teen Titans
Mego

RELEASE DATE: **1976**
SCALE: **7 inches**
ARTICULATION: **16 points**
ACCESSORIES: **Removable cloth costume, boots, and necklace**
VARIANTS: **Early releases featured costume with flesh-tone "sleeves"**

WHAT A WONDERFUL WORLD

The Mego Corporation capitalized on the popular *Wonder Woman* television series by producing twelve-inch fashion dolls targeting the Barbie set. Based on actress Lynda Carter's likeness and featuring packaging touting thus, the company's *Wonder Woman* line included various interchangeable cloth outfits and wardrobe accessories for the Amazing Amazon, as well as the first-ever toy representations of Amazon princess Diana's beautiful mother, Queen Hippolyte [sic]; her Amazon sister, Nubia; and her paramour, Steve Trevor. In addition, Mego produced a "three-way" playset, featuring Diana Prince's apartment, Paradise Island, and Wonder Woman's secret headquarters on its various sides, with furniture and accessories included for each.

WONDER GIRL (DONNA TROY)

Identity Crisis (Series 2)
DC Direct

RELEASE DATE: **2007**
SCALE: **6½ inches**
ARTICULATION: **11 points**
ACCESSORIES: **Display base and lasso**

WONDER GIRL II

Contemporary Teen Titans (Series 1)
DC Direct

RELEASE DATE: **2004**
SCALE: **6½ inches**
ARTICULATION: **11 points**
ACCESSORIES: **Golden Lasso and TEEN TITANS logo display base**

WONDER WOMAN

Super Queens
Ideal

RELEASE DATE: **1967**
SCALE: **11½ inches**
ARTICULATION: **5 points**
ACCESSORIES: **Cloth costume and shield**

> Cassie Sandsmark's wondrous superpowers were a gift from the Greek god Zeus, who may or may not be her real father.
>
> **FIRST APPEARANCE**
> *Wonder Woman* Vol. 2, No. 105

WONDER WOMAN

World's Greatest Super-Heroes!
Mego

RELEASE DATE: **1972-82**
SCALE: **8 inches**
ARTICULATION: **21 points**
ACCESSORIES: **Removable cloth costume and boots**
VARIANTS: **Early releases featured screen-printed boots.**

WONDER WOMAN

Comic Action Heroes
Mego

RELEASE DATE: **1975-78**
SCALE: **3¾ inches**
ARTICULATION: **5 points**
ACCESSORIES: **Golden Lasso and display base**
VEHICLE/PLAYSET: **Collapsing tower with invisible plane, plus activator**

> Wonder Woman was created by psychologist William Moulton Marston, inventor of the polygraph, which is also known as the lie detector.
>
> **FIRST APPEARANCE**
> *All-Star Comics* No. 8

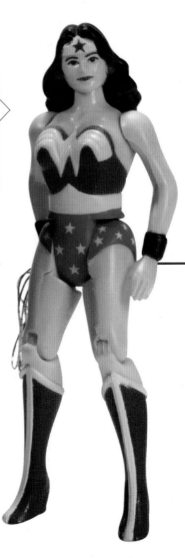

WONDER WOMAN

Wonder Woman
Mego

RELEASE DATE: **1977-80**
SCALE: **12 inches**
ARTICULATION: **5 points**
ACCESSORIES: **Golden Lasso, removable cloth costume, boots, and tiara**
VARIANTS: **Early releases featured a painted halter top.**

WONDER WOMAN

Pocket Super Heroes
Mego

RELEASE DATE: **1979-82**
SCALE: **3¾ inches**
ARTICULATION: **5 points**
ACCESSORIES: **Golden Lasso**

WONDER WOMAN

Super Powers (Series 1)
Kenner

RELEASE DATE: **1984**
SCALE: **3¾ inches**
ARTICULATION: **7 points**
ACCESSORIES: **Golden Lasso**
ACTION FEATURE: **Power-action deflector bracelets**

WONDER WOMAN

DC Super Heroes
Toy Biz

RELEASE DATE: **1989**
SCALE: **3¾ inches**
ARTICULATION: **7 points**
ACCESSORIES: **Golden Lasso**
ACTION FEATURE: **Power arm**

WONDER WOMAN AND THE STAR RIDERS

Mattel's first attempt at DC Comics toys occurred in 1992, when the company developed a potential line based on the Amazing Amazon and her super-powered "sisters." *Wonder Woman and the Star Riders* would have targeted the young girls' market with action-oriented fashion dolls on an eco-conscious mission to save Earth from the plots of the evil Purrsia. A teenaged Wonder Woman traded her Golden Lasso for a Wonder Wand and was joined by Dolphin, Ice, Solara, and Star Lily. Unfortunately, the Star Riders never made it past the proposal stage and remain lost on a Paradise Island of misfit toys.

WONDER WOMAN
JLA (Series 4)
Hasbro

RELEASE DATE: **1999**
SCALE: **5 inches**
ARTICULATION: **5 points**
ACCESSORIES: **Golden Lasso and JLA logo display base**

WONDER WOMAN
Wonder Woman
DC Direct

RELEASE DATE: **1999**
SCALE: **6½ inches**
ARTICULATION: **9 points**
ACCESSORIES: **Golden Lasso, shield, and battle-axe**

WONDER WOMAN
Wonder Woman (variant)
DC Direct

RELEASE DATE: **1999**
SCALE: **6½ inches**
ARTICULATION: **9 points**
ACCESSORIES: **Golden Lasso, helmet (nonremovable), and spear**

WONDER WOMAN
Justice Society of America (Series 1)
DC Direct

RELEASE DATE: **2000**
SCALE: **6½ inches**
ARTICULATION: **5 points**
ACCESSORIES: **Golden Lasso, sword, shield, removable cloth skirt, and WONDER WOMAN logo display stand**

WONDER WOMAN
Wonder Woman Masterpiece Edition
Chronicle Books

RELEASE DATE: **2001**
SCALE: **8½ inches**
ARTICULATION: **7 points**
ACCESSORIES: **Golden Lasso**

WONDER WOMAN
The Silver Age Wonder Woman and Wonder Girl
DC Direct

RELEASE DATE: **2001**
SCALE: **6½ inches**
ARTICULATION: **7 points**
ACCESSORIES: **Golden Lasso, toga, interchangeable hands, and display base**
VARIANT: **Redecoed figure included with *First Appearance: JLA (The Brave and the Bold No. 28)* gift set; re-released as single-carded *ReActivated* (Series 1) figure in 2006.**

WONDER WOMAN
Pocket Super Heroes (Exclusive)
DC Direct

RELEASE DATE: **2002**
SCALE: **3¼ inches**
ARTICULATION: **6 points**
NOTE: **Packaged w/ full-size Solomon Grundy action figure as a 2002 Toy Fair promotional giveaway.**

WONDER WOMAN
Pocket Super Heroes (Series 1)
DC Direct

RELEASE DATE: **2002**
SCALE: **3¼ inches**
ARTICULATION: **6 points**
ACCESSORIES: **Display base**

WONDER WOMAN
Super Friends!
DC Direct

RELEASE DATE: **2003**
SCALE: **6½ inches**
ARTICULATION: **9 points**
ACCESSORIES: **Invisible Plane miniature and SUPER FRIENDS! logo display base**

WONDER WOMAN
Pocket Super Heroes (JLA Box Set)
DC Direct

RELEASE DATE: **2003**
SCALE: **3¼ inches**
ARTICULATION: **6 points**

WONDER WOMAN
Kingdom Come (Series 1)
DC Direct

RELEASE DATE: **2003**
SCALE: **6½ inches**
ARTICULATION: **7 points**
ACCESSORIES: **Golden Lasso**

WONDER WOMAN
JLA (Series 1)
DC Direct

RELEASE DATE: **2003**
SCALE: **6½ inches**
ARTICULATION: **9 points**
ACCESSORIES: **Golden Lasso and JLA logo display base**
VARIANT: **Redecoed figure included in JLA gift set (2005)**

WONDER WOMAN
Justice League
Mattel

RELEASE DATE: **2003**
SCALE: **4¾ inches**
ARTICULATION: **5 points**
ACCESSORIES: **Display base**

WONDER WOMAN
Kingdom Come (Series 3)
DC Direct

RELEASE DATE: **2003**
SCALE: **6½ inches**
ARTICULATION: **7 points**
ACCESSORIES: **Golden Lasso, shield, spear, and display base**

WONDER WOMAN
First Appearance (Series 1)
DC Direct

RELEASE DATE: **2004**
SCALE: **6½ inches**
ARTICULATION: **12 points**
ACCESSORIES: **Golden Lasso, cloth skirt, mini comic, and FIRST APPEARANCE logo display base**

WONDER WOMAN
Justice League: Mission Vision
Mattel

RELEASE DATE: **2004**
SCALE: **4¾ inches**
ARTICULATION: **6 points**
ACCESSORIES: **Mission Vision Shield, crossbow, breathing apparatus, and cape (nonremovable)**

WONDER WOMAN
Justice League
Mattel

RELEASE DATE: **2004**
SCALE: **10 inches**
ARTICULATION: **5 points**
ACCESSORIES: **Golden Lasso and display base**

RED SON WONDER WOMAN
Elseworlds (Series 1)
DC Direct

RELEASE DATE: **2005**
SCALE: **6½ inches**
ARTICULATION: **11 points**
ACCESSORIES: **Golden Lasso and display base**

WONDER WOMAN
Justice League Unlimited
Mattel

RELEASE DATE: **2005**
SCALE: **4¾ inches**
ARTICULATION: **6 points**
ACCESSORIES: **Golden Lasso (single-carded only), sword, removable cloak, and space mask**

JUSTICE LORDS WONDER WOMAN
DC Super Heroes: Justice League Unlimited
Mattel

RELEASE DATE: **2005**
SCALE: **4¾ inches**
ARTICULATION: **6 points**

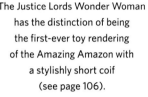

The Justice Lords Wonder Woman has the distinction of being the first-ever toy rendering of the Amazing Amazon with a stylishly short coif (see page 106).

WONDER WOMAN
JLA Classified (Series 1)
DC Direct

RELEASE DATE: **2006**
SCALE: **6½ inches**
ARTICULATION: **11 points**
ACCESSORIES: **Golden Lasso and display base**

WONDER WOMAN
Justice (Series 3)
DC Direct

RELEASE DATE: **2006**
SCALE: **7 inches**
ARTICULATION: **11 points**
ACCESSORIES: **Golden Lasso and display base**

WONDER WOMAN
DC: The New Frontier (Series 1)
DC Direct

RELEASE DATE: **2006**
SCALE: **6½ inches**
ARTICULATION: **11 points**
ACCESSORIES: **Alternate head, sword, shield, and display base**

WONDER WOMAN
Infinite Crisis (Series 2)
DC Direct

RELEASE DATE: **2007**
SCALE: **6½ inches**
ARTICULATION: **11 points**
ACCESSORIES: **Display base, sword, sheath, and lasso**

WORLD'S GREATEST SUPER-HEROES!

For many toy collectors, Mego's long-running *World's Greatest Super-Heroes!* lineup truly lived up to its own hype. The first toy collection devoted to DC Comics characters since Ideal's *Justice League* figurines, *WGSH!* debuted in 1972 and featured multiarticulated poseable figures with removable cloth costumes. Vehicles included the Batmobile, Batcycle, Batcopter, Mobile Bat Lab, Joker Mobile, and the first-ever Green Arrowcar. Mego's Hall of Justice, Batcave, and Wayne Foundation playsets offered maximum play value, with dynamic art and accessories. It's no wonder then that the *WGSH!* occupied store shelves for a full decade and are among the most sought-after collectible toys today.

X, Y & Z

X-RATED

While *The DC Comics Action Figure Archive* spans the letters A to Z, this toy tome is bereft of entries for just two letters of the alphabet. To date, there have been no DC action figures having names beginning with either X or Y. Of course, there is a dearth of major DC characters with either letter as a first (or last) initial. Thus, collectors still wait for action figures devoted to Starfire's patron goddess X'Hal, the hero XerO, or even thirty-first-century Legionnaire speedster XS. Of course, even Yankee Poodle and the Yellow Peri suffer the same indignity—for now.

YOUNG INJUSTICE

Hasbro's continuation of *Total Justice* as a JLA-themed line of action figures had the added benefit of allowing DC Comics' *Young Justice*—a *JLA* comic book spin-off—to see its own mini collection in 1999. In addition to a redecoed *Total Justice* Robin, the *JLA*-carded *Young Justice* action figures included newly sculpted versions of Superboy and Impulse, a toy-first for the latter. In addition, the *YJ* mini collection featured team mentor Red Tornado, only the second action figure for the cyclonic-powered android. Unfortunately, the *JLA* line dwindled well before the *Young Justice* boys' female teammates could be added to the mix.

ZATANNA
Mages, Mystics & Magicians
DC Direct

RELEASE DATE: **2000**
SCALE: **6½ inches**
ARTICULATION: **9 points**
ACCESSORIES: **Real fishnet tights and display base**

ZATANNA
Identity Crisis (Series 1)
DC Direct

RELEASE DATE: **2006**
SCALE: **6½ inches**
ARTICULATION: **11 points**
ACCESSORIES: **IDENTITY CRISIS logo display base (w/ foot pegs)**

ZATANNA
Justice (Series 4)
DC Direct

RELEASE DATE: **2006**
SCALE: **7 inches**
ARTICULATION: **12 points**
ACCESSORIES: **Removable hand, real fishnet tights, and display base**

ZATANNA
DC Super Heroes:
Justice League Unlimited
Mattel

RELEASE DATE: **2006**
SCALE: **4¾ inches**
ARTICULATION: **5 points**

Before joining the JLA as a replacement "wingman" for Hawkman, Zauriel was an angel of Heaven's Eagle Host.

FIRST APPEARANCE
JLA No. 6

ZAURIEL
JLA (Series 2)
Hasbro

RELEASE DATE: **1999**
SCALE: **5 inches**
ARTICULATION: **7 points (including wings)**
ACCESSORIES: **Flaming sword and JLA logo display base**

Zatanna is the daughter of magician/adventurer John Zatara, a descendant of Leonardo da Vinci. Like her father before her, Zatanna casts her magical spells by speaking the incantations backward.

FIRST APPEARANCE
Hawkman Vol. 1, No. 1

ACKNOWLEDGMENTS

The author would like to especially thank DC Comics editor Steve Korté and, at Chronicle Books, Matt Robinson, Sarah Malarkey, Doug Ogan, Evan Hulka, Beth Steiner, and Brooke Johnson for their enduring patience in seeing this book to completion.

Thanks to Marc Witz and Mike Essl, collaborators in every sense of the word.

Special thanks to Georg Brewer and the staff of DC Direct: Jim Fletcher, Iris Goudjabidze, Shawn Knapp, Evan Metcalf, and Ashly Powell. Thanks, too, to these DC staffers: Chris Cerasi, Marilyn Drucker, William Eng, Tonya Henderson, Gary Holling, Bob Joy, Jim King, Kevin Kiniry, Emily Ryan Lerner, John Morgan, Cheryl Rubin, Kyle Slepinski, and Mike Zagari.

Thanks also to the following real-life "action figures," without whose help this book would not be possible: Aaron Archer; John Bonavita; Bethel Caram; Chuck Dixon; Peter Dupree and Paul Lazo at Amok Time; Joseph Figured at America's Most Wanted Collectibles; Matt Golding, Cathy Odem, and Valerie Amans at Bandai; Chris Griffy, Cale Paige, and Cully Waggoner at Batman: Yesterday, Today, and Beyond; Jennifer Holzapfel; Arturo Interian; Linda Lum at Dreams & Visions; Pat McCallum; Matt MacNabb at Legions Of Gotham; Nick and Mint at St. Mark's Comics; Daniel Pickett; Gus Poulakis at Silver Age; Dave Romeo Jr. at Comics on the Green; David Scothon, Steed Sun, Jim Murphy, Jason Horowitz, Binh Luong, Scott Neitlich, Brandon Sopinsky, Frank Varela, and Geoff Walker at Mattel; Steve Younis at Superman Homepage.

Thanks to *ToyFare* magazine for starting me down this plastic path.

And thanks to Jennifer Myskowski for accepting my "hobby."

This book is dedicated to Finnegan Scott Beatty, who believes FLAVOR is every bit as important to action figures as ARTICULATION and ACCESSORIES.